RON

The L. Ron Hubbard Series

BRIDGE PUBLICATIONS, INC.
5600 E. Olympic Blvd.
Commerce, California 90022 USA

ISBN 978-1-4031-9888-4

The L. Ron Hubbard Series

WRITER
THE SHAPING OF
POPULAR
FICTION

PUBLICATIONS, INC. ®

CONTENTS

An Introduction to
L. Ron Hubbard

OR ALL THE NAME L. RON HUBBARD REPRESENTS AS THE Founder of Dianetics and Scientology, let us never lose sight of the man as an author—specifically, among the world's most enduring and widely read authors of popular fiction—with international sales of some fifty million translated into better than thirty languages.

Then, too, he is legitimately credited with helping to reshape whole genres and laying the foundation for much of what we know as modern speculative literature. While just for good measure, his eleven consecutive *New York Times* bestsellers from the mid-1980s marked an unequaled event in publishing history. Finally, and even more to the point of this publication is all he brought to aspiring writers and those who would better their command of the craft—which is to say, all that is presented here as L. Ron Hubbard addresses the art of writing.

Included are essays, articles and notes from the whole of those fifty years as a leading light of popular fiction. That we find L. Ron Hubbard devoted so much in explanation of creative writing is typical of a man who authored the singularly most influential philosophic statement on artistic creativity,

ART. It is likewise typical of a man who founded the singularly most prestigious program for the discovery of young talent

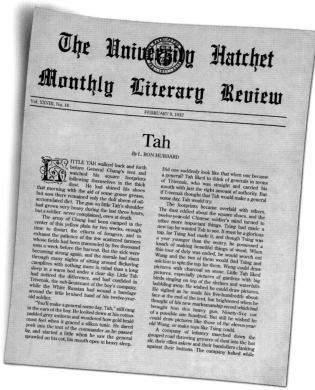

Below
Tah, Ron's first published fiction story, February 1932

Left At the start of a fifty-year career

within speculative fiction, the internationally acclaimed Writers of the Future Contest. Then again, it is typical of an American Fiction Guild president who worked so doggedly on behalf of emerging talent through the Great Depression, as the voice of new authors from the Pacific Northwest and as a regular voice of encouragement to colleagues in need. But quite apart from all other efforts to instruct and inspire, we are about to discover how L. Ron Hubbard himself approached the blank page—how he conceived of ideas, executed those ideas and otherwise attended to what he first and foremost described as "this business of writing."

It would prove a lifelong occupation. His earliest published stories date from 1932, or his sophomore year at George Washington University, where three LRH works appear among the pages of the student quarterly: two tragic tales drawn from travels across Asia, and the existential narrative of a sailor who has glimpsed his own death in a San Diego movie house. For whatever it's worth, the stories are miles better than the maudlin stuff from fellow undergraduates and, arguably, the finest work to emerge from the George Washington literary department. Beyond university, and following much in the way of raw adventure through the course of two Caribbean expeditions, he

set himself to a fully professional literary pursuit—in particular, supplying short stories to that legendary vehicle of popular fiction, the rough-stock periodicals otherwise known as the pulps.

The pulps—name alone still conjures images of high adventure in exotic realms: Tarzan and Doc Savage stalking crazed killers through beast-infested jungles, the Shadow and Phantom hunting equally nefarious creatures through a grim urban netherworld. And if critics of the day generally dismissed it all as lowbrow escapism, the best of those pulps represented a lot more. For example, with the likes of Dashiell Hammett, Raymond Chandler

and Tennessee Williams all setting forth from the pages of pulps, those pages finally gave as much to the modern American novel as a Hemingway or Fitzgerald. (Chandler probably described it best as that literature reflecting "a sharp, aggressive attitude towards life...spare, frugal, hard-boiled...") Then, too, with a full quarter of the American population regularly turning to those crudely cut pages, the pulps did far more than a Henry James or a Stephen Crane to introduce a nation to the sheer joy of reading.

What L. Ron Hubbard wrought in that great pulp kingdom was ultimately just as significant and just as transcendent. "As perfect a piece

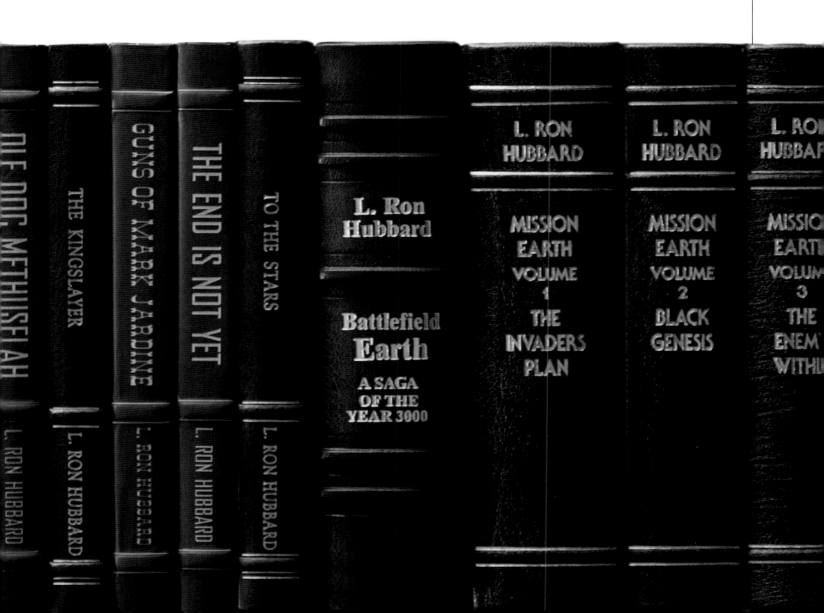

of science fiction as has ever been written," declared Robert Heinlein of the apocalyptic *Final Blackout,* while elsewhere we find that LRH tale of a war without end repeatedly described as surpassing all science fiction offered as of 1940. Representing no less to the realm of modern fantasy is the perennially popular *Fear,* broadly acknowledged as a pillar of all modern horror and, as master of the genre,

exceptional contribution to the genre. Similarly honored was the ten-volume *Mission Earth* series, each topping international bestseller lists in what amounted to a publishing phenomenon and cumulatively earning both the Cosmos 2000 Award from French readers and Italy's Nova Science Fiction Award. Then again, one could cite all L. Ron Hubbard represents as the model author in many a university and all

"...trying harder to make every word live and breathe."—L. Ron Hubbard

Stephen King, proclaimed, one of the few in the genre "which actually merits employment of the overworked adjective 'classic,' as in 'This is a classic tale of creeping, surreal menace and horror.'"

One could say more, particularly regarding the extraordinary critical and popular success of the later LRH. The internationally bestselling *Battlefield Earth: A Saga of the Year 3000,* for example, not only stands as the largest single volume of science fiction to date, but among the most honored. In addition to both the Academy of Science Fiction, Fantasy and Horror Films' Golden Scroll and Saturn Awards, the work earned Italy's Tetradramma d'Oro Award (in recognition of the story's inherent message of peace) and a special Gutenberg Award as an

else he represents to modern fiction as a whole: "one of the most prolific and influential writers of the twentieth century," to quote critic and educator Stephen V. Whaley. But it is finally not the purpose of this publication to merely celebrate the author, L. Ron Hubbard; our purpose is to learn from him.

Among the various essays to follow, LRH makes reference to a certain "professor of short story...[who] knew nothing about the practical end of things." We happen to know that professor was Douglas Bement of George Washington University—apparently well-meaning, but fairly obsessed with all the claptrap of academic criticism, including the intentional foreshadow, the timely *denouement,* the pervasive mood and carefully wrought allegory. As an undergraduate, Ron confesses to learning nothing, while as a later guest at the lectern, he tells of inciting a virtual revolt when defining a viable production rate in terms of a hundred thousand words a month. (So much for the carefully wrought allegory.) But in any case, and for all that is indeed carefully wrought in the LRH short story, he offers none of the Bement verbiage.

The fact is, no one addresses the world of an author with greater candor and authenticity than L. Ron Hubbard. Moreover, his pronouncements are timeless—every bit as pertinent to authorship today as when he originally fought his way into that vibrant pulp jungle. True, the paperback has long replaced the pulp: the advance-against-royalties, the penny-a-word and the mass-market novelette are virtually no more. But the rest remains: the agents and editors, the markets and percentages, the scathing critics, the checkless Fridays, the "trying harder to make every word live and breathe." Then, too, the passion remains unchanged: "to write, write and then write some more. And never to allow weariness, lack of time, noise, or any other thing to throw me off my course."

In addition to instructional essays from his formative years, we include working notes on the shaping of the monumental *Battlefield Earth* and *Mission Earth* and the same again from the crafting of his later screenplays. Also included are incidental remarks on life as a "manuscript factory" and much else following from the statement "Somehow I got started in the writing business." ■

CHAPTER ONE

About the
MANUSCRIPT FACTORY

About the Manuscript Factory

"**I** STARTED OUT WRITING FOR THE PULPS, WRITING THE BEST I knew, writing for every mag on the stands, slanting as well as I could."—L. Ron Hubbard

To which we might add: The earliest of his stories date from the summer of 1933, and a passing residence along the California coast just north of San Diego. He still suffered periodic chills from the touch of malaria contracted through the course of his Puerto Rican Mineralogical Expedition, and would later describe his financial predicament as classically grim—literally down to a last loaf of bread. Then, too, among the first submissions were several western sagas, soundly rejected as lacking authenticity—a particularly frustrating comment given those stories came straight from the heart of his Helena, Montana, home. (While Max Brand, then undisputed king of the Wild West adventure, was actually a failed New York poet by the name of Frederick Schiller Faust, and he churned out his implausible six-shooter tales from the terrace of an Italian villa.)

As Ron further explains, however, with half a million words shotgunned out to a dozen markets, he actually saw sales from the start. The first to see print was a white-knuckled story of Asian intrigue entitled *The Green God*. If the work was not especially memorable—a fairly stock tale of a Western intelligence officer in search of a stolen idol, it is notable on one exceptional count: The young L. Ron Hubbard had, indeed, walked the gloomy streets of Tientsin *and* in the company of a Western intelligence officer—specifically, a Major Ian Macbean of the British Secret Service. Similarly, the young LRH had actually served aboard a working schooner not unlike those described in *The Pearl Pirate,* had actually helped engineer a road through subtropical jungles as described in his highly atmospheric *Sleepy McGee,* while the chilling portrayal of voodoo rites in *Dead Men Kill* had been drawn from genuine adventures on Haiti.

The point, and one he would repeatedly stress:

"You must have raw material. It gives you the edge on the field."

Still, that field was extremely competitive. Notwithstanding

In New York City, circa 1935

THE UNDERWOOD NO. 3: Featuring an early shifting carriage for capitalization, the Underwood served as Ron's first typewriter. The earliest stories from his freshman year at George Washington University bore the stamp of this machine, as did the manuscripts from Encinitas, California, where he initially "started out writing for the pulps, writing the best I knew."

the great pulp appetite—approximately a million stories were said to have been published through the sixty-year pulp reign—the vast majority of those stories were actually authored by some two hundred hard-line professionals. Moreover, at a penny a word, those tales were pounded out pretty quickly. LRH friend and colleague Richard Sale (generally remembered for his "Daffy Dill" series and the Clark Gable vehicle *Strange Cargo*) would later tell of penning a story a day—three thousand words and more, every day. Then there was the legendary Arthur J. Burks, a.k.a. "Mr. Pulps," who regularly topped two million words a year—an astonishing feat for a typist, let alone a creative writer. While if the LRH rate of seventy thousand words a month (eventually a

hundred thousand) seems rather less impressive, one must understand that wordage sprang from but three days a week at his Remington manual.

Yet even from the most accelerated prose comes a sense of something more enduring than the hammering of keys "until I am finger worn to the second joint," as Ron so vividly phrased it. Later critics would speak of a "hard but brittle truth" and point to the work of pulpateer Horace McCoy and all he brought to French Existentialists André Gide and Jean-Paul Sartre. They would also speak of that "unvarnished realism" and point to a Chandler and Hammett who "took murder out of the Venetian vase and dropped it into the alley," as Chandler himself would describe it. Similarly, they would point to an L. Ron Hubbard who was soon to

REMINGTON NOISELESS PORTABLE, A.K.A. "SUPER SEVEN": According to Robert Heinlein, it was upon this Remington Noiseless Portable (en route from New York City by train) that Ron revised his legendary *Fear*. The Heinlein remark is, of course, apocryphal, but Ron's Super Seven most definitely saw a lot of mileage.

accomplish the same for the supernatural novel, lifting it out of an unreal Gothic and weaving it into the fabric of Anytown, USA.

The point here, as LRH so appropriately phrased it, and a point reiterated in one way or another by both Chandler and Hammett:

"If you write insincerely, if you think the lowest pulp can be written insincerely and still sell, then you're in for trouble unless your luck is terribly good. And luck rarely strikes twice."

All this and more is the stuff of Ron's first instructional essay on the business of writing for the pulps. Aptly entitled *The Manuscript Factory*, it dates from late 1935, or his formal admittance into the professional fold as president of New York's American Fiction Guild chapter. His residence stood at the 44th Street Hotel in

Manhattan, augmented with a rented desk from the Wholey Office Equipment Company on Madison Avenue. Notwithstanding the continual clamor of "ten thousand taxi drivers," he continued to work much as before: "plotted the yarn in my sleep, rose and wrote it." Meals were generally taken at Rosoff's, unofficial Guild headquarters and watering hole for the likes of Lester "Doc Savage" Dent and Walter "The Shadow" Gibson. In addition to regular duties—enlisting the New York City coroner to enlighten members on strange forms of murder—Ron's tenure as Guild president was largely devoted to the neophyte author. In particular, he sought their admittance to the Guild in the status of "novice" and otherwise worked to ease their entrance into the stables of

The genres spanned by L. Ron H
included westerns, which have a rem
provocative power and driving i
of action that re-created for mi
readers the sense of the real C

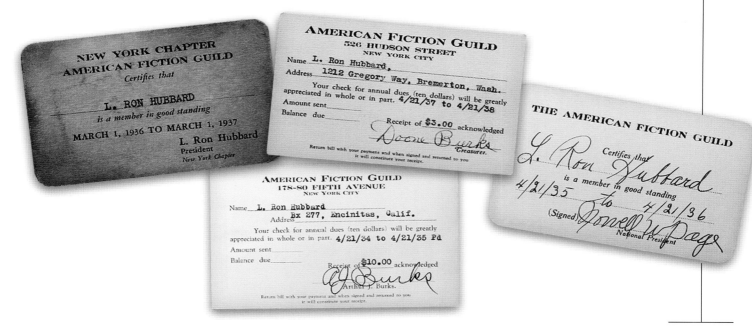

a *Five-Novels Monthly* or a *Thrilling Adventures*. He also passed on more than a few worthy names to his own agent extraordinaire, the wildly eccentric Ed Bodin, who boasted $20,000 in annual sales but still shared an office with a button broker and bill collector. Then, too, we find what is reprinted here for the education of all.

Considering what those "gentlemen of the craft" typically offered in the way of advice, Ron's *Manuscript Factory* is remarkably candid and enlightening. For the fact is the two or three hundred hard-line pulpateers were generally a guarded lot and particularly suspicious of those who would encroach upon their markets. There are accounts—possibly apocryphal, possibly not—of authors who actually came to blows over stolen plot twists. Then again, one hears of raging jealousies over half-a-penny advances in pay. In either case, here is what L. Ron Hubbard initially "learned about this writing business." ■

Above
As American Fiction Guild president, Ron devoted much time in assisting the neophyte author

Below
L. Ron Hubbard, center second row, with members of the New York chapter of the American Fiction Guild, of which he served as president in 1936

Left In San Diego, California, 1929

THE MANUSCRIPT FACTORY

by L. RON HUBBARD

S O YOU WANT TO be a professional.

Or, if you are a professional, you want to make more money. Whichever it is, it's certain that you want to advance your present state to something better and easier and more certain.

Very often I hear gentlemen of the craft referring to writing as the major "insecure" profession. These gentlemen go upon the assumption that the gods of chance are responsible and are wholly accountable for anything which might happen to income, hours or pleasure. In this way, they seek to excuse a laxity in thought and a feeling of unhappy helplessness which many writers carry forever with them.

But when a man says that, then it is certain that he rarely, if ever, takes an accounting of himself and his work, that he has but one yardstick. You are either a writer or you aren't. You either make money or you don't. And all beyond that rests strictly with the gods.

I assure you that a system built up through centuries of commerce is not likely to cease its function just because your income seems to depend upon your imagination. And I assure you that the overworked potence of economics is just as applicable to this business of writing as it is to shipping hogs.

You are a factory. And if you object to the word, then allow me to assure you that it is not a brand, but merely a handy designation which implies nothing of the hack, but which could be given to any classic writer.

Yes, you and I are both factories with the steam hissing and the chimneys belching and the machinery clanging. We manufacture manuscripts, we sell a stable product, we are quite respectable in our business. The big names of the field are nothing more than the name of Standard Oil on gasoline, Ford on a car, or Browning on a machine gun.

And as factories, we can be shut down, opened, have our production decreased, change our product, have production increased. We can work full blast and go broke. We can loaf and make money. Our machinery is the brain and the fingers.

And it is fully as vital that we know ourselves and our products as it is for a manufacturer to know his workmen and his plant.

Few of us do. Most of us sail blithely along and blame everything on chance.

Economics, taken in a small dose, are simple. They have to do with price, cost, supply, demand and labor.

If you were to open up a soap plant, you would be extremely careful about it. That soap plant means your income. And you would hire economists to go over everything with you. If you start writing, ten to one, you merely write and let everything else slide by the boards. But your writing factory, if anything, is more vital than your soap factory. Because if you lose your own machinery, you can never replace it—and you can always buy new rolls, vats and boilers.

The first thing you would do would be to learn the art of making soap. And so, in writing, you must first learn to write. But we will assume that you already know how to write. You are more interested in making money from writing.

It does no good to protest that you write for the art of it. Even the laborer who finds his chief pleasure in his work tries to sell services or products for the best price he can get. Any economist will tell you that.

You are interested in income. In net income. And "net income" is the inflow of satisfaction from economic goods, estimated in money, according to Seligman.

I do not care if you write articles on knitting, children's stories, snappy stories or gag paragraphs, you can still apply this condensed system and make money.

When you first started to write, if you were wise, you wrote anything and everything for everybody and sent it all out. If your quantity was large and your variety wide, then you probably made three or four sales.

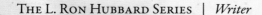

With the field thus narrowed and you had, say, two types of markets to hammer at, you went ahead and wrote for the two. But you did not forget all the other branches you had first aspired to. And now and then you ripped off something out of line and sent it away, and perhaps sold it, and went on with the first two types regardless.

Take my own situation as an example—because I know it better than yours. I started out writing for the pulps, writing the best I knew, writing for every mag on the stands, slanting as well as I could.

I turned out about a half a million words, making sales from the start because of heavy quantity. After a dozen stories were sold, I saw that things weren't quite right. I was working hard and the money was slow.

Now, it so happened that my training had been an engineer's. I leaned toward solid, clean equations rather than guesses, and so I took the list which you must have: stories written, type, wordage, where sent, sold or not.

My list was varied. It included air-war, commercial air, western, western love, detective and adventure.

On the surface, that list said that adventure was my best bet, but when you've dealt with equations long, you never trust them until you have the final result assured.

I reduced everything to a common ground. I took stories written of one type, added up all the wordage and set down the wordage sold. For instance:

DETECTIVE .... 120,000 words written
30,000 words sold

$$\frac{30,000}{120,000} = 25\%$$

ADVENTURE .... 200,000 words written
36,000 words sold

$$\frac{36,000}{200,000} = 18\%$$

13

1933

7/15/33	Tailwind Willies Sportsman Pilot	20 00
4/15/33	Sans Power " "	23 43
8/10/33	Langley Day " "	30 00
8/29/33	Navy Pets Star Suppl.	9 45
10/13/33	The Green God Thrilling Advs.	52 50
12/10/33	Sea Fang Five Novels	250 00
		45 00

Ron's 1933 "Record Book" recording sales of manuscripts, to whom and for how much

According to the sale book, adventure was my standby, but one look at 18 percent versus 25 percent showed me that I had been doing a great deal of work for nothing. At a cent a word, I was getting $0.0018 for adventure and $0.0025 for detective.

A considerable difference. And so I decided to write detectives more than adventures.

I discovered from this same list that, whereby I came from the West and therefore should know my subject, I had still to sell even one western story. I have written none since.

I also found that air-war and commercial air stories were so low that I could no longer afford to write them. And that was strange as I held a pilot's license.

Thus, I was fooled into working my head off for little returns. But things started to pick up after that and I worked less. Mostly I wrote detective stories, with an occasional adventure yarn to keep up the interest.

But the raw materials of my plant were beginning to be exhausted. I had once been a police reporter and I had unconsciously used up all the shelved material I had.

And things started to go bad again, without my knowing why. Thereupon, I took out my books, which I had kept accurately and up to date—as you should do.

Astonishing figures. While detective seemed to be my mainstay, here was the result.

$$\text{DETECTIVE} \dots\dots\dots \frac{95{,}000 \text{ words sold}}{320{,}000 \text{ words written}} = 29.65\%$$

$$\text{ADVENTURE} \dots\dots\dots \frac{21{,}500 \text{ words sold}}{30{,}000 \text{ words written}} = 71.7\%$$

Thus, for every word of detective I wrote I received $0.002965 and for every adventure word $0.00717. A considerable difference. I scratched my head in perplexity until I realized about raw materials.

I had walked some geography, had been at it for years and, thus, my adventure stories were beginning to shine through. Needless to say, I've written few detective stories since then.

About this time, another factor bobbed up. I seemed to be working very, very hard and making very, very little money.

But, according to economics, no one has ever found a direct relation between the value of a product and the quantity of labor it embodies.

A publishing house had just started to pay me a cent a word and I had been writing for their books a long time. I considered them a mainstay among mainstays.

Another house had been taking a novelette a month from me. Twenty thousand words at a time. But most of my work was for the former firm.

Dragging out the accounts, I started to figure up on words written for this and that, getting percentages.

I discovered that the house which bought my novelettes had an average of 88 percent. Very, very high.

And the house for which I wrote the most was buying 37.6 percent of all I wrote for them.

Because the novelette market paid a cent and a quarter and the others a cent, the average pay was: House A, $0.011 for novelettes on every word I wrote for them. House B, $0.00376 for every word I wrote for *them*.

I no longer worried my head about House B. I worked less and made more. I worked hard on those novelettes after that and the satisfaction increased.

That was a turning point. Released from drudgery and terrific quantity and low quality, I began to make money and to climb out of a word grave.

That, you say, is all terribly dull, disgustingly sordid. Writing, you say, is an art. What are you, you want to know, one of these damned hacks?

No, I'm afraid not. No one gets a keener delight out of running off a good piece of work. No one takes any more pride in craftsmanship than I do. No one is trying harder to make every word live and breathe.

But, as I said before, even the laborer who finds his chief pleasure in his work tries to sell services or products for the best price he can get.

> *"The competition is keener in the writing business than in any other. Therefore, when you try to skid by with the gods of chance, you simply fail to make the grade. It's a brutal selective device."*

And that price is not word rate. That price is satisfaction received, measured in money.

You can't go stumbling through darkness and live at this game. Roughly, here is what you face. There are less than two thousand professional writers in the United States. Hundreds of thousands are trying to write—some say millions.

The competition is keener in the writing business than in any other. Therefore, when you try to skid by with the gods of chance, you simply fail to make the grade. It's a brutal selective device. You can beat it if you know your product and how to handle it. You can beat it on only two counts. One has to do with genius and the other with economics. There are very few men who sell and live by their genius only. Therefore, the rest of us have to fall back on a fairly exact science.

If there were two thousand soap plants in the country and a million soap plants trying to make money and you were one of the million, what would you do? Cutting prices, in our analogy, is not possible, nor fruitful in any commerce. Therefore you would tighten up your plant to make every bar count. You wouldn't produce a bar if you knew it would be bad. You'd think about such things as reputation, supply, demand, organization, the plant, type of soap, advertising, sales department, accounting, profit and loss, quality versus quantity, machinery, improvements in product, raw materials and labor employed.

And so it is in writing. We're factories working under terrific competition. We have to produce and sell at low cost and small price.

Labor, according to economics in general, cannot be measured in simple, homogenous units of time such as labor hours. And laborers differ, tasks

differ, in respect to amount and character of training, degree of skill, intelligence and capacity to direct one's work.

That for soap making. That also for writing. And you're a factory whether your stories go to *Saturday Evening Post, Harper's* or an upstart pulp that pays a quarter of a cent on publication. We're all on that common level. We must produce to eat and we must know our production and product down to the ground.

Let us take some of the above-mentioned topics, one by one, and examine them.

Supply and Demand

You must know that the supply of stories is far greater than the demand. Actual figures tell nothing. You have only to stand by the editor and watch him open the morning mail. Stories by the truckload.

One market I know well is publishing five stories a month. Five long novelettes. Dozens come in every week from names which would make you sit up very straight and be very quiet. And only five are published. And if there's a reject from there, you'll work a long time before you'll sell it elsewhere.

That editor buys what the magazine needs, buys the best obtainable stories from the sources she knows to be reliable. She buys impersonally as though she bought soap. The best bar, the sweetest smell, the maker's name. She pays as though she paid for soap, just as impersonally, but many times more dollars.

That situation is repeated through all the magazine ranks. Terrific supply, microscopic demand.

Realize now that every word must be made to count?

Organization and the Plant

Do you have a factory in which to work? Silly question, perhaps, but I know of one writer who wastes his energy like a canary wastes grain just because he has never looked at a house with an eye to an office. He writes in all manner of odd places. Never considers the time he squanders by placing himself where he is accessible. His studio is on top of the garage, he has no light except a feeble electric bulb and yet he has to turn out seventy thousand a month. His nerves are shattered. He is continually going elsewhere to work, wasting time and more time.

Whether the wife or the family likes it or not, when the food comes out of the roller, a writer should have the pick and choice, say what you may. Me? I often take the living room and let the guests sit in the kitchen.

A writer needs good equipment. Quality of work is surprisingly dependent upon the typewriter. One lady I know uses a battered, rented machine which went through the world war, judging by its looks. The ribbon will not reverse. And yet, when spare money comes in, it goes on anything but a typewriter.

Good paper is more essential than writers will admit. Cheap, unmarked paper yellows, brands a manuscript as a reject after a few months, tears easily and creases.

Good typing makes a good impression. I have often wished to God that I had taken a typing course instead of a story writing course far back in the dim past.

Raw Materials

Recently, a lady who once wrote pulp detective stories told me that, since she knew nothing of detective work, she went down to Centre Street and sought information. The detective sergeant there gave her about eight hours of his time. She went through the gallery, the museum, looked at all their equipment and took copious notes.

And the sergeant was much surprised at her coming there at all. He said that in fifteen years, she was the third to come there. And she was the only one who really wanted information. He said that detective stories always made him squirm. He wished the writers would find out what they wrote.

And so it is with almost every line. It is so easy to get good raw materials that most writers consider it quite unnecessary.

Hence the errors which make your yarn unsalable. You wouldn't try to write an article on steel without at least opening an encyclopedia, and yet I'll wager that a fiction story which had steel in it would never occasion the writer a bit of worry or thought.

You must have raw material. It gives you the edge on the field. And so, one tries to get it by honest research. For a few stories, you may have looked far, but for most of your yarns, you took your imagination for the textbook.

After all, you wouldn't try to make soap when you had no oil.

The fact that you write is a passport everywhere. You'll find very few gentlemen refusing to accommodate your curiosity. Men in every and any line are anxious to give a writer all the data he can use because, they reason, their line will therefore be truly represented. You're apt to find more enmity in not examining the facts.

Raw materials are more essential than fancy writing. Know your subject.

Type of Work

It is easy for you to determine the type of story you write best. Nothing is more simple. You merely consult your likes and dislikes.

But that is not the whole question. What do you write and sell best?

A writer tells me that she can write excellent marriage stories, likes to write them and is eternally plagued to do them. But there are few markets for marriage stories. To eat, she takes the next best thing—light love.

My agent makes it a principle never to handle a type of story which does not possess at least five markets. That way he saves himself endless reading and he saves his writers endless wordage. A story should have at least five good markets because what one editor likes, another dislikes and what fits here will not fit there. All due respect to editors, their minds change and their slant is never too iron-bound. They are primarily interested in good stories. Sometimes they are overbought. Sometimes they have need of a certain type which you do not fill. That leaves four editors who may find the desired spot.

While no writer should do work he does not like, he must eat.

Sales Department

If you had a warehouse filled with sweet-smelling soap and you were unable to sell it, what would you do? You would hire a man who could. And if your business was manufacturing soap, your selling could not wholly be done by yourself. It's too much to ask. This selling is highly complex, very expensive.

Therefore, instead of wasting your valuable manufacturing time peddling your own manuscripts, why not let another handle the selling for you?

There's more to selling than knowing markets. The salesman should be in constant contact with the buyer. A writer cannot be in constant contact with his editors. It would cost money. Luncheons, cigars, all the rest. An agent takes care of all that and the cost is split up among his writers so that no one of them feels the burden too heavily.

An agent, if he is good, sells more than his ten percent extra. And he acts as a buffer between you and the postman. Nothing is more terrible than the brown envelope in the box. It's likely to kill the day. You're likely to file the story and forget it. But the agent merely sends the yarn out again, and when it comes home, out again it goes. He worries and doesn't tell you until you hold the check in your hand.

The collaborating agent and the critic have no place here. They are advisers and doctors. Your sales department should really have no function except selling—and perhaps when a market is going sour, forward a few editorial comments without any added by your agent. This tends for high morale and a writer's morale must always be high. When we started, we assumed that you already could write.

By all means, get an agent. And if you get one and he is no good to you, ditch him and try another. There are plenty of good agents. And they are worth far more than 10 percent.

Advertising

Your agent is your advertising department. He can tell the editor things which you, out of modesty, cannot. He can keep you in the minds of the men who count.

But a writer is his own walking advertisement. His reputation is his own making. His actions count for more than his stories. His reliability is hard won and, when won, is often the deciding factor in a sale. Editors must know you can produce, that you are earnest in your attempt to work with them.

To show what actions can do, one writer recently made it a habit to bait an editor as he went out to lunch. This writer met this editor every day, forced his company on the editor and then, when they were eating, the writer would haul out synopsis after synopsis. The answer is, the writer doesn't work there anymore.

If a check is due, several writers I know haunt the office. It fails to hurry the check and it often puts an end to the contact when overdone. Many harry their editors for early decisions, make themselves nuisances in the office. Soon they stop selling there. Others always have a sob story handy.

Sob stories are pretty well taboo. It's hitting below the belt. And sob stories from writer to writer are awful. One man I know has wrecked his friendship with his formerly closest companions simply because he couldn't keep his troubles to himself. It's actually hurt his sales. You see, he makes more money than anyone I know and he can't live on it. Ye gods, ALL of us have troubles, but few professionals use them to get checks or sympathy.

Reputation is everything.

It does not hurt to do extra work for an editor. Such as department letters. Check it off to advertising. Answer all mail. Do a book for advertising. Write articles. Your name is your trademark. The better known, the better sales.

Quality versus Quantity

I maintain that there is a medium ground for quantity and quality. One goes up, the other comes down.

The ground is your own finding. You know your best wordage and your best work. If you don't keep track of both, you should.

Write too little and your facility departs. Write too much and your quality drops. My own best wordage is seventy thousand a month. I make money at that, sell in the upper percentage brackets. But let me do twenty thousand in a month and I feel like an old machine trying to turn over just once more before it expires. Let me do a hundred thousand in a month and I'm in possession of several piles of tripe.

The economic balance is something of your own finding. But it takes figures to find it. One month, when I was used to doing a hundred thousand per, I was stricken with some vague illness which caused great pain and sent me to bed.

For a week I did nothing. Then, in the next, I laid there and thought about stories. My average, so I thought, was shot to the devil. Toward the last of the month, I had a small table made and, sitting up in bed, wrote a ten thousand worder and two twenty thousand worders. That was all the work I did. I sold every word and made more in eight days than I had in any previous month.

That taught me that there must be some mean of average. I found it and the wage has stayed up. There is no use keeping the factory staff standing by and the machinery running when you have no raw material.

You can't sit down and stare at keys and wish you could write and swear at your low average for the month. If you can't write that day, for God's sakes don't write. The chances are, when tomorrow arrives, and you've spent the yesterday groaning and doing nothing, you'll be as mentally sterile as before.

Forget what you read about having to work so many hours every day. No writer I know has regular office hours. When you can't write, when it's raining and the kid's crying, go see a movie, go talk to a cop, go dig up a book of fairy stories. But don't sweat inactively over a mill. You're just keeping the staff standing by and the machinery running, cutting into your overhead and putting out nothing. You're costing yourself money.

Come back when you're fresh and work like hell. Two in the morning, noon, eight at night, work if you feel like it and be damned to the noise you make. After all, the people who have to hear you are probably fed by you and if they can't stand it, let them do the supporting. I take sprees of working at night and then sleep late into the day. Once in the country, farmers baited me every day with that unforgivable late slumber. It didn't worry me so much after I remembered that I made in a month what they made in a year. They think all writers are crazy. Take the writer's license and make the best of it.

But don't pretend to temperament. It really doesn't exist. Irritation does and is to be scrupulously avoided.

When all the arty scribblers (who made no money) talked to a young lady and told her that they could not write unless they were near the mountains, or unless they had the room a certain temperature, or unless they were served tea every half hour, the young lady said with sober mien, "Me? Oh, I can never write unless I'm in a balloon or in the Pacific Ocean."

One thing to remember: It seems to work out that your writing machine can stand just so much. After that the brain refuses to hand out plots and ideas.

It's like getting a big contract to sell your soap to the navy. You make bad soap, ruin the vats with a strong ingredient and let the finer machinery rust away in its uselessness. Then, when the navy soap contract ceases to supply the coffee and cakes, you discover that the plant is worthless for any other kind of product.

Such is the case of the writer who sees a big living in cheap fiction, turns it out to the expense of his vitality and, finally, years before his time, discovers that he is through. Only one writer of my acquaintance can keep a high word output. He is the exception and he is not burning himself out. He is built that way.

> *"If you write insincerely, if you think the lowest pulp can be written insincerely and still sell, then you're in for trouble unless your luck is terribly good. And luck rarely strikes twice."*

But the rest of us shy away from too cheap a brand. We know that an advanced wage will only find us spending more. Soon, when the target for our unworthy efforts is taken down, we discover that we are unable to write anything else. That's what's meant by a rut.

As soon as you start turning out stories which you do not respect, as soon as you start turning them out wholesale over a period of time, as soon as your wordage gets out of control, then look for lean years.

To get anywhere at all in the business, you should turn out the best that's in you and keep turning it out. You'll never succeed in pulp unless you do, much less in the slicks.

If you start at the lowest rung, do the best job of which you are capable. Your product, according to economic law, will do the raising for you. Man is not paid for the amount of work in labor-hours, he is paid for the quality of that work.

Improvement of Product

With experience, your stories should improve. If they do not, then you yourself are not advancing. It's impossible not to advance, it's impossible to stand still. You must move, and you must slide back.

Take a story published a month ago, written six months ago. Read it over. If it seems to you that you could have done better, that you are doing better, you can sit back with a feline smile and be secure in the knowledge that you are coming up. Then sit forward and see to it that you do.

If you write insincerely, if you think the lowest pulp can be written insincerely and still sell, then you're in for trouble unless your luck is terribly good. And luck rarely strikes twice. Write sincerely and you are certain to write better and better.

So much for making soap and writing. All this is merely my own findings in an upward trail through the rough paper magazines. I have tested these things and found them to be true and if someone had handed them to me a few years ago, I would have saved myself a great deal of worry and more bills would have been paid.

Once, a professor of short story in a university gave me a course because I was bored with being an engineer. The course did not help much outside of the practice in writing. Recently I heard that professor address the radio audience on the subject "This Business of Writing." It was not until then that I realized how much a writer had to learn. He knew nothing about the practical end of things and I told him so. He made me give a lecture to his class and they did not believe me.

But none of them, like you and I, have to make the bread and butter someway in this world. They had never realized that competition and business economics had any place whatever in the writing world. They were complacent in some intangible, ignorant quality they branded ART. They did not know, and perhaps will someday find out, that art means, simply:

"The employment of means to the accomplishment of some end; the skillful application and adaptation to some purpose or use of knowledge or power acquired from Nature, especially in the production of beauty as in sculpture, etc.; a system of rules and established methods to facilitate the performance of certain actions."

They saw nothing praiseworthy in work well done. They had their hearts fixed on some goal even they did not understand. To them, writing was not a supreme source of expression, not a means of entertaining, not a means of living and enjoying work while one lived. If you wrote for a living, they branded you a hack. But they will never write.

Poor fools, they haven't the stamina, the courage, the intelligence, the knowledge of life's necessity, the mental capacity to realize that whatever you do in this life you must do well and that whatever talent you have is expressly given you to provide your food and your comfort.

My writing is not a game. It is a business, a hardheaded enterprise which fails only when I fail, which provides me with an energy outlet I need, which gives me the house I live in, which lets me keep my wife and boy. I am a manuscript factory but *not*—and damn those who so intimate it—an insincere hack, peddling verbal belly-wash with my tongue in my cheek. And I eat only so long as my factory runs economically, only so long as I remember the things I have learned about this writing *business.*

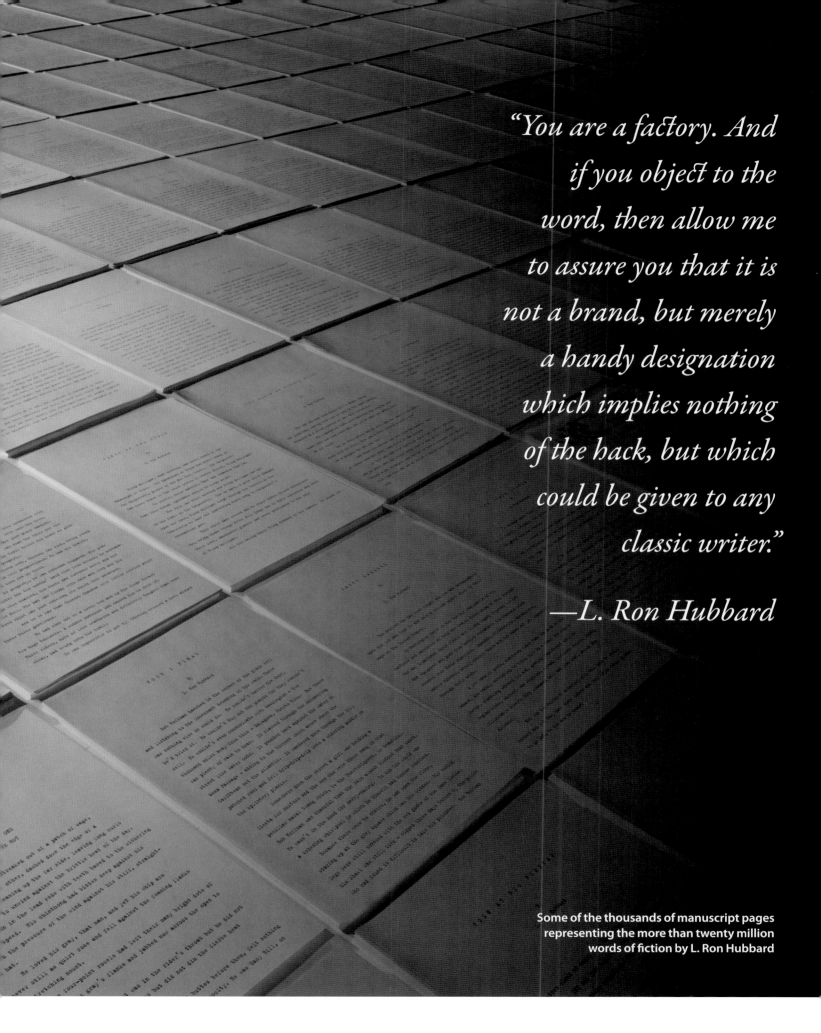

"You are a factory. And if you object to the word, then allow me to assure you that it is not a brand, but merely a handy designation which implies nothing of the hack, but which could be given to any classic writer."

—L. Ron Hubbard

Some of the thousands of manuscript pages representing the more than twenty million words of fiction by L. Ron Hubbard

CHAPTER TWO

The Art of
WRITING

The Art of
Writing

NOTWITHSTANDING HIS HABITUAL WARNING ON THE perils of a New York residence—"Chances are a hundred to one that you won't be able to turn out a line when the subway begins to saw into your nerves"—by February 1936 Ron had taken a basement apartment in that perennial artistic enclave, Greenwich Village.

By all accounts, it was an interesting place, with an ancient piano in the sitting room and a fresco of pink cherubs (appropriately peeking from clouds) on the ceiling. As we shall see, it was also routinely filled with some fairly interesting characters.

There are dozens of telling anecdotes from Ron's stay in his King Street apartment: the afternoon he took control of a speeding subway in the name of research, the evening he slipped on an old tweed jacket and a porkpie hat for a black-tie reception at the Museum of Modern Art's first Picasso exhibition, the Paul Ernst mystery parties where guests were required

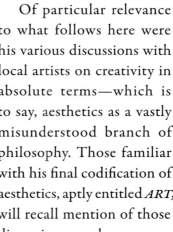

to solve a mock murder and talk of dastardly deeds finally grew so heated two neighboring matrons actually telephoned the police.

Of particular relevance to what follows here were his various discussions with local artists on creativity in absolute terms—which is to say, aesthetics as a vastly misunderstood branch of philosophy. Those familiar with his final codification of aesthetics, aptly entitled *ART,* will recall mention of those discussions, as when:

"I used to buy breakfasts for Greenwich Village artists (which they ate hungrily, only stopping between bites to deplore my commercialism and

Left
This charcoal sketch of a twenty-five-year-old L. Ron Hubbard by friend and artist Richard Albright hung above the editor's desk at *Five-Novels Monthly*

Left In New York City, 1936: a Pulp Fiction King in the heyday of the pulps

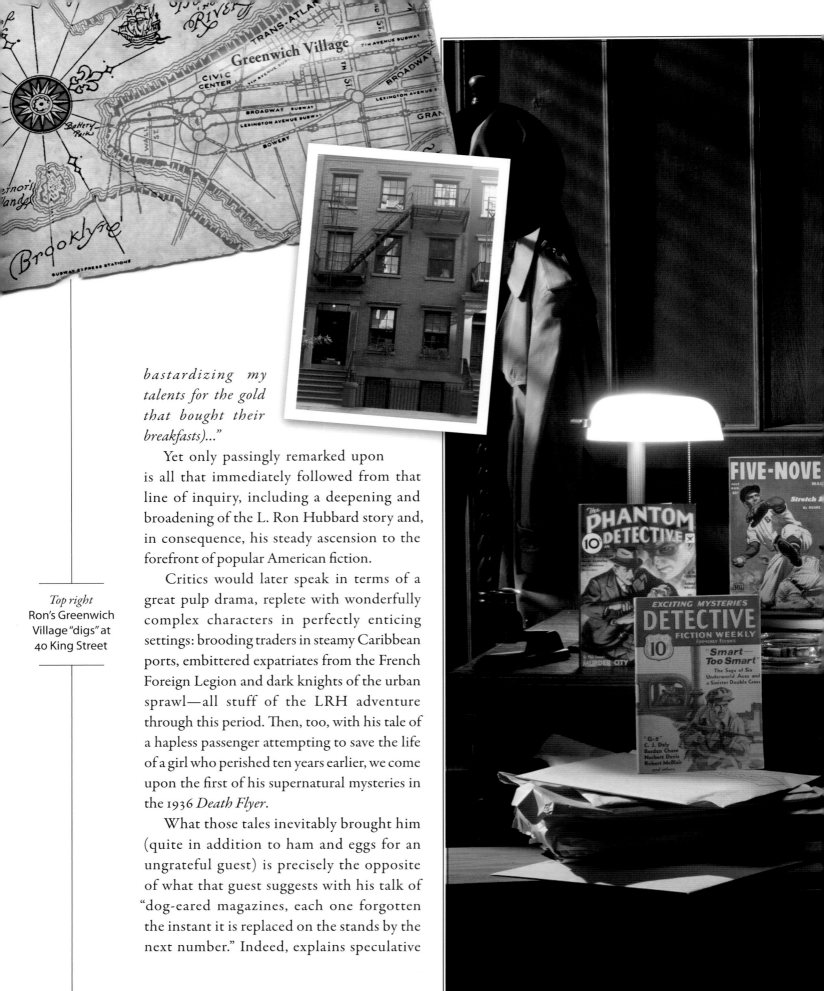

bastardizing my talents for the gold that bought their breakfasts)…"

Yet only passingly remarked upon is all that immediately followed from that line of inquiry, including a deepening and broadening of the L. Ron Hubbard story and, in consequence, his steady ascension to the forefront of popular American fiction.

Critics would later speak in terms of a great pulp drama, replete with wonderfully complex characters in perfectly enticing settings: brooding traders in steamy Caribbean ports, embittered expatriates from the French Foreign Legion and dark knights of the urban sprawl—all stuff of the LRH adventure through this period. Then, too, with his tale of a hapless passenger attempting to save the life of a girl who perished ten years earlier, we come upon the first of his supernatural mysteries in the 1936 *Death Flyer*.

What those tales inevitably brought him (quite in addition to ham and eggs for an ungrateful guest) is precisely the opposite of what that guest suggests with his talk of "dog-eared magazines, each one forgotten the instant it is replaced on the stands by the next number." Indeed, explains speculative

Top right
Ron's Greenwich Village "digs" at 40 King Street

Through his many detective and mystery novels readers experienced the hard-edged reality of police and crime

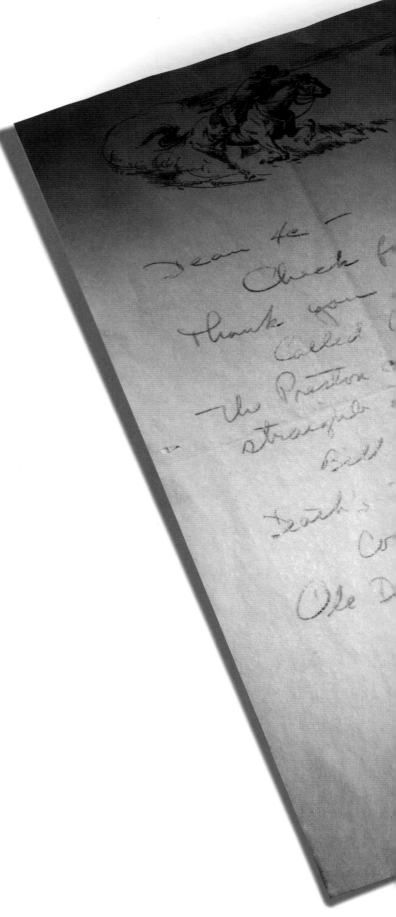

fiction master Frederik Pohl, "The instant Ron's stories appeared on the newsstands, they were part of every fan's cultural heritage." Moreover, the fact those fans included "vapid stenogs...garbage collectors and housemaids"—to cite another stock gibe—is very much to the point of all L. Ron Hubbard represented as of 1936 and, for that matter, what the pulps in general represented as a literary force across the whole of American society.

Finally, we might also consider this: When Ron speaks of an invitation to lecture on "the writing and marketing of short stories," he is referencing his eventual talks at Harvard University, while to appreciate his search for a central truth with which to explain the whole of this writing business "in one grand sweep," one need only turn to the pages of *ART*. ∎

"A writer needs good equipment," including this collection of LRH ballpoint and fountain pens

L. Ron Hubbard

ART VS. EATS

by L. RON HUBBARD

IT WAS MIDNIGHT IN the Village—or maybe three or four. The long-haired exponent of the moderns stabbed a slab of ham and somehow navigated the torturous course through uncombed shoals and to his mouth. He pointed his fork at me.

"But it's tripe! You know it's tripe. You aren't creating anything. You are taking a predetermined plot and garnishing it to suit the puerile taste of fatuous editors. You are shoveling out words as though they were so many beans. Ugh!" And he speared some scrambled eggs.

"My wares are read anyway," said I with wicked malice.

"Read! By whom, pray tell? Taxi drivers and whitewings and vapid stenogs! By garbage collectors and housemaids…"

"And doctors and lawyers and merchants and thieves," I snapped.

"Why not? But what of it?" He emptied his fork into his bottomless cavern and again waved it before my nose. "What of it, I say? You'll end up your days by never writing anything truly great. All you'll have to show for it is a stack of dog-eared magazines, each one forgotten the instant it is replaced on the stands by the next number."

"Is there anything wrong with that?" I said. "Is it so different to lay away magazines than to stow unpublished manuscripts? When it comes to that, my pro-nothing friend, I think it far better to have been read and forgotten than never to have been read at all."

"You dissemble. At least I am earnest. At least I am striving to write something truly great. At least my wares are not beneath my dignity and if those few I have published went unpaid, they at least added their small bit to the true literature of the day. You fictioneers make my hair crawl. You prostitute a God-given gift for the sake of your stomachs. Mark my words," he said, ominously striving to put out my eyes with his useful fork, "you will live to regret it."

At the time I was quite amused, for it was I who paid for that ration of ham and eggs he had so manfully mauled. For a long time afterwards I related the story to my brethren amid much applause. It was so funny, you see, for this shaggy half-bake to berate the source of the money which had paid for his much-needed meal. But through the din of laughter, there still hovered a small doubt. What he had said was perfectly true. In fact it was so true that I was made very uneasy. To write millions and millions of words for the magazines was wonderful from a financial standpoint. But money isn't everything—or is it?

"I think it far better to have been read and forgotten than never to have been read at all."

Now it so happens that this argument started long before two of the Pharaoh's chief poets fanned it into the raging flame which has carried it so far down the ages. On one hand, there is the fellow who consoles himself with the thought that his work, unread, is too great; and on the other, the man who says that though his work is not great, it is widely read.

In such a way do we all maunder. If we write "trash," we apologize for it. If we write "art," we bellicosely defend our right to starve. In such a way do all writers put themselves on the tilt field with their resulting wounds. Few indeed are the fellows who feel neither one way or the other about it.

This argument of art vs. eats is without foundation. It is a chimera. According to Voltaire, if one must argue, one must define his terms and, certainly, it is impossible to draw a line between art and trash—for where one ends and the other begins is wholly dependent upon the taste of the man who makes the distinction.

Unless, then, it is possible to discover some generality whereby these matters can be reconciled, we will continue to stumble and stagger and apologize.

Quite accidentally I discovered what appears to be such a generality. Occasionally, in this business of writing, a fellow is called upon to stand up before aspirants to the profession and utter magic words. Rarely are the words very magic; usually the writer states that it is a fine business, that editors read manuscripts and that one has to produce to sell. Beyond that the wise speaker never ventures—for he would find himself as lonely as an eagle in the blue so far as understanding is concerned. Unless one has experienced editorial reactions, he cannot understand them. Unless one has been confronted with the woes of technique in their most Inquisitorial form, he cannot discourse upon relative merits. Unless one has a rather mysterious gift in the first place, he cannot write at all. And so it goes.

But on this one particular occasion I was confronted with the epitome of impossibility. In so many words, it was requested that I "talk for forty-five minutes and tell all about the writing and marketing of short stories." And as one could talk for forty-five years without getting deeper than the surface of the subject, the cue was for laughter. Anytime men find themselves confronted with impossibles, they laugh.

Still, the thing was a challenge. To tell *all* about the writing and selling of short stories in forty-five minutes would be an alp to climb. And that I refused to climb it irked me. I dislike the acknowledgment of impossibilities. It couldn't be done and it never had been done and it never would be done...unless I could figure out some generality which would cover the whole subject in one grand sweep.

CHAPTER THREE

Notes on
RESEARCH

Notes on
Research

WITH HIS CONTINUED ADVANCE TO THE FOREFRONT OF popular fiction, Ron found himself increasingly pressed for instructional lectures and articles—particularly those articles "in which there was a great deal of sound advice about writing and a number of examples," as he so simply described it. Among other topics eventually considered were the rarely discussed editorial canons: "The heroine must always be as pure as snowdrifts, unsullied, unsoiled, and the greatest worry is about the intentions of the big, bad, sneering, leering, rasping, grating, snarling villain." Then again, we find him offering a few choice remarks on the consequences of ignoring canons: "What courage it takes to break free! You stare at a vision of an empty cupboard. You seem to feel your toes peeping through your shoes, you already listen to the angry words of the landlord as he helps the sheriff toss your writing desk out into the street."

Of particular stress through LRH instructional articles, however, was the never-ending business of research.

The matter is not as obvious as one might imagine, and what Ron addresses has rarely been so plainly stated—namely, the actual process of conceiving a story. Of course, the dozen or more periodicals aimed at would-be wordsmiths of the day were forever offering "tips to inspire." The most interesting, if only as a curiosity, was the Plot Genie. Described as an "infallible" aid to the plotting of stories, the mail-order contraption featured two cardboard wheels with every conceivable literary contrivance matched with every conceivable stock character, as in: the rancher's daughter enraptured with the lonesome drifter, or the disinherited stepson on the trail of lost treasure. Yet having plotted "three infallibles from that Genie," Ron explained, "I hated myself for days and days."

What he instead provides is the actual stuff of literary grist—and not merely for that great pulp mill. For example, when LRH speaks of the "slim, forgotten fact," he is actually touching upon a critical element in much of what we

Amidst the Washington State wilderness where he authored so many of his greatest adventures

> "Mr. Hubbard has reversed a time-honored formula and has given a thriller to which, at the end of every chapter or so, another paleface bites the dust... an enthusiasm, even a freshness and sparkle, decidedly rare in this type of romance."
> — New York Times Book Review

LEFT: *Buckskin Brigades,* original edition, 1937   **RIGHT:** Subsequent editions of what has become a perennial classic and repeated bestseller through ensuing decades

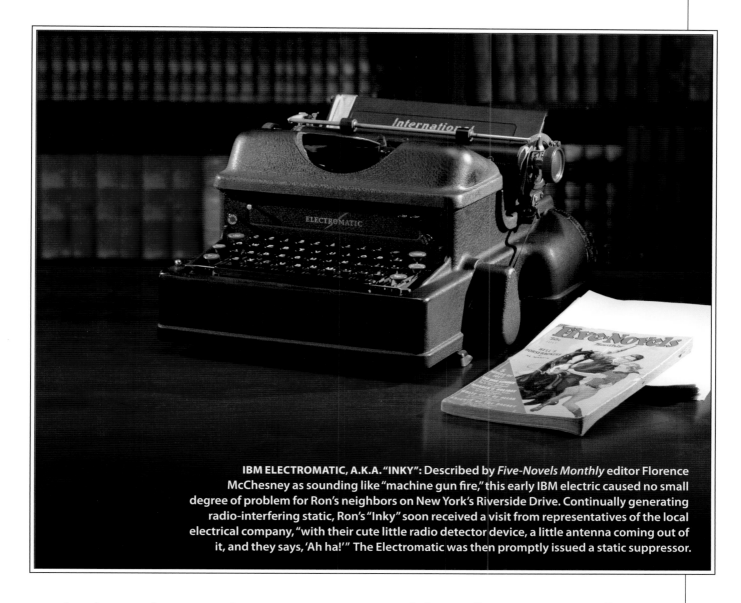

IBM ELECTROMATIC, A.K.A. "INKY": Described by *Five-Novels Monthly* editor Florence McChesney as sounding like "machine gun fire," this early IBM electric caused no small degree of problem for Ron's neighbors on New York's Riverside Drive. Continually generating radio-interfering static, Ron's "Inky" soon received a visit from representatives of the local electrical company, "with their cute little radio detector device, a little antenna coming out of it, and they says, 'Ah ha!'" The Electromatic was then promptly issued a static suppressor.

regard as the most fascinating of stories, e.g., the slim, forgotten history of Alexander Selkirk, inspiration for Daniel Defoe's *The Adventures of Robinson Crusoe*. Those works discussed here, as following from Ron's own examination of the slim and forgotten, are just as engaging.

The first, his "decidedly rare" and accurate portrayal of the Blackfeet, *Buckskin Brigades,* has enjoyed a long and respected history of reprint and review. The work has further received much acclaim from the Blackfeet themselves, whom a young Ron had known from the Montana of his youth and his ceremonial induction as a tribal blood brother at the age of six. Likewise memorable was his impelling adventure with Admiral Nelson on the Nile, *Mr. Tidwell, Gunner.*

By way of a few ancillary notes: The Norvell Page encountered among the New York City Library stacks was none other than Norvell "The Spider" Page, occasionally glimpsed through the Manhattan streets in a black cloak and sloping fedora—rather like his menacing hero. Those stories concerning the world's most dangerous professions were eventually known as the "Hell Job" series and appeared in that original and most respected of all pulp periodicals, *Argosy*. In addition to what Ron relates on the shaping of *Test Pilot,* he would elsewhere describe scaling rooftops with steeplejacks, plunging into a dark and chilled Puget Sound with navy divers and rolling bone-crushing logs with lumberjacks—all in the name of a continuing "search for research." ∎

The authenticity and perceptions in
L. Ron Hubbard's adventure stories are
drawn from his extensive travels and
broad cultural research. His literature
is part of an intensely and genuinely
American idiom of literary expression
and thought. His influence has stayed
with us and does now, perhaps even
more forcefully, shaping the direction
of things to come. Between 1934 and
1950, L. Ron Hubbard wrote more than
fifteen million words of fiction in some
two hundred classic publications. To
span the many genres for which he
wrote, he employed more than two
dozen pseudonyms, some of which are
Winchester Remington Colt, Lt. Jonathan
Daly, Capt. Charles Gordon, Bernard
Hubbel, Michael Keith, Rene Lafayette,
Legionnaire 148, Legionnaire 14830, Ken
Martin, Scott Morgan, Lt. Scott Morgan,
Kurt von Rachen, Barry Randolph, Capt.
Humbert Reynolds and John Seabrook.

SEARCH FOR RESEARCH

by L. RON HUBBARD

ALL OF US WANT to sell more stories and write better ones. It is hard to believe that there exists a writer with soul so dead that he would not. But, from careful observation, I have come to the heartbreaking conclusion that while writers usually *want* to do this, they generally fail to try.

Writers are the laziest people on earth. And I know I'm the laziest writer. In common with the rest of the profession, I am always searching for the magic lamp which will shoot my stories genie-like into full bloom without the least effort on my part.

This is pure idiocy on my part as I have long ago found this magic lamp, but not until a couple years ago did I break it out and use the brass polish to discover that it was solid gold.

This lamp was so cobwebby and careworn that I am sure most of us have not looked very long at it in spite of its extreme age and in spite of the fact that it is eternally being called to our attention.

The name of this magic lamp is RESEARCH.

Ah, do I hear a chorus of sighs? Do I hear, "Hubbard is going to spring that old gag again." "What, another article on research? I thought LRH knew better."

In defense, I instantly protest that I am neither the discoverer nor the sole exploiter of research. But I do believe that I have found an entirely new slant upon an ancient object.

In Tacoma, a few months ago, I heard a writer sighing that he washavingahelluvatimegettingplots. This acute writing disease had eaten deeply into his sleep and bankbook. It had made him so alert that he was ruined as a conversationalist, acting, as he did, like an idea sponge. Hanging on and hoping, but knowing that no ideas could possibly come his way.

As usual, I injected my thoughts into his plight—a habit which is bad and thankless.

I said, "Here's an idea. Why not go out and dig around in the old files at the library and the capitol at Olympia and find out everything you can on the subject of branding? There should be a lot of stories there."

He raised one eye and leered, "What? Do all that work for a cent and a half a word?"

And just to drive the idea home, I might remark that one day I happened into the New York Public Library. Crossing the file room, I slammed into a heavy bulk and ricocheted back to discover I had walked straight into Norvell Page and he into me.

I gaped. "Page!"

"Hubbard!" he whispered in awed tones.

Solemnly we shook each other by the hand.

CHORUS: Well, this is the first time I ever saw a writer in a library!

These two instances should serve to illustrate the fact that research does not rhyme with writer no matter what kind of mill you pound.

> "Research is a habit which is only acquired by sheer force of will. The easy thing to do is guess at the facts—so thinks the writer. When, as a matter of facts, the easy thing to do is go find the facts if you have to tear a town to pieces."

Research is a habit which is only acquired by sheer force of will. The easy thing to do is guess at the facts—so thinks the writer. When, as a matter of facts, the easy thing to do is go *find* the facts if you have to tear a town to pieces.

Witness what happened last summer.

Staring me in the face were a stack of dangerous-profession stories which have since appeared in *Argosy*. At that time they were no more than started and I sighed to see them stretching forth so endlessly.

I chose *Test Pilot* as the next on the list and started to plot it. I thought I knew my aviation because the Department of Commerce tells me so. Blithely, thinking this was easy, I started in upon a highly technical story without knowing the least thing about that branch of flying—never having been a test pilot.

For one week I stewed over the plot. For another week I broiled myself in the scorching heat of my self-accusation. Two weeks and nothing written.

Was I losing money fast!

There wasn't anything for it then. I had to find out something about test pilots.

Across the bay from my place in Seattle is the Boeing plant. At the Boeing plant there would be test pilots. I had to go!

And all for a cent and a half a word.

I went. Egtvedt, the Boeing president, was so startled to see a real live writer in the place that he almost talked himself hoarse.

Minshall, the chief engineer, was so astounded at my ignorance that he hauled me through the plant until I had bunions the size of onions.

I sighed.

All for a cent and a half a word!

I went home.

About that time it occurred to me that I used to write a lot for the *Sportsman Pilot* and as long as I had the dope and data, I might as well fix the details in my head by writing them an article.

That done, I suddenly saw a fine plot for my *Argosy* yarn and wrote that in a matter of a day and a half.

Two months went by. Arthur Lawson came in as editor of Dell and promptly remembered *Test Pilot* in *Argosy* and demanded a story along similar lines.

In two days I wrote that.

A month after that, Florence McChesney decided that she needed a twenty-thousand-word flying story.

"Test Pilot," says I, "do your stuff!"

Each and every one of those yarns sold first crack out. Article for the *Sportsman Pilot,* short for *Argosy,* short for *War Birds,* twenty-thousand worder for *Five Novels.*

One day of research = several hundred bucks in stories.

This naturally made me think things over and, not being quite as foolish as editors think writers are, I added up the account book and promptly went to work. Thus, the moral is yet to come.

On the dangerous-profession stories which followed, I almost lost my life and broke my neck trying to make them authentic. On each one I kept a complete list of notes and a list of plots which occurred to me at the time. There is

> *"I wanted information and nothing else. I wanted to know how the people used to think here, how the land lay there. Given one slim fact for a background, I have found it easy to take off down the channel of research and canal-boat out a cargo of stories."*

enough writing material in that file to last me at least a year. It is the finest kind of copy because it is risky in the extreme, full of drama and high tension. I haven't any fears about mentioning this as any writer who is crazy enough to go down in diving suits and up in spar trees deserves all the help he can get.

But research does not end there and that is not the point of this article.

A short time ago I began to search for research on the theory that if I could get a glimmering of anything lying beyond a certain horizon, I could go deep enough to find an excellent story.

I stopped doing what I used to do. There was a time when I expected a story to blaze up and scorch me all of its own accord. I have found, however, that there is a premium on divine fire and it is not very bright when used by a pulpateer. This gentleman has to write an immortal story about once every three days to keep eating.

On this plan I began to read exhaustively in old technical books, ancient travel books, forgotten literature. But not with the idea of cribbing. I wanted information and nothing else. I wanted to know how the people used to think here, how the land lay there. Given one slim fact for a background, I have found it easy to take off down the channel of research and canal-boat out a cargo of stories.

In other words, I have no use for an obvious story idea as laid out in *Popular Mechanics* or *Forensic Medicine*. I want one slim, forgotten fact. From there a man can go anywhere and the story is very likely to prove unusual.

In one old volume, for instance, I discovered that there was such a thing as a schoolmaster aboard Nelson's ships of the line.

That was a weird one. Why should Nelson want a schoolmaster?

Answer: Midshipmen.

When did this occur?

Answer: The Napoleonic Wars.

Ah, now we'll find out how those old ships looked. We'll discover how they fought, what they did.

And there was the schoolmaster during battle. Where? In the "cockpit" helping hack off arms and legs.

Next lead indicated: Surgery during the Napoleonic Wars.

Wild guess in another allied field: Gunnery.

Again: Nelson.

A battle: On the Nile.

A ship or something strange about this battle: *L'Orient,* monster French flagship which mysteriously caught fire and blew up, throwing the weight of guns to Nelson.

Incidental discovery: "The Boy Stood on the Burning Deck" was written about the son of *L'Orient*'s skipper.

Back to midshipmen, the King's Letter Boys: They were hell on wheels, arrogant, ghastly urchins being trained as officers.

And with all this under my mental belt, I girded up my mental loins. Complete after a few days of search, I had *Mr. Tidwell, Gunner,* which appeared in *Adventure.*

All that because I chanced to find there was a schoolmaster aboard Nelson's ships of the line.

This is now happening right along because I haven't let the idea slide as my laziness dictated I should.

The final coup d'état arrived last winter.

Boredom had settled heavily upon me and I sat one evening staring vacantly at a shelf of books. They were most monotonous. Whole sets stretched out along the shelves with very little change in color or size. This annoyed me and I bent forward and took one out just to relieve the regularity.

It proved to be Washington Irving's *Astoria,* his famous epic of the fur-trading days.

It had never been brought home to me that Irving had written such a book and to find out why, I promptly started to read it. The result was, of course, a fur-trading story. But the method of arriving at this story was so indirect that it merits a glance.

Irving only served to call to my attention that I was out in the fur-trading Northwest and that I had certainly better take advantage of the history of the place.

I roved around, found very little because I had no direct starting point. I went to the *Encyclopaedia Britannica* to discover a bibliography of such source books and started out again to ferret them out.

All these books were contemporary with fur-trading days, all of them written, of course, by white men. But everywhere I kept tripping across the phrases, "The Warlike Blackfeet," "The Bloodthirsty Blackfeet."

This finally penetrated my thick skull. I did not like it because I thought I knew something about the Blackfeet.

Were they as bad as they were represented?

Into the records. The real records. Into Alexander Henry's journal. Into this and out of that until I had a stack of material higher than my desk.

And then I capped the climax by locating a young chap in Seattle who happens to be a blood brother of the Blackfeet. Lewis and Clark's Journal contained about five pages concerning the circumstances which surrounded the killing of a Blackfoot brave by Lewis.

The way this suddenly shot down the groove is remarkable to remember. The Hudson's Bay Company, the Nor'Westers, the Blackfeet, John Jacob Astor... The story pieces dovetailed with a click.

Coupled with years of experience in the northwest, these hundred sources jibed to make the story.

The result was *Buckskin Brigades,* a novel being put out this summer by Macaulay.

Buckskin Brigades came to life because I happened to be bored enough one evening to sit and stare at a line of books on a shelf.

This account of researching is not complete unless I mention a certain dogging phobia I have and which I suspect is deeply rooted in most of us.

H. Bedford Jones mentioned it long ago and I did not believe him at the time. But after rolling stacks of it into the mags, I know that B-J was right as a check.

He said that it was hard for a person to write about the things he knew best.

This gives rise to an ancient argument which says pro and con that a writer should write about the things he knows.

Witnesseth: I was born and raised in the West and yet it was not until last year that I sold a couple westerns. And I only sold those because somebody said I couldn't.

Know ye: The Caribbean countries know me as El Colorado and yet the only Caribbean stories I can write are about those countries which I have touched so briefly that I have only the vaguest knowledge of them and am therefore forced to depend upon researching the books and maps for my facts.

Hear ye: I wrote fine Hollywood stories until I came down here and worked in pictures. I wrote one while here and the editor slammed it back as a total loss.

THE
JOURNALS
OF THE EXPEDITION

UNDER THE COMMAND OF
Capts. LEWIS and CLARK

to the sources of the MISSOURI, thence across
the ROCKY MOUNTAINS and down
the river COLUMBIA to the PACIFIC Ocean,
performed during the YEARS 1804–5–6
by ORDER of the Government of the United States.

EDITED BY
NICHOLAS BIDDLE
with an introduction by JOHN BAKELESS

VOLUME ONE

There are only a few exceptions to this. I have been able to cash in heavily upon my knowledge of North China because the place appealed to me as the last word in savage, romantic lore. The last exception seems to be flying stories, though after flying a ship, I can't write an aviation story for a month.

The final proof of this assertation came in connection with my Marine Corps stories. Most of my life I have been associated with the Corps one way or another in various parts of the world and I should know something about it.

But I have given up in dark despair.

He Walked to War in *Adventure* was branded as technically imperfect.

Don't Rush Me in *Argosy,* another Marine story, elicited anguished howls of protest.

And yet if there is any story in the world I should be qualified to write, it is a Marine story.

> *"I believe that the only way I can keep improving my work and my markets is by broadening my sphere of acquaintanceship with the world and its people and professions."*

These are my woes. The reason for them is probably very plain to everyone. But I'll state my answer anyway.

A man cannot write a story unless he is deeply interested in it. If he thinks he knows a subject, then he instantly becomes careless with his technical details.

The only way I have found it possible to sidetrack these woes is by delving into new fields constantly, looking everywhere for one small fact which will lead me on into a story field I think I'll like.

This is not very good for a writer's reputation, they tell me. A writer, it is claimed, must specialize to become outstanding. I labored trying to build up a converse reputation, hoping to be known as a writer of infinite versatility.

I did not know until two years ago that the specializing writer is *persona non grata* with an editor. Jack Byrne, for instance, rebuilt *Argosy* with variety as a foundation. And once I heard Bloomfield sigh that he wished some of his top-notchers would stop sending him the same background week in and week out.

Maybe I am right, possibly I am wrong.

But I believe that the only way I can keep improving my work and my markets is by broadening my sphere of acquaintanceship with the world and its people and professions.

Providing yet another angle on how an author might improve his work and broaden his markets is "Circulate." That Ron specifically cites Jack London (of *White Fang* and *Call of the Wild* fame) is apt. For here, too, was a thoroughly adventurous writer who wrote of what he had witnessed. That, between frozen Klondike wastes and sultry Pacific ports, London had witnessed a lot is quite beside the point. Indeed, as Ron further confides: "Adventure, I well know, is in the heart, not in the view."

CIRCULATE

by L. RON HUBBARD

JACK LONDON POSSESSED A secret and he put it to a use which amounted to little less than alchemy. He knew the magic formula which permitted him to write about the things he knew best—a bag of tricks in itself.

Like the rest of us, Jack had his ups and sub-zeros, but unlike many of us he knew the correct way to combat them. He knew that work was the only solution and, far more than that, he knew how to get to work. He knew what to do when his pockets sagged with emptiness. He knew that sitting around bewailing a writer's lot was a poor method of creation.

Down on the San Francisco waterfront, there was a bookshop which handled mildewed volumes and secondhand pulps. It was close to the Embarcadero and the ships and the saloons, and its proprietor was close to the heart of Jack London. At those trying times when the checks were few and small, Jack would drop around for the purpose of borrowing half a dollar.

It was not that he was hungry. That fifty-cent piece was much more necessary than that. For with it, Jack London would head for the nearest saloon. Straight for the swinging doors and the barflies.

Sailors would be there. Sailors from Alaska and China and the South Seas. Sailors whose ships were lately on the bottom or whose crews were lately serving time for mutiny. And from that crowd, Jack London would select himself a tough old salt who looked garrulous. And then the fifty-cent piece would diminish across the mahogany and the old salt would pour out his heart. Perhaps the things he said were lies, perhaps divine truth. But whatever they were, they stimulated.

With the half-dollar gone, Jack would depart with a quick stride and end up at his writing desk. Seldom would he write what he had heard. It was enough that his mental wheels were revolving once more and that he could again taste salt spray and listen to the singing of wind aloft.

The infamously treacherous Inside Passage between British Columbia and the Alaskan Panhandle: such were the waters Ron plied through the autumn of 1940 and from whence he drew material for many a tale of Northwest adventure à la Jack London; photograph by L. Ron Hubbard

That was his trade secret. By applying it, he was soon enabled to place a silver dollar in the cash drawer at the bookshop.

"But I only lent you fifty cents!" protested the proprietor.

"I know, but I'll be wanting it again. Take it while I've got the money."

Jack London never allowed his interest in men to lag. And because of that, he grew to know men and could write about them and what they did and why.

Circulate was his motto and circulate he did. Everyone on the Embarcadero knew him and liked him and brought stories to him.

Often our ears are filled with the advice "Write about the things you know. The things close to you." And in despair, we wail that there is nothing of interest in our surroundings or in the lives we lead. We say that and we believe it. And in despair, we pound out a bloody thunderer, using the other side of the world as our locale.

———

The reason we cannot write about the things at hand is apparent. If we *knew* our surroundings well enough, we could put them on paper. Someone else comes around, looks us over and studies our environment for a brief period and then goes off to write a novel. Why, we moan, didn't we write that book? Surely we knew more about it than the lucky one.

But did we? To know a thing, we must first find it interesting. And it's certain that we can never see the hovel next door while we yearn for the picturesque scene hundreds of miles away.

People pass our houses to and from their work each day. We know their names and what they do, but we are not really interested in them. Even though each is a potential story, we pass them all up because, as with the postman, we never really see them.

Down on the corner is a drugstore. Occasionally we enter to buy copies of our prospective markets, but do we ever get to know the clerk? Or the loafers out front? Or the cop who parks his motorcycle at the curb? Or the fireman just off duty? Or the high-school seniors who suck up sodas in the booth? Or...?

No, probably and sadly not. Even while we look at them we're probably thinking about the story we are going to write about the north woods and the girl caught in the outlaw's cabin. The outsider comes in and looks our people over, goes off and writes about them, and then, quite reasonably, we get sore about his stealing our neighbors for material.

Jack London's environment was the sea. He knew it well. Too well, in fact. He knew he had to work hard to keep up his interest. As a boy he was an oyster pirate. Then a member of the fish patrol. Later he was a seaman on a sealing vessel. From there he went to the Klondike, to Japan, to Mexico and finally around the world in the *Snark*. No wonder, you say, he wrote about the sea. It was fascinating. No wonder he dealt with wild animals. They had attacked him. His environment, you say, was intensely interesting.

Jack London, strangely enough, didn't think so. He had to work hard to whip up flagging interest in the things he knew so well. He aspired to be, and became, the best-known American Socialist. His finest works, so he and the literati thought, were *The Iron Heel, War of the Classes, Revolution, Martin Eden* and *The People of the Abyss*.

But he made his money on adventure and sea stories. And to write them, he found that he must know them better than he did. He circulated among the men who were to become his characters. Long after he had given up the sea, he still forced himself to study his subject. He too wanted to graze in greener fields. He said that he wrote his adventure novels solely for the money.

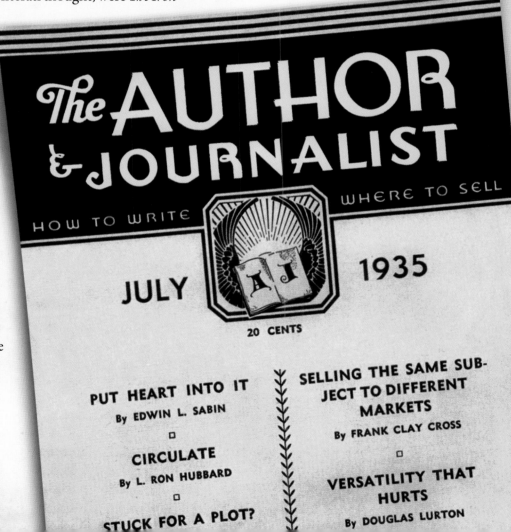

In other words, he did not revel in his environment any more than we do in ours. Yet he forced himself to study it thoroughly and write about it because it was his means of livelihood. He never allowed himself to go stale. He circulated constantly.

And now, how about our drugstore? The clerk knows all about the trouble Mrs. Smith is having with her back and why young Smith had to come home from college. The loafers out front have fought wars and excavated ditches. The fireman can tell why the mansion on the hill went up in smoke and just how that affected his little boy's schoolwork. The cop leaning on his motorcycle played a big part in the late kidnapping. He knows the inside story and he'll tell it. He also knows a hundred rackets which are worked right under your nose. And those high-school seniors could fill a novel with their hidden adventures.

> *"The only real solution lies in circulating. In moving around and talking. In studying our neighbors and associates as closely as if we were about to transfer their likenesses to canvas."*

But most of us just walk up to the magazine rack and thumb the copies and wish to goodness we could think of something worthwhile to write about. We wish we could be in New York or Texas or Tahiti so that we could gather some real material.

Photograph by
L. Ron Hubbard

The point of it is, we'll never be able—most of us—to shed our present environment unless we can make the well-known bucks. And if we can't sell, we can't earn. And if we can't think up stories, we therefore can't move on. In short, we're trapped.

It is not that our present locale is the best, but that it will have to do—emphatically. And the only real solution lies in circulating. In moving around and talking. In studying our neighbors and associates as closely as if we were about to transfer their likenesses to canvas.

If we don't *know* the average man, we can't write about him or for him and our assets will shrink in direct ratio to the pile of cancelled stamps on the return envelopes.

In other words: CIRCULATE!

Photograph by
L. Ron Hubbard

How exactly does a writer translate experience into stories? How does one spin fiction from fact and thereby ground tales in reality? The answer lies in L. Ron Hubbard's "Story Vitality." Likewise offered in the name of turning rejection slips into acceptance checks, here is the definitive word on writing from experience. Here is also the substantive word behind what Ron elsewhere termed "borrowing from the Bank of the World in ideas and knowledge and experience." That is: "The writer who has drawn much from the world will find that his mind is filled with material that can be used to make the payments. The more the writer throws himself into debt, the more he will have with which to repay."—L. Ron Hubbard

EVERY STORY COMPLETE

Five Novels

20c

5 NOVELS for JANUARY

Outlaws' Round-Up
Vengeance Takes the Trail
By C. B. Glasscock

The Phantom Patrol
Adventure with the Coast Guard
By L. Ron Hubbard

Mistress Headlong
Romance in the Hungarian Hills
By F. V. W. Mason

King Coal's Luck
A Stirring Story of the Turf
By Philip L. Scruggs

The Murray Affair
Novel

STORY VITALITY

by L. RON HUBBARD

IT VAGUELY IRRITATES ME to hear that a pulp writer need not know anything about his scene, that he should have no preoccupation with accuracy, that a beginning action scene and plenty of fight are the only requisites.

Many moons ago I wrote a story called *The Phantom Patrol*. I wrote it with an old-timer's remarks in mind. I said to myself, "M'boy, you're writing tripe, why slave over it? Why go to all the trouble of researching the thing? Your readers won't know the difference anyway."

And so *The Phantom Patrol* cruised the markets, collected copious rejects.

When it at last came limping home, abashed and whipped, I gazed sternly at it. It would seem that it had all the things required for a good story. It had action, it had unusual situations, it had lots of thud and blunder. Why, then, didn't it sell?

To understand the evolution of *The Phantom Patrol,* some of the plot is necessary. It concerns a Coast Guard boat, a dope runner and piracy.

The hero is a lieutenant, chasing a cargo of heroin. He gets cast ashore in the blow, his crew is all drowned, he wakes on the beach in the morning to discover that his vessel is still serviceable. But before he can board the boat, the dope runners shoot him down and steal the ship before his eyes.

He recovers from the wound, escapes to the C.G. base only to discover that he is tagged with the name of pirate. Unknown to him, the villains have taken his boat, have stopped liners in the name of the Coast Guard and have robbed them.

He has no way of proving his innocence, so he goes to jail, escapes, returns and wipes out the dope runners.

Ah, yes, I know. That story has always been good. I felt it would sell, but I could think of no way to pep it up.

I threw it in the ashcan and rewrote it all the way through. It went out again—and came home, more battered than ever.

Certainly there was something wrong, but I didn't have time to waste on it and I threw it in the files.

It might well have stayed there forever, had I not been faced with one of those sudden orders which leave you cold and trembling for want of a plot.

The second rewrite of *The Phantom Patrol* was ten thousand words. The order was for twenty thousand. And all I could find in the files was *The Phantom Patrol*. Something had to be done about it. I had a few days to spare and I decided that maybe the Coast Guard might be able to slip me some data which would lengthen it.

Then and there, I learned something. The scene of the yarn was laid in the Gulf and Louisiana. In my rambles I seem to have missed both places. The theme was the Coast Guard and, outside of watching some of the C.G. boats, I knew little or nothing about the outfit.

But hadn't an old-timer said that accurate data was unnecessary? Why did I have to go to all this trouble?

It happened at the moment that I was writing aviation articles for about twenty-five bucks a throw. The price of the twenty-thousand worder was to be two hundred and fifty dollars.

Thinking about that, I reasoned that maybe I ought to spend a little time on the latter, if I always spent a day on an aviation article.

With the bare thought that maybe I could get some data for stretching purposes, I hied myself down to the city and looked around. A Coast Guard tug was tied to the dock.

Summoning up my nerve, I walked up the plank and rapped on the commanding officer's door. He was engaged in changing his uniform, but he bade me enter.

I sat down on a transom and plied him with a few questions. He informed me with some heat that lieutenants were never in charge of seventy-five-foot patrol boats. Only chief petty officers captained them.

I asked him about the Gulf and service there, but he was rather ungracious about it. A little miffed, I started to go.

As a parting broadside, he said, "I always laugh when I read stories about the Coast Guard."

And I stamped down the gangway, vowing that this would be one story which wouldn't make the so-and-so laugh, yea man!

Another C.G. boat was in, a slim greyhound. I decided I ought to board her and see what I could discover there. No officers were aboard. The deck watch was headed by a chief petty officer, a grizzled soul with a salt tang to his speech.

"You wanna see the old tub, do you?" said the C.P.O. "All right, Johnny here will take you around."

Johnny, another C.P.O., escorted me through the vessel. He explained about engines in terms which made me squirm. He showed me everything, including how to fire a one-pounder. He told me that dope runners were bad eggs. Why, once up in Maine he had...

And so passed the afternoon.

I skittered homeward, mentally afire. I blessed the C.P.O. and cursed the officer in the same breath.

Right
The Phantom Patrol by L. Ron Hubbard as originally published in *Five-Novels Monthly* in January 1935

ANTOM PATROL by L. RON HUBBARD

Bilbo sank back on his haunches, grinning. Slowly he lowered another cartridge into his rifle.

"We've got to forget Georges Coquelin," Johnny replied. "This makes the third time in a row. Why can't these Two-Continents pilots take care of themselves?"

Heinie Swartz eyed the dripping foredeck of the lunging seventy-five footer. Green seas topped with froth were breaking. The one-pound gun was alternately swallowed and disgorged by water. The two 200 h.p. Sterling Diesels throbbed under the deck, pounding out their hearts against the blow. For five hours the Coast Guard Patrol Boat *1004* had barely held her own.

Heinie turned back to Trescott, noting the wild look in the C.P.O.'s sea-blue eyes.

By God, those officers weren't so hot. My hero was the chief petty officer, beleaguered by officers and dope runners, battered by hurricanes in the Gulf, patrolling the sea with a keen salt wind nipping at him.

The new *Phantom Patrol* began:

> Crisp and brittle, the staccato torrent ripped out from the headphones, "S.O.S.... S.O.S.—Down in storm 20 miles south of Errol Island. Hull leaking. Starboard wing smashed... Cannot last two hours.... Transport plane New Orleans bound sinking 20 miles...!"

> Johnny Trescott's opinion of the matter was amply summed in the single word, "Damn!"

And there I had it. Johnny is trailing the dope runners, but because saving life comes before stopping crime, he must leave his course and rescue the transport plane.

But the runner, Georges Coquelin, hears the SOS too and, as there's wealth aboard that plane, Johnny walks straight into Coquelin when he tries to rescue the transport.

The atmosphere began to crackle in the yarn. I was still listening to that C.P.O. telling me about these trips, these escapes:

> Heinie Swartz eyed the dripping foredeck of the lunging 75-footer. Green seas topped with froth were breaking. The one-pound gun was alternately swallowed and disgorged by water. The two 200 h.p. Sterling Diesels throbbed under the deck, pounding out their hearts against the blow.

I knew what made the boat tick and I could visualize it. I was suddenly so secure in my data that I felt able to tinker with the effect of situations.

The wordage went up like a skyrocket. I had so much at my command that I was hard put to hold the stuff down.

And then when Johnny came back to the base, he's up against the officers. And are those officers a bunch of thick-witted, braid-polishing bums? I hope to tell you:

> Lieutenant Maitland, counsel for the defense, entered with stiff, uncompromising strides. He had been appointed to the task much against his will, and the fact was clearly etched in his sunburned face. He sparkled with gold braid and distaste.

> When he entered the cell, he eyed his two "clients" with disgust. Garbed as they were in prison dungarees, they were two uninteresting units which comprised a sordid case.

Johnny and Heinie stood up, in deference to his rank, but Maitland either forgot or refused to give the order, "At ease!"

In those first two stories, the patrol boat had merely been a method of conveyance. Now it began to live and snort and wallow in the trough.

The plight of Johnny, meeting up with Georges Coquelin and losing his ship, was capped by the attitude of the officers. He was in trouble and no mistake. When I started thinking about what would actually happen in such a case, I began to feel very, very sorry for my hero. He was really on the spot.

And then, I had a little personal interest in the case too. Somebody thought they'd laugh when they read the yarn, eh? Well, let them try to laugh now.

With a very clear picture of Coast Guard armament in my mind, I was able to give the final scenes the reality, the zip they needed. And those final scenes, when you're tired, need something outside to give them life.

Johnny Trescott sighted the lighted hut they had first seen. A harsh streak of lightning showed that the clearing was empty. The door of the hut swung to and fro in the wind.

Johnny pulled back the loading handle of the machine gun. The belt dangled over his shoulder, drooling water from its brace studded length.

"To hell with insubordination!" —*The Phantom Patrol*

Collected data changed the plot, pepped up the writing, gave the story an undercurrent of vitality which made the yarn. The wild implausibility of the original was there because I had no actual vision of what the Coast Guard tried to do and how it did it.

The first two drafts were laughable, worthless. But my writing hadn't changed so terribly much. Nothing had changed but the subject.

And the subject had changed because I could feel it.

The Phantom Patrol was published in the January *Five Novels*. The illustrator made a slight error in making the pictures those of officers.

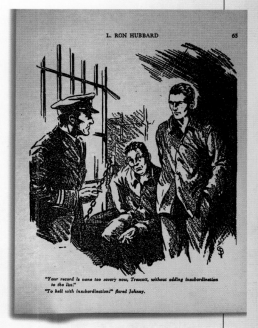

L. RON HUBBARD 65

"Your record is none too savory now, Trescott, without adding insubordination to the list."
"To hell with insubordination!" flared Johnny.

But even then the Coast Guard did not laugh. They read the story and wrote me about it and I felt that I had succeeded.

Adventure is as difficult as you want to make it. The way to make it difficult is to sail blithely along, listening to the words of wisdom dropped by the old-timers about how the knowledge of the subject is unnecessary. One should listen and then promptly forget.

Oh well, maybe when I've been in the game twenty-five years, I'll go around pooh-poohing everything, especially accuracy. But if I do, I hope some young feller will take me for a buggy ride. Maybe I'll remember then how I used to sell.

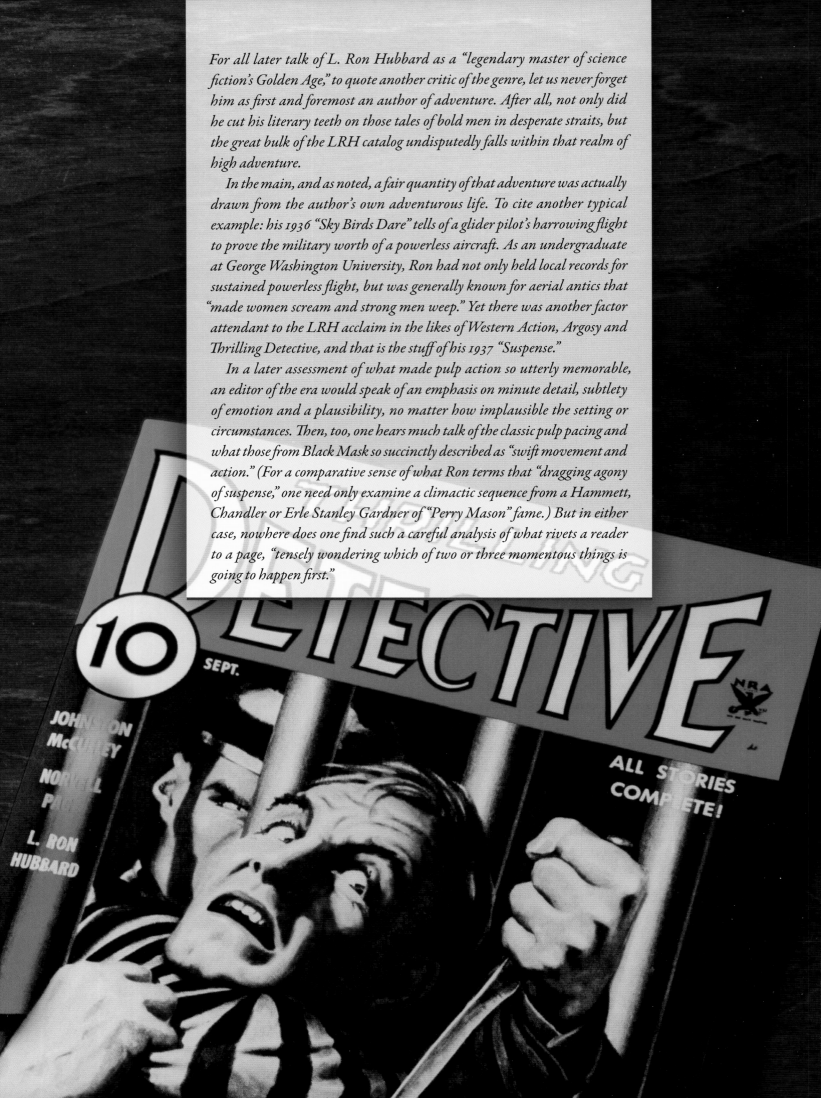

For all later talk of L. Ron Hubbard as a "legendary master of science fiction's Golden Age," to quote another critic of the genre, let us never forget him as first and foremost an author of adventure. After all, not only did he cut his literary teeth on those tales of bold men in desperate straits, but the great bulk of the LRH catalog undisputedly falls within that realm of high adventure.

In the main, and as noted, a fair quantity of that adventure was actually drawn from the author's own adventurous life. To cite another typical example: his 1936 "Sky Birds Dare" tells of a glider pilot's harrowing flight to prove the military worth of a powerless aircraft. As an undergraduate at George Washington University, Ron had not only held local records for sustained powerless flight, but was generally known for aerial antics that "made women scream and strong men weep." Yet there was another factor attendant to the LRH acclaim in the likes of Western Action, Argosy and Thrilling Detective, and that is the stuff of his 1937 "Suspense."

In a later assessment of what made pulp action so utterly memorable, an editor of the era would speak of an emphasis on minute detail, subtlety of emotion and a plausibility, no matter how implausible the setting or circumstances. Then, too, one hears much talk of the classic pulp pacing and what those from Black Mask so succinctly described as "swift movement and action." (For a comparative sense of what Ron terms that "dragging agony of suspense," one need only examine a climactic sequence from a Hammett, Chandler or Erle Stanley Gardner of "Perry Mason" fame.) But in either case, nowhere does one find such a careful analysis of what rivets a reader to a page, "tensely wondering which of two or three momentous things is going to happen first."

SUSPENSE

by L. RON HUBBARD

NEXT TO CHECKS, THE most intangible thing in this business of writing is that quantity "Suspense."

It is quite as elusive as editorial praise, as hard to corner and recognize as a contract writer.

But without any fear of being contradicted, I can state that suspense, or rather, the lack of it, is probably responsible for more rejects than telling an editor he is wrong.

You grab the morning mail, find a long brown envelope. You read a slip which curtly says, "Lacks suspense."

Your wife starts cooking beans, you start swearing at the most enigmatic, unexplanatory, hopeless phrase in all that legion of reject phrases.

If the editor had said, "I don't think your hero had a tough enough time killing Joe Blinker," you could promptly sit down and kill Joe Blinker in a most thorough manner.

But when the editor brands and damns you with that first cousin to infinity, "Suspense," you just sit and swear.

Often the editor, in a hurry and beleaguered by stacks of manuscripts higher than the Empire State, has to tell you something to explain why he doesn't like your wares. So he fastens upon the action, perhaps. You can tell him (and won't, if you're smart) that your action is already so fast that you had to grease your typewriter roller to keep the rubber from getting hot.

Maybe he says your plot isn't any good, but you know doggone well that it is a good plot and has been a good plot for two thousand years.

Maybe, when he gives you those comments, he is, as I say, in a hurry. The editor may hate to tell you you lack suspense because it is something like B.O.—your best friends won't tell you.

But the point is that, whether he says that your Mary Jones reminds him of *The Perils of Pauline*, or that your climax is flat, there's a chance that he means suspense.

Those who have been at this business until their fingernails are worn to stumps are very often overconfident of their technique. I get that way every now and then, until something hauls me back on my haunches and shows me up. You just forget that technique is not a habit, but a constant set of rules to be frequently refreshed in your mind.

And so, in the scurry of getting a manuscript in the mail, it is not unusual to overlook some trifling factor which will mean the difference between sale and rejection.

This suspense business is something hard to remember. You know your plot (or should, anyway) before you write it. You forget that the reader doesn't. Out of habit, you think plot is enough to carry you through. Sometimes it won't. You have to fall back on none-too-subtle mechanics.

Take this, for example:

> He slid down between the rocks toward the creek, carrying the canteens clumsily under his arm, silently cursing his sling. A shadow loomed over him.

> "Franzawi!" screamed the Arab sentinel.

There we have a standard situation. In the Atlas. The hero has to get to water or his wounded legionnaires will die of thirst. But, obviously, it is very, very flat except for the slight element of surprising the reader.

Surprise doesn't amount to much. That snap-ending tendency doesn't belong in the center of the story. Your reader knew there were Arabs about. He knew the hero was going into danger. But that isn't enough. Not half.

> Legionnaire Smith squirmed down between the rocks clutching the canteens, his eyes fixed upon the bright silver spot which was the water hole below. A shadow loomed across the trail before him. Hastily he slipped backward into cover.

The AUTHOR & JOURNALIST

HOW TO WRITE WHERE TO SELL

JUNE A J 1937

20 Cents

Suspense
By L. RON HUBBARD

Can You Express It?
By ELTON STERRETT

The Spot is the Thing
By AL BARNES

An Arab sentinel was standing on the edge of the trail, leaning on his long gun. The man's brown eyes were turned upward, watching a point higher on the cliff, expecting to see some sign of the besieged legionnaires.

Smith started back again, moving as silently as he could, trying to keep the canteens from banging. His sling-supported arm was weak. The canteens were slipping.

He could see the sights on the Arab's rifle and knew they would be lined on him the instant he made a sound.

The silver spot in the ravine was beckoning. He could not return with empty canteens. Maybe the sentinel would not see him if he slipped silently around the other side of this boulder.

He tried it. The man remained staring wolfishly up at the pillbox fort.

Maybe it was possible after all. That bright spot of silver was so near, so maddening to swollen tongues....

Smith's hand came down on a sharp stone. He lifted it with a jerk.

A canteen rattled to the trail.

For seconds nothing stirred or breathed in this scorching world of sun and stone.

Then the sentry moved, stepped a pace up the path, eyes searching the shadows, gnarled hands tight on the rifle stock.

Smith moved closer to the boulder, trying to get out of sight, trying to lure the sentry toward him so that he could be silently killed.

The canteen sparkled in the light.

A resounding shout rocked the blistered hills.

"Franzawi!" cried the sentinel.

The surprise in the first that a sentinel would be there and that Smith was discovered perhaps made the reader blink.

The dragging agony of suspense in the latter made the reader lean tensely forward, devour the page, gulp....

Or at least, I hope it did.

But there's the point. Keep your reader wondering which of two things will happen (i.e., will Smith get through or will he be discovered) and you get his interest. You focus his mind on an intricate succession of events and that is much better than getting him a little groggy with one swift sock to the medulla oblongata.

"The dragging agony of suspense in the latter made the reader lean tensely forward, devour the page, gulp...."

That is about the only way you can heighten drama out of melodrama.

It is not possible, of course, to list all the ways this method can be used. But it is possible to keep in mind the fact that suspense is better than fight action.

And speaking of fight action, there is one place where Old Man Suspense can be made to work like an Elkton marrying parson.

Fights, at best, are gap fillers. The writer who introduces them for the sake of the fight itself and not for the effects upon the characters is a writer headed for eventual oblivion even in the purely action books.

Confirmed by the prevailing trend, I can state that the old saw about action for the sake of action was right. A story jammed and packed with blow-by-blow accounts of what the hero did to the villain and what the villain did to the hero, with fists, knives, guns, bombs, machine guns, belaying pins, bayonets, poison gas, strychnine, teeth, knees and calks is about as interesting to read as the Congressional Record and about twice as dull. You leave yourself wide open to a reader comment, "Well, what of it?"

But fights accompanied by suspense are another matter.

Witness the situation in which the party of the first part is fighting for possession of a schooner, a girl or a bag of pearls. Unless you have a better example of trite plotting, we proceed. We are on the schooner. The hero sneaks out of the cabin and there is the villain on his way to sink the ship. So we have a fight:

> Jim dived at Bart's legs, but Bart was not easily thrown. They stood apart. Jim led with his left, followed through with his right. Black Bart countered the blows. Bone and sinew cracked in the mighty thunder of conflict.... Jim hit with his right.... Bart countered with a kick in the shins....

There you have a masterpiece for wastebasket filing. But, believe it, this same old plot and this same old fight look a lot different when you have your suspense added. They might even sell if extracted and toned like this:

Jim glanced out of the chart room and saw Black Bart. Water dripping from his clothes, his teeth bared, his chest heaving from his long swim, Bart stood in a growing pool which slid down his arms and legs. In his hand he clutched an axe, ready to sever the hawser and release them into the millrace of the sweeping tide....

This is Jim's cue, of course, to knock the stuffing out of Black Bart, but that doesn't make good reading nor very much wordage, for thirty words are enough in which to recount any battle as such, up to and including wars. So we add suspense. For some reason Jim can't leap into the fray right at that moment. Suppose we add that he has these pearls right there and he's afraid Ringo, Black Bart's henchman, will up and swipe them when Jim's back is turned. So first Jim has to stow the pearls.

This gets Bart halfway across the deck toward that straining hawser which he must cut to wreck the schooner and ruin the hero.

Now, you say, we dive into it. Nix. We've got a spot here for some swell suspense. Is Black Bart going to cut that hawser? Is Jim going to get there?

Jim starts. Ringo hasn't been on his way to steal the pearls but to knife Jim, so Jim tangles with Ringo, and Black Bart races toward the hawser some more.

Jim's fight with Ringo is short. About like this:

Ringo charged, eyes rolling, black face set. Jim glanced toward Bart. He could not turn his back on this charging demon. Yet he had to get that axe.

Jim whirled to meet Ringo. His boot came up and the knife sailed over the rail and into the sea. Ringo reached out with his mighty hands. Jim stepped through and nailed a right on Ringo's button. Skidding, Ringo went down.

Jim sprinted forward toward Bart. The blackbearded Colossus spun about to meet the rush, axe upraised.

Now, if you want to, you can dust off this scrap. But don't give it slug by slug. Hand it out, thus:

The axe bit down into the planking. Jim tried to recover from his dodge. Bart was upon him, slippery in Jim's grasp. In vain Jim tried to land a solid blow, but Bart was holding him hard.

"Ringo!" roared Bart. "Cut that hawser!"

Ringo, dazed by Jim's blow, struggled up. Held tight in Bart's grasp, Jim saw Ringo lurch forward and yank the axe out of the planking.

"That hawser!" thundered Bart. "I can't hold this fool forever!"

Now, if you wanted that hawser cut in the first place (which you did, because that means more trouble and the suspense of wondering how the schooner will get out of it), cut that hawser right now before the reader suspects that this writing business is just about as mechanical as fixing a Ford.

Action suspense is easy to handle, but you have to know when to quit and you have to evaluate your drama and ladle it out accordingly.

Even in what the writers call the psychological story you have to rely upon suspense just as mechanical as this.

Give your reader a chance to wonder for a while about the final outcome.

There is one type of suspense, however, so mechanical that it clanks. I mean foreshadowing.

To foreshadow anything is weak. It is like a boxer stalling for the bell. You have to be mighty sure that you've got something outstanding to foreshadow or the reader will nail up your scalp.

It is nice to start ominously like this:

I knew that night as I sloshed through the driving rain that all was not well. I had a chilly sense of foreboding as though a monster dogged my steps....

> *"Give your reader a chance to wonder for a while about the final outcome."*

Brass Keys to Murder by Michael Keith—one of some two dozen L. Ron Hubbard pseudonyms under which he penned two-fisted, high-action thrillers

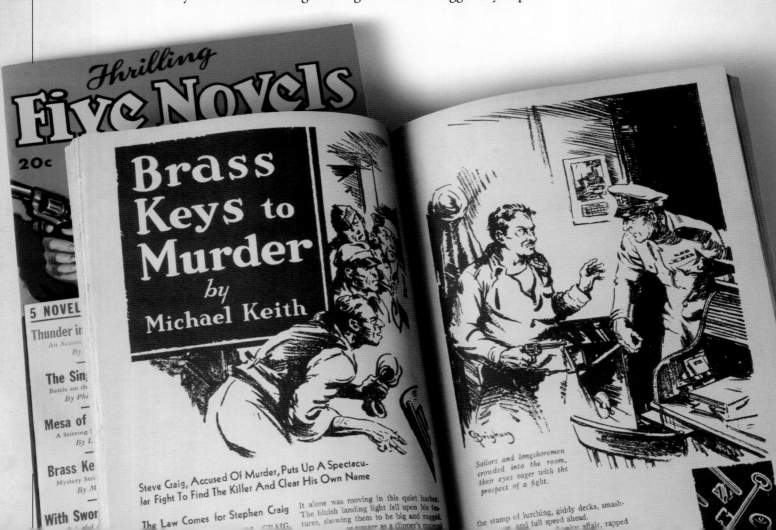

Thrilling Five Novels
20c

5 NOVEL
Thunder in
An Action
By

The Sin
Battle on th
By Phi

Mesa of
A Stirring
By L

Brass Ke
Mystery Stri
By M

With Swor

Brass Keys to Murder by Michael Keith

Steve Craig, Accused Of Murder, Puts Up A Spectacular Fight To Find The Killer And Clear His Own Name

The Law Comes for Stephen Craig

it alone was moving in this quiet harbor. The bluish landing light fell upon his features, showing them to be big and rugged, square as a clipper's mains'l

Sailors and longshoremen crowded into the room, their eyes eager with the prospect of a fight.

the stamp of lurching, giddy decks, smash- and full speed ahead.

If I only had known then what awaited me when the big chimes in the tower should strike midnight, I would have collapsed with terror....

Very good openings. Very, very good. Proven goods, even though the nap is a bit worn. But how many times have writers lived up to those openings? Not very many.

You get off in high, but after you finish you will probably tear out these opening paragraphs—even though Poe was able to get away with this device. Remember the opening of "The Fall of the House of Usher"? You know, the one that goes something like this: "Through the whole of a dark and dismal afternoon."

That is foreshadowing. However, few besides Poe have been able to get away with suspense created by atmosphere alone.

One particular magazine makes a practice of inserting a foreshadow as a first paragraph in every story. I have come to suspect that this is done editorially because the foreshadow is always worse than the story gives you.

It's a far cry from the jungles of Malaysia to New York, and there's a great difference between the yowl of the tiger and the rattle of the L, but in the city that night there stalked the lust of the jungle killers and a man who had one eye....

I have been guilty of using such a mechanism to shoot out in high, but I don't let the paragraph stand until I am pretty doggone sure that I've got everything it takes in the way of plot and menace to back it up.

If you were to take all the suspense out of a story, no matter how many unusual facts and characters you had in it, I don't think it would be read very far.

If you were to take every blow of action out of a story and still leave its suspense (this is possible, because I've done it), you might still have a fine story, probably a better story than before.

There is not, unhappily, any firm from which you can take out a suspense insurance policy. The only way you can do it is to make sure that the reader is sitting there tensely wondering which of two or three momentous things is going to happen first. If you can do that, adroitly, to some of those manuscripts which have come bouncing back, they may be made to stay put.

Despite all the pulps offered as a passport to far-flung adventure, one persistent link to ordinary life remained: the single-column advertisement on front and back pages. Why those advertisements so often tended towards the oddball or salacious is a difficult question but apparently followed from yet another pulp paper myth—that the typical reader was both low-class and gullible. In fact, the pulps pervaded the whole of American society. To wit: while future Nobel laureate Sinclair Lewis provided editorial assistance to *Adventure*, readers included none other than President Franklin Roosevelt. But in either case, the first and final pages remained filled with ads for false teeth, eczema ointment and the rest of what Ron describes in his wry commentary on "The Pulp Paper Puzzle."

THE PULP PAPER PUZZLE

by L. RON HUBBARD

IF YOU'RE BASHFUL AND easily embarrassed, please lay this thing aside.

If I had good sense, I wouldn't write this or even mention it because, as a cautious friend once said, "Many a man has been noosed for less." But if I'm doing wrong, please keep in mind that this is *not* a slam against editors, only an attempt to help them and myself and our brethren. And it isn't a slam against publishers, because publishers can't do anything about it either, at the moment. And it isn't a slam against pulps, because I like pulps and I write pulps and I think many of them are vastly underrated as literature.

I speak, and God help me, about pulp advertising, and I speak about it in the terms two thousand writers speak about it and I think it's about time somebody said something, and right now I happen to be all burned up.

In a recent issue, a novelette of mine was carried over into the back of one of our pulps. Right at the point where the heroine was being very shy and where the hero was being good and pure and saving her virtue, I saw this ad:

> THE FORBIDDEN SECRETS OF SEX ARE DARINGLY REVEALED.
> Away with false modesty. At last a famous doctor has told all the secrets of sex in frank, daring language. No prudish beating about the bush, no veiled hints, but TRUTH...

Imagine my gentle heroine's embarrassment when she was confronted with that!

It has been said before and often that the pulps have to have advertising of some kind, but no one has bothered to explain to me just why a group with half a million guaranteed circulation has to take that kind.

And somebody has said someplace that these ads have to appear somewhere and there's really nothing wrong with the ads, either. They're just out of place.

Pulps, bless 'em, print the cleanest stories which appear on the stands as a whole. Pulps have taboos which are the run-of-the-mill in a lot of slick offices.

Take the hero. He has to be red-blooded, plenty tough, virile, clean-minded, active, pure, good and a model any boy might be glad to emulate.

It follows, then, that the people reading the pulps want to read about fine fellows. These people buy the pulps because of the stories. Why, then, must an advertising man insist that the pulp paper book is the place for such an ad?

Maybe I'm dumb, I dunno. But the whole pulp code is built upon one fact. One book, one dish. The taboos run the same, the stories run in the same channel. Every editorial effort is based upon that one thing.

Then why doesn't the same method apply to the ads?

Two and two, in my day, made four. In pulps ads, they make me sick.

I am generally very broad minded. In fact, my mind, they tell me, is simply a wide-open-space.

I read the pulps for amusement, the same as anyone else, not entirely for business. And when I read about red-blooded men, I am seeking escape and more escape. I want to be right out there in the jungle knocking the hell out of the natives with the hero. I feel like I'm big and tough, too, and that I can climb mountains, get wounded, climb mountains and still be so virile that I can still climb more mountains. I want to be like the hero and these heroes aren't too far drawn at that.

But in the midst of my reading, the page turns, right while I'm in my glory of being tough with Mr. Hero and I read:

STOP YOUR RUPTURE WORRIES.
Learn about my perfected rupture invention.

Swell thought while I'm busy being tough.

But, they tell me, ads pay writers indirectly. That's why I can't understand it. If ads pay me at all, then why the devil don't they pay me big?

In the waiting room of a big pulp publisher I heard an ad man—and God knows they have their troubles too—selling a man on an inch spread.

"We have, in these books," said the ad man—poor devil—"a guaranteed circulation of one million. Your ad will be run in each book and it will reach all these people. Now if you don't get results, you'll get your money back. And if you don't get the guaranteed circulation, you'll get a rebate."

Well, I guess he had to tell that guy something, but it's puzzled me ever since. One million circulation for that string of books. There's less duplication than you think. A western reader snarls and snaps at your hand when you offer him an air book. And a love pulp reader isn't likely to be caught reading horror stories.

But now, with one million circulation, which is what a few slicks boast and a lot of them far less, a slick goes out and gets swell drawings and full color and good copy. They advertise soap and furniture and cars and electric iceboxes of fine make. They get plenty of money for those ads, otherwise they'd have to get more money for their books.

I dunno, I'm just a writer. I'm not supposed to worry my head about such things. But my pulp rates aren't anything to brag about and neither are yours, so don't sneer, and sometimes I get funny ideas about word rates, thinking in my dumb way that, after all, my wife deserves to eat *once* in a while.

And so we come back to the ads and the pulps. The pulps—so one well-known publisher whose name would surprise you—are known for their advertising and are damned for it. He said that was the main trouble with the pulps—this big man with his million circulation—and that the ads held the pulps back.

But I haven't seen him doing anything about it in his books.

Maybe he can't do anything about it. Certainly there is no agency to handle pulp ads, although one had vaguely given a statement upon this to…

Let's take the grand old man of the pulps, the book which is greater than all the other books and which has a fine type of readers.

Fine, convincing stories, no woman interest. A book I'd like to have my boy read when he grows up.

The copy here, opened at random, begins with:

THE FIRST GIRL I EVER LIKED AND THESE PIMPLES HAD TO COME!

Swell ad, but it so happens that this book, this granddaddy of pulps, has no woman interest whatever and it got there through lack of it. Its readers want nothing at all to do with women. They are seekers beyond the horizon and their thoughts are far away, in lands where tom-toms mutter and where a man can be a man and has to be a man to live—and to hell with the dames.

The company which runs this ad is a fine firm. It runs the same ad in the comic strips and I dare say the thing might work there. But there seems to be a gap, a lack of…

Next!

This is more to the point in this book, as it happens to deal with far lands:

BE A DETECTIVE. Experience unnecessary.

Another:

BE A DETECTIVE. Follow this man.

Again:

BE A DETECTIVE.

We'll take a good western book which has no woman interest at all. A book which is read by a lot of people I know who are very intelligent people. I like the book, too. But it so happens that the wide-open-space appeal is capped by:

PILES, DON'T BE CUT.

By:

BE A DETECTIVE.

And in the midst of a column which says that the next issue will contain Explosive Action, we read:

DON'T DYNAMITE KIDNEYS.

I mean, these things are not in step somehow.
It's not that people shouldn't be warned that you must:

WAKE UP YOUR LIVER BILE.

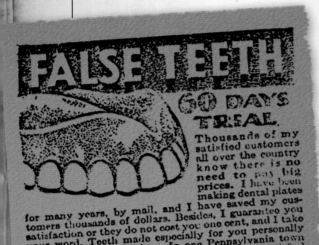

It's that the reader wants to forget all about it, escape it or he wouldn't be reading the book. After all, when a specter of liver bile is hanging over your head and you want to get away from it all...

The detective book is fine in its choice of ads. Detectives are notorious for their disguises and:

FALSE TEETH, 60 Day Trial.

Going on from the defendant teeth we are informed that:

KIDNEYS CAUSE MUCH TROUBLE.

Of course, this is perfectly all right and I'm not making fun of the pulps at all. I'm trying to defend them. It isn't the editor's fault that his book is filled with such stuff, and it isn't the advertising man's either. Both these boys are on the spot and they would do something about it I know if they could. Of course…

When my stories are published, I don't feel bad about having them appear on wood pulp paper. Why should I? I'm doing a sincere, honest task. I am nothing more or less than an entertainer. But I cringe a little when my friends read them because, invariably, along about the climax, this jumps up:

PROSTATE GLAND WEAKNESS.

Hell's bells, fellow craftsmen, we wouldn't mention it in polite society if we had it, would we?

Now let's take a cruise into the love pulp field.

I have seen an odd survey of the readers of one of the best of these mags. Surprised, I learned that the readers are not added up to an average age. I thought that high-school people and gum-chewing stenos ate them up. I was wrong.

The people that read love pulp are anywhere from sixteen to sixty in any walk of life. They are respectable matrons, schoolteachers, cashiers, wives and the girl who lives in the swank apartment down the hall with her mom and pop. A varied, intelligent audience, when you come to think of it, and if they aren't, then you're slamming America.

You and I have their equals in our own friends. They are the ladies who buy and buy and buy some more. They wear the latest and they use the best lipstick and they influence the old man when he buys his car and they use soap and electric iceboxes and what the devil do they care about:

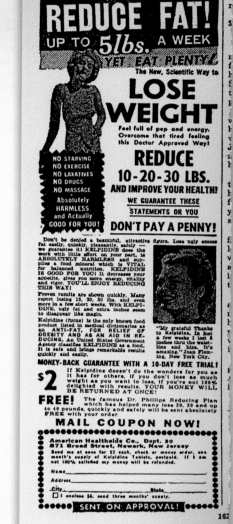

IF YOU DO NOT ADD AT LEAST THREE INCHES TO YOUR CHEST, IT WON'T COST YOU ONE CENT!
Mold a Mighty Chest and amaze your friends.

And then, remembering that this is a love pulp, we read:

A TIP GOT BILL A GOOD JOB.
Train in spare time at home
for radio work.

This is presented in the light that a tip comes from a girl. He wins the job and the jane and everybody is happy and the idea is that the girl will read it and tell Bill and they won't have any more money worries and he won't be out of a job and they can feed the kiddies.

When the whole doggone book is busy putting the man in romance, stressing the beauty of a cozy nest for two, this doesn't seem to jibe somehow. The gals will probably shudder when they read it and say, "So that's the price of marriage." Anticlimax for ten happy-ending stories when *he* gives *her* the ring.

With no alibi to qualify its presence in a woman's book:

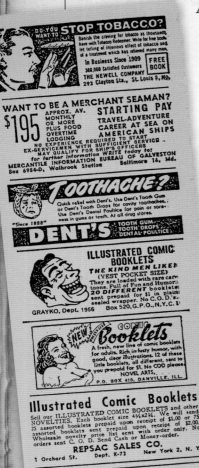

A MONEY-MAKING OPPORTUNITY FOR MEN OF CHARACTER.
Be a traveling salesman for us.
Endless opportunities for the right man.

And also:

MR. SALESMAN! WHAT'S WRONG?

That's subtle, that one is. But we go on, still in the love book, read by all these nice people as that survey testifies:

GET ON AVIATION'S PAYROLL.

Also very subtle, if you know what I mean. Fact is, I know the chap who runs this last outfit and he's a prince. But he's paying a little money in this book for that ad and I don't think he could spot it anywhere else and I don't think he'd want to pay a big price for it.

And still in the love pulp, we have:

FOLLOW THIS MAN!

Not bad, I guess, but it's about being a detective.
But when we run into this one, we wonder:

FOREST JOBS.
Hunt, trap, cabin.

Dear, dear me, am I blushing about all this. But I think the ladies must love:

SEE ABOUT MY TEETH BEFORE ORDERING ELSEWHERE.
False teeth at lowest prices.

And, of course, this too is right in line:

SAVE ON TIRES.

These things are all flattering, I suppose, but take a look at this:

QUIT WHISKEY.

This is another one I get the creeps reading in this book devoted to sweet, gentle adoration:

PROSTATE GLAND WEAKNESS.

And:

EPILEPSY—EPILEPTICS.

And this, of course, has a definite place in the book:

STRONG MEN AT ALL TIMES HAVE USED DUMBBELLS TO GAIN THEIR GREAT STRENGTH.

And again:

GET RID OF YOUR PIMPLES.

I assure you it goes on and on, and I'm taking all the ads as I come to them. How about:

ITCHING STOPPED QUICKLY.

And:

JOBLESS MEN, READ THIS!

All in a love mag too. Well, well, well.

By this time you have probably stopped reading or you're gagged beyond all help. But just listen at me a second. This is the stuff which appears beside your story and mine. This is the thing our readers have to read the instant they open the book the first time. A fine introduction.

We see "Joe Writer's smashing story, 'Bilgewater Bill's Mistake'" and then, right against that announcement, we'll see:

Do You Suffer From
PSORIASIS??
ECZEMA, ACNE CURED.

I can never quite reconcile myself and tell myself that the reader of that announcement won't go through life associating Joe Writer with a pimply face.

But I grow lengthy over this. Actually, I cannot quite bring myself to write up three or four of these ads for fear that I'd blush for days. I leave them out. You can find them in your own pulps.

Other ads I have omitted are those dealing with time-payment jewelry, which is okay, with typewriters (showing that typewriter people have sense) and with tap dancing. Nor do I mention these fake offers of information where you expect one thing and get another and a request for more dough.

In connection with that last, the funniest thing I have seen this month is a column in a detective mag which exposes rackets for the readers. This month the columnist is exposing a certain concern and right there in the ad across the page is the whole copy, word for word, which he is exposing.

I omit, too, the pen-pal clubs and old money. I omit the one saving grace—those swell-looking cigarette ads on the back and a couple furniture ads.

But those are all. Just those, no more. I have the field covered.

The argument against big companies advertising in the pulps is twofold. The big company doesn't want to be in such companionship and the returns from these pulp ads is not sufficient. Good arguments against it.

But here is what I'm driving at. You and I are writers. We are supposed to know nothing about such things. But if you have snickered or blushed while reading this article, then please realize that your friend, the reader, does exactly the same thing. He's no different from us, except that we're probably a little dumber than he is.

I am taking a lead upon myself in writing this at all. Don't think I shoot off my face for my health, because it isn't at all healthy.

Up in the advertising offices of the Big Five, angry advertising men, I suppose, will take this in to the boss and swear at it. And then word will come through the office that every time L. Ron Hubbard has a story in *Dashing Stories,* or in *Gun-Slingers,* or in *Gun Novels,* the circulation goes down. Please don't give us no more Hubbard nohow.

The men have a right to be sore about it. In one way such things as this take the bread out of the mouths of babes (I've got two, thanks).

But nobody will boycott a chap who tries like hell to make the magazine pay. Well, indirectly though it seems, I'm trying to up my own rates and your rates and the profit on the book.

This idea is not original with me. I take no credit for it and I am not speaking with authority for any organization.

However, I've named no solutions. That's for the other chap, that's the business of this one outfit of which I speak, helping writers and publishers alike. One of these days the solution will be advanced and everybody will be very happy, especially you and I with a big check in the pocket instead of a small check.

Publishers look with suspicion upon writers and their organization. They think the purpose they have in mind is forcing more money per word out of the tottering editorial budget.

That doesn't happen to be the truth. If a writer can boost sales of a book and if he can give real, material help and if he has any ideas what makes the dough come in, then he should be allowed to speak his piece in peace. That he is not, is true to many a man's everlasting sorrow and it probably will be to mine.

But somebody has to say something about this first and I'm saying it right here. Soon, if you and you and you give it moral support, we will see all the big advertising agencies paying attention and—what is more important—cold cash to the pulps.

The first step has been taken. I am not the crusader, only the recorder. Since starting this article I have been told that I can tell you this. I wanted to be sure.

Through the American Fiction Guild, the key man of a large advertising firm has become interested in pulp ads. The Guild offered to conduct a reader survey, offered to bring all publishers together. The Guild is meeting with some success in this and even those publishers who have not bothered to take the course through the Guild (which is all the same to the outfit) are gradually working out the problem.

They are afraid, those publishers (and this is strictly my idea), that their big accounts will be jerked away from them by other houses. Each house is working separately under this delusion, failing to see this evident fact.

National advertising will become a concrete fact, raising profit and rates, only when every good pulp on the stands, whether it be published by POPULAR, STANDARD, MUNSEY, DELL, or STREET AND SMITH, banishes this foolish copy forever and does away with the only bugaboo which is keeping national advertising from their pages.

All houses have to pull together in this. No dog-eat-dog about it.

The Guild's part in the affair was merely starting the ball rolling and the program is already becoming an accomplished fact.

It takes nerve to go at this thing. One house has already gone at it and I haven't permission to mention its name. It found, in the first real survey it ever conducted, that their readers averaged thirty-five years of age. Not fourteen to nineteen.

This house banished all the ads it could (though a lot of their copy is still bad because of contracts which they cannot break). For a long time, advertising brought in nothing although specialists were hired.

But just when this house was about to throw up its hands, several good, national accounts fell their way. They are on the road. Gradually they'll put a little more dignity into the space and quit this comic strip attack advertisers think they have to use in pulp.

Several accounts, big money and the other houses will soon be following. This first house will realize more money on their space when other houses do follow suit.

And so, from the stand of the crusader, I become a prosaic reporter. But the fight is not won, it has to go on. Someday we hope that you won't be ashamed of the pages in which your yarns appear. They're good yarns, they're excellent books. Men with intelligence read them and thrill to them.

Things are still slow. But shortly you'll see steam roaring out of the kettle and we'll be in better shape, all of us.

Given the sheer quantity of copy required for survival in that menacing pulp jungle, authors of the realm were frequently hard-pressed for ideas. The highly stylized, and thus comparatively slow, Raymond Chandler regularly cannibalized his own work if only to keep himself fed at a penny a word. While reasoning that what's sauce for the gander will also serve the goose, others tell of recycling plots from arctic adventures as Sahara tales, and aerial twists as deep-sea thrillers. Even more to the point here, fellow pulpateer Richard Sale tells of drawing inspiration from whatever object in his office seemed to suggest a story: an empty whiskey bottle, a dented cigarette lighter, a handful of nickels. Similarly, we come to A. J. Burks's common wastebasket and Ron's "Magic Out of a Hat."

MAGIC OUT OF A HAT

by L. Ron Hubbard

WHEN ARTHUR J. BURKS told me to put a wastebasket upon my head, I knew that one of us—probably both—was crazy. But Burks has a winning way about him—it's said he uses loaded dice—and so I followed his orders and thereby hangs a story. And what a story!

You know, of course, how all this pleasant lunacy started. Burks bragged that he could give six writers a story apiece if only they would name an article in a hotel room. Considering the way New York furnishes its hotels—and remember Burks lived there—that doesn't sound so remarkable. And so six of us, he tells me, took him up on it and trooped in.

The six were Fred "Par" Painton, George "Sizzling Air" Bruce, Norvell "Spider" Page, Walter "Curly-top" Marquiss, Paul "Haunted House" Ernst and myself. An idiotic crew if I do say it, wholly in keeping with such a scheme to mulch editors with alleged stories.

So Burks told me to put a wastebasket on my head, told me that it reminded me of a *kubanka* (Ruski lid, if you aren't a Communist) and ordered me to write the story. I won't repeat here the story he told me to write. It was clean, that's about all you can say for it—although that says a great deal coming from an ex-Marine like Art.

This wastebasket didn't even look faintly like a *kubanka*. A *kubanka* is covered with fur, looks like an ice-cream cone minus its point and is very nice if you're a Ruski. I wrote the story and I'll tell you all about the right way to develop it, so don't go wrong and find Art's article (in that issue with the putrid-pink cover and bilge-green head) and see how he did it. I'll show you the *right* way.

Burks told me to write about a Russian lad who wants his title back and so an American starts the wheels rolling, which wheels turn to gun wheels or some such drivel—and there's a lot of flying in the suggestion too. Now I saw right there that Art had headed me for a cheap action story not worth writing at all. He wanted to do some real fighting in it and kill off a lot of guys.

But I corrected the synopsis so I didn't have to save more than the Russian Empire and I only bumped about a dozen men. In fact, my plot was real literature.

The conversation which really took place (Burks fixed it in his article so he said everything) was as follows:

Burks: I say it looks like a hat. A *kubanka*.

Hubbard: It doesn't at all. But assuming that it does, what of it?

Burks: Write a story about it.

Hubbard: Okay. A lot of guys are sitting around a room playing this game where you throw cards into a hat and gamble on how many you get in. But they're using a fur wastebasket for the hat.

Burks: A fur wastebasket? Who ever heard of that?

Hubbard: You did just now. And they want to know about this fur wastebasket, so the soldier of fortune host tells them it's a *kubanka* he picked up and he can't bear to throw it away although it's terrible bad luck on account of maybe a dozen men getting bumped off because of it. So he tells them the story. It's a "frame" yarn, a neat one.

Burks: But you'll make me out a liar in my article.

Hubbard: So I'll make you a liar in mine.

So I started to plot the story. This hat is a very valuable thing, obviously, if it's to be the central character in a story. And it is a central character. All focus is upon it. Next I'll be writing a yarn in second person.

Anyway, I was always intrigued as a kid by an illustration in a book of knowledge. Pretty red pictures of a trooper riding, a fight, a dead trooper.

You've heard the old one: For want of a nail the shoe was lost, for want of a shoe the horse was lost, for want of a horse the rider was lost, for want of a rider the message was lost, for want of a message the battle was lost and all for the want of a horseshoe nail.

So, it's not to be a horseshoe nail but a hat that loses a battle or perhaps a nation. I've always wanted to lift that nail plot and here was my chance to make real fiction out of it. A hat. A lost empire.

Pretty far apart, aren't they? Well, I'd sneak up on them and maybe scare them together somehow. I made the hat seem ominous enough and when I got going, perhaps light would dawn.

> "The others eyed the object and Stuart turned it around in his hands, gazing thoughtfully at it."

"That's a funny-looking hat," I remarked.

The others eyed the object and Stuart turned it around in his hands, gazing thoughtfully at it.

"But not a very funny hat," said Stuart, slowly. "I don't know why I keep it around. Every time I pick it up I get a case of the jitters. But it cost too much to throw away."

That was odd, I thought. Stuart was a big chap with a very square face and a pocket full of money. He bought anything he happened to want and money meant nothing to him. But here he was talking about cost.

"Where'd you get it?" I demanded.

Still holding the thing, still looking at it, Stuart sat down in a big chair. "I've had it for a long, long time, but I don't know why. It spilled more blood than a dozen such hats could hold, and you see that this could hold a lot."

"I can't have my hero killed, naturally, as this is a first-person story, so I pass the torch to another..."

Something mournful in his tone made us take seats about him. Stuart usually joked about such things.

Well, there I was. Stuart was telling the story and I had to give him something to tell. So I told how he came across the hat.

This was the world war, the date was July 17, 1918, Stuart was a foreign observer trying to help Gajda, the Czech general, get Russia back into fighting shape. Stuart is in a clearing.

...and the rider broke into a clearing.

From the look of him, he was a Cossack. Silver cartridge cases glittered in the sun and the fur on his *kubanka* rippled in the wind. His horse was lathered, its eyes staring with exertion. The Cossack sent a hasty glance over his shoulder and applied his whip.

Whatever was following him did not break into the clearing. A rifle shot roared. The Cossack sat bolt upright as though he had been a compressed steel spring. His head went back, his hands jerked, and he slid off the horse, rolling when he hit the ground.

I remember his *kubanka* bounced and jumped and shot in under a bush....

Feebly, he motioned for me to come closer. I propped him up and a smile flickered across his ashy face. He had a small, arrogant mustache with waxed points. The blackness of it stood out strangely against the spreading pallor of death.

"The...*kubanka*...Gajda..."

That was all he would ever say.

Fine. The *kubanka* must get to General Gajda. Here I was, still working on the horseshoe nail and the message.

The message, the battle was lost. The message meant the *kubanka*. But how could a *kubanka* carry a message? Paper in the hat? That's too obvious. The hero's still in the dark. But here a man has just given his life to get this hat to the Czechs and the hero at least could carry on, hoping General Gajda would know the answer.

He was picking up the one message he knew the hat must carry. He had killed three men in a rifle battle at long range in an attempt to save the Cossack. There's suspense and danger for you. A white man all alone in the depths of Russia during a war. Obviously somebody else is going to get killed over this hat. The total is now four.

I swore loudly into the whipping wind. I had had no business getting into this fight in the first place. My duty was to get back to the main command and tell them that Ekaterinburg was strongly guarded. Now I had picked up the Cossack's torch. These others had killed the Cossack. What would happen to me?

"What's the most startling thing I can think of? The empire connected with the fate of the kubanka. So..."

So my story was moving along after all. The fact that men would die for a hat seems too ridiculous that, when they do die, it's horrible by contrast, seemingly futile.

But I can't have my hero killed, naturally, as this is a first-person story, so I pass the torch to another, one of the hero's friends, an English officer.

This man, as the hero discovers later, is murdered for the *kubanka* and the *kubanka* is recovered by the enemy while the hero sleeps in a hut of a *muzjik* beside the trail.

The suspense up to here and even further is simple. You're worried over the hero, naturally. And you want to know, what's better, why a hat should cause all this trouble. That in itself is plenty of reason for writing a story.

Now while the hero sleeps in the loft, three or four Russian Reds come in and argue over the money they've taken from the dead Englishman, giving the hero this news without the hero being on the scene.

The hat sits in the center of the table. There it is, another death to its name. Why?

So they discover the hero's horse in the barn and come back looking for the hero. Stuart upsets a lamp in the fight, the hut burns, but he cannot rescue the hat. It's gone.

Score nine men for the hat. But this isn't an end in itself. Far from it. If I merely went ahead and said that the hat was worth a couple hundred kopeks, the reader would get mad as hell after reading all this suspense and sudden death. No, something's got to be done about that hat, something startling.

What's the most startling thing I can think of? The empire connected with the fate of the *kubanka*. So the Russian Empire begins to come into it more and more.

The allies want to set the tsar back on the throne, thinking that will give Russia what it needs. Germany is pressing the Western Front and Russia must be made to bear its share.

But I can't save Russia by this hat. Therefore I'll have to destroy Russia by it. And what destroyed it? The tsar, of course. Or rather his death.

The Czech army moves on Ekaterinburg, slowly because they're not interested so much in that town. They could move faster if they wanted. This, for a feeling of studied futility in the end.

They can't find the tsar when they get there. No one knows where the tsar is or even if he's alive. This must be solved. Stuart finds the hat and solves it.

He sees a Red wearing a *kubanka*. That's strange because Cossacks wear *kubankas* and Reds don't. Of all the hats in Russia this one must stand out, so I make the wrong man wear it.

Stuart recovers the *kubanka* when this man challenges him. He recognizes the fellow as one of the Englishman's murderers. In the scrap, seconded by a sergeant to even up the odds, Stuart kills three men.

Score twelve for one secondhand hat. Now about here the reader's patience is tried and weary. He's had enough of this. He's still curious, but the thing can't go any farther. He won't have it.

That's the same principle used in conversation. You've got to know enough to shut up before you start boring your listeners. Always stop talking while they're still interested.

I could have gone on and killed every man in Russia because of that hat and to hell with history.

History was the thing. It thrust up its ugly head and shook a warning finger at me. People know now about the tsar, when and where he was killed and all the rest. So that's why I impressed dates into the first of the story. It helps the reader believe you when his own knowledge tells him you're right. And if you can't lie convincingly, don't ever write fiction.

Now the hero, for the first time (I stressed his anxiety in the front of the story) has a leisurely chance to examine this hat. He finally decides to take the thing apart, but when he starts to rip the threads he notices that it's poorly sewn.

This is the message in the hat, done in Morse code, around the band:

"*Tsar* held at Ekaterinburg, house of Ipatiev. Will die July 18. Hurry."

Very simple, say you. Morse code, old stuff. But old or not, the punch of the story is not a mechanical twist.

The eighteenth of July has long past, but the hero found the hat on the seventeenth. Now had he been able to get it to Gajda, the general's

Price of a Hat,
March 1936

staff could have exhausted every possibility and uncovered that message. They could have sent a threat to Ekaterinburg or they could have even taken the town in time. They didn't know, delayed, and lost the Russian tsar and perhaps the nation.

Twelve men, the tsar and his family and an entire country dies because of one hat.

Of course, the yarn needs a second punch, so the hero finds the jewels of the tsar in burned clothing in the woods and knows that the tsar is dead for sure and the Allied cause for Russia is lost.

The double punch is added by the resuming of the game of throwing cards into this hat.

But after a bit we started to pitch the cards again. Stuart sent one sailing down the room. It touched the brim and teetered there. Then, with a flicker of white, it coasted off the side and came to rest some distance away, face up.

We moved uneasily. I put my cards away.

The one Stuart had thrown, the one which had missed, was the king of spades.

Well, that's the *Price of a Hat*. It sold to Leo Margulies' *Thrilling Adventures* magazine of the Standard Magazines, Inc., which, by the way, was the magazine that bought my first pulp story. It will appear in the March issue, on sale, I suppose, in February. Leo is pretty much of an adventurer himself and, without boasting on my part, Leo knows a good story when he sees it. In a letter to my agent accepting my story, Leo Margulies wrote: "We are glad to buy Ron Hubbard's splendid story *Price of a Hat*. I read the DIGEST article and am glad you carried it through."

Art Burks is so doggoned busy these days with the American Fiction Guild and all, that you hardly see anything of him. But someday I'm going to sneak into his hotel anyway, snatch up the smallest possible particle of dust and make him make me write a story about that. I won't write it, but he will. I bet when he sees this, he'll say:

"By golly, that's a good horror story." And sit right down and make a complete novel out of one speck of dust.

Anyway, thanks for the check, Art. I'll buy you a drink, plenty of pay, at the next luncheon. What? Well, didn't I do all the work?

Among the more revealing notes on this business of writing and of particular significance to anyone who has faced a fickle editor is Ron's "How to Drive a Writer Crazy."

Although undated, it would seem to fit the infamously difficult John W. Campbell, Jr.—forever bombarding authors with contradictory ideas and frightening more than a few into mental paralysis "by showing his vast knowledge of a field...especially on subjects where nothing is known anyway." In either case, what Ron describes is not merely amusing; it is also the ruin of many a young literary talent.

HOW TO DRIVE A WRITER CRAZY

by L. Ron Hubbard

1. When he starts to outline a story, immediately give him several stories just like it to read and tell him three other plots. This makes his own story and his feeling for it vanish in a cloud of disrelated facts.

2. When he outlines a character, read excerpts from stories about such characters, saying that this will clarify the writer's ideas. As this causes him to lose touch with the identity he felt in his character by robbing him of individuality, he is certain to back away from ever touching such a character.

3. Whenever the writer proposes a story, always mention that his rate, being higher than other rates of writers in the book, puts up a bar to his stories.

4. When a rumor has stated that a writer is a fast producer, invariably confront him with the fact with great disapproval, as it is, of course, unnatural for one human being to think faster than another.

5. Always correlate production and rate, saying that it is necessary for the writer to do better stories than the average for him to get any consideration whatever.

6. It is a good thing to mention any error in a story bought, especially when that error is to be editorially corrected, as this makes the writer feel that he is being criticized behind his back and he wonders just how many other things are wrong.

7. Never fail to warn a writer not to be mechanical, as this automatically suggests to him that his stories are mechanical and, as he considers this a crime, wonders how much of his technique shows through and instantly goes to much trouble to bury mechanics very deep—which will result in laying the mechanics bare to the eye.

8. Never fail to mention and then discuss budget problems with a writer, as he is very interested.

9. By showing his vast knowledge of a field, an editor can almost always frighten a writer into mental paralysis, especially on subjects where nothing is known anyway.

10. Always tell a writer plot tricks, as they are not his business.

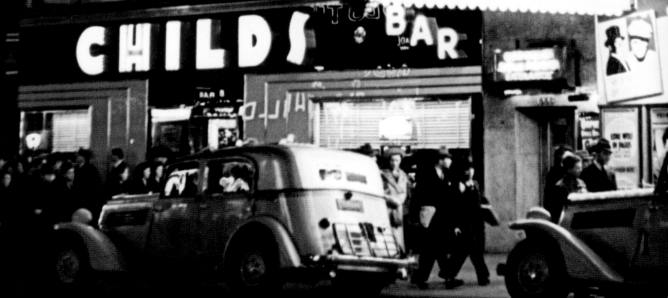

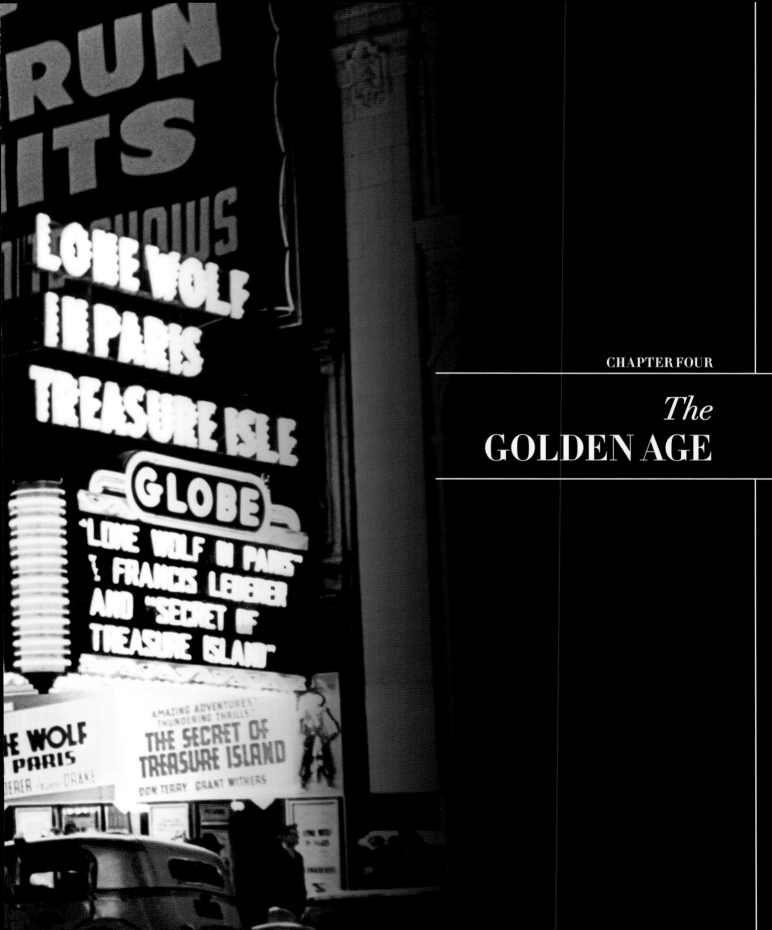

CHAPTER FOUR

The GOLDEN AGE

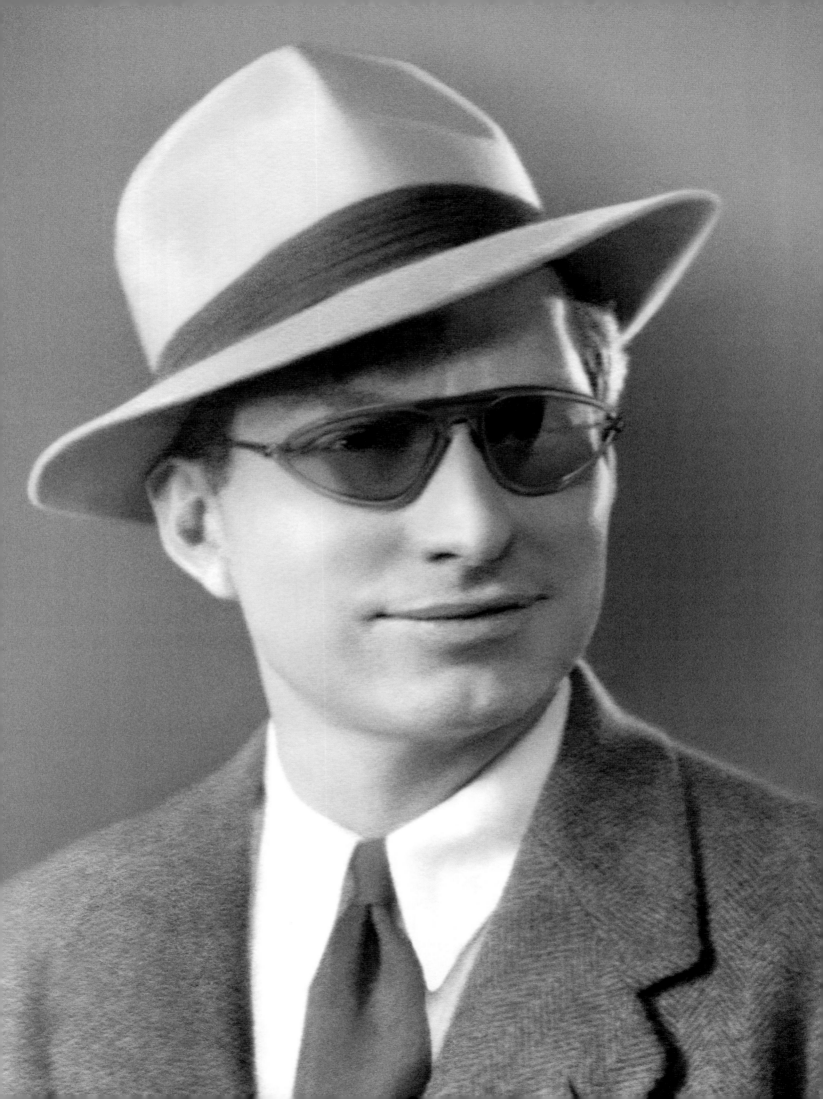

The
Golden Age

"**I**T WILL PROBABLY BE BEST TO RETURN TO THE DAY IN 1938 when I first entered this field, the day I met John W. Campbell, Jr., a day in the very dawn of what has come to be known as The Golden Age of science fiction."—L. Ron Hubbard

In addition to what is told of that day in Ron's frequently quoted introduction to *Battlefield Earth,* let us provide the following: John W. Campbell, Jr., was then twenty-eight years old, and not quite a graduate of the Massachusetts Institute of Technology. (He had failed to master the requisite languages, and so finally earned a Bachelor of Science degree from Duke University.) He had nonetheless proven himself a capable enough author of the genre with a spaceship-driven epic, appropriately entitled *The Machine* series. In suggesting Campbell had originally resisted publishing L. Ron Hubbard and Arthur J. Burks, however, Ron is touching upon a highly significant point of science fiction history, i.e., Campbell was *not* initially that *force majeure* behind the genre's Golden Age; it was the far less scientifically minded F. Orlin Tremaine, who had then held an editorial directorship over Street & Smith's *Astounding* and had indeed invited LRH and A. J. Burks into the fold because he wished an infusion of *character*-driven stories. Or as Ron himself explains: "He was going to get *people* into his stories and get something going besides *machines.*"

Nevertheless, and despite all inherent differences, L. Ron Hubbard and John W. Campbell, Jr., soon set forth beneath the banner of a new science fiction. The first LRH offering, and not one Campbell would

Left L. Ron Hubbard, New York City, 1940

have necessarily published had F. Orlin Tremaine left him unfettered, was entitled *The Dangerous Dimension*. In contrast to the typical Campbell setting amidst gleaming spaceports off the rings of Saturn, that most startling "dangerous dimension" opens in the utterly prosaic office of Yamouth University's Professor Henry Mudge. Nor do we find the usual ranks of simmering beakers or curiously blinking contraptions. Rather, here is nothing more exotic than a "snowdrift of wasted paper" and strewn texts from shelves of arcane metaphysics. What ultimately emerges from that heap of "limp-leaved" texts is a tale of purely intellectual exploration, or what Tremaine had previously described as "thought variant." In this case, it seems Professor Mudge has stumbled upon a mathematical door to a "negative dimension" and has only to think of some distant location in order to physically transport himself. That he cannot control his thoughts finally proves his undoing and so raises the recurring LRH theme involving failures to harness technological advancement.

Although indisputably astounding, this tale of a teleporting professor was not, strictly

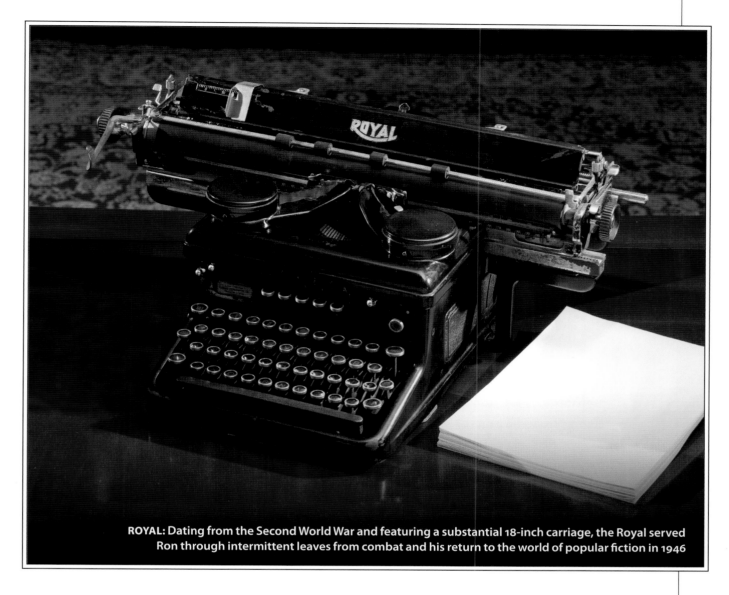

ROYAL: Dating from the Second World War and featuring a substantial 18-inch carriage, the Royal served Ron through intermittent leaves from combat and his return to the world of popular fiction in 1946

speaking, science fiction. Ron himself would describe the work as fantasy and essentially inspired from an Asian tradition of astral projection, i.e., that one's physical location may be altered by mere thought. Much more to the point of *Astounding* was the second LRH offering, *The Tramp*. Telling of a hobo endowed with extraordinary mental powers after experimental brain surgery, *The Tramp* is finally the tale of a Frankenstein's monster or experimentation gone awry. In that regard, the theme again involves a failure to harness technological advancement and so stood quite at odds with Campbell's equation of hard science as our sole salvation. With the advent of atomic weapons, however, more than a few from *Astounding* circles would

join Ron at the Hollywood home of Robert Heinlein for discussions on ways of inspiring a peaceable space race instead of a nuclear arms race.

It is only with *Final Blackout,* however, that we come to the most fully realized LRH statement on this matter of a technological advance into oblivion. Initially appearing in April of 1940 and originally entitled "The Unkillables," the novel is consistently ranked among the ten greatest works of science fiction's Golden Age, rightfully compared to Orwell's *1984,* and certainly just as chilling. Yet again, *Final Blackout* is probably not science fiction as Campbell conceived it. Rather, the setting is a Europe just beyond Dunkirk—but a Europe so thoroughly battered, it finally

> *"Final Blackout is as perfect*
> *a piece of science fiction*
> *as has ever been written."*
>
> —*Robert Heinlein*

resembles nothing less than a moonscape. The central figure, known only as The Lieutenant, is arguably the most fully mythic character to ever emerge from the pages of *Astounding:*

"He was born in an air-raid shelter—and his first wail was drowned by the shriek of bombs, the thunder of falling walls and the coughing chatter of machine guns raking the sky.

"He was taught in a countryside where A was for Antiaircraft and Z was for Zeppelin. He knew that the improved Vickers Wellington bombers had flown clear to Moscow, but nobody thought to tell him about a man who had sailed a carrack twice as far in the opposite direction—a chap called Columbus.

"War-shattered officers had taught him the arts of battle on the relief maps of Rugby. Limping sergeants had made him expert with rifle and pistol, light and heavy artillery. And although he could not conjugate a single Latin verb, he was graduated as wholly educated at fourteen and commissioned the same year."

Once in the field, commands were lost to "all causes and connections," with faith in nothing beyond their Lieutenant. Yet "he was, after all, a highly satisfactory god. He fed them, clothed them, and conserved their lives—which was more than any other god could have done." If

the enemy is clearly fascist, the socialists are no ally. Nevertheless, the work is not a political statement; it is antiwar and inevitably sparked no small controversy on that eve of international mobilization.

Concurrently, or nearly so, we find another sort of LRH work from the period, the mature fantasy. If the genre was tentatively approached by that teleporting Professor Mudge, it is first fully realized with *The Ultimate Adventure.* Telling of a thoroughly modern trek into the realm of *A Thousand and One Nights,* the story was the first of several to tap the world of Arabian myth and played no small part in Street & Smith's founding of *Unknown*—that most memorable of all fantasy vehicles, and expressly launched to accommodate the likes of the LRH tale.

On the heels of *The Ultimate Adventure* and also for the pages of *Unknown* came the similarly inspired *Slaves of Sleep.* Again the setting is that never-never world of *The Arabian Nights,* and again the protagonist is thoroughly modern—in this case, a shipping clerk condemned to a simultaneous existence in parallel realms. Described as a prototypic tale of alternate dimensions, the work inspired much imitation. Hence, the J. W. Campbell, Jr.,

"*A landmark classic! It has been remembered through the decades as one of the all-time memorable classics of the science fiction field.*"

—Robert Bloch

LEFT: *Final Blackout* as originally serialized in *Astounding Science Fiction* through April, May and June 1940   **RIGHT:** Subsequent editions, each achieving bestseller status as succeeding generations discovered what original readers declared to be the greatest tale of science fiction ever authored

"Slaves of Sleep became a sort of buzzword. There are bits and pieces from Ron's work that became a part of the language in ways that very few other writers imagined."
—Frederik Pohl

LEFT: *Slaves of Sleep* as originally published in *Unknown,* July 1939, and *The Masters of Sleep* as originally published in *Fantastic Adventures,* October 1950 **RIGHT:** Later editions featuring both tales in a single volume and enthralling successive generations in emphasis of what science fiction legend Frederik Pohl described as a work that was indelibly part of the culture

note to LRH: "I've been telling a few of the boys to read Washington Irving as an example of pure fantasy...and adding that they aren't to do *Arabian Nights* because the field is preempted by you." As of midsummer, 1940, however, LRH sights had already settled on still higher ground, and a literary trail not easily followed.

As an introductory word, let us briefly consider a continuing topic of LRH interest extending from his ethnological work in the Caribbean and elsewhere—namely, the primitive's belief in unseen but "jealous beings anxious to undermine the happiness of man." The subject proved particularly fascinating owing to its universality: Virtually all tribal communities subscribe to a cosmology of animistic demons. Of interest here, however, is what followed from that research in a purely literary sense—namely, the extraordinary tale of ethnologist James Lowry, who must find four missing hours from his life. Originally entitled "Phantasmagoria" and rightly described as a story of "metaphysical unease," it is a landmark work in every way and remembered today as *Fear.*

"If I handle it properly," reads an LRH note on the work-in-progress, "it will be something Dostoyevsky might have done." He was correct, and particularly when considering the

"An adventure story written in the great style adventure should be written in."
—*Clive Cussler*

LEFT: *Typewriter in the Sky* as it appeared in the November and December 1940 editions of Street & Smith's *Unknown,* a publication inaugurated in part to carry L. Ron Hubbard's tales of fantasy   **RIGHT:** Ensuing editions enchanted successive waves of readers with the tale of a character caught inside a novel and concluded with an unforgettable conceit of a "whimsical god in a dirty bathrobe"

hauntingly surreal *Notes from the Underground.* The work has also been compared to the best of Edgar Allan Poe and legitimately so:

"Clouds, hard driven high up, occasionally flashed shadows over the pavement and lawns; the breeze close to earth frisked with the remnants of autumn, chasing leaves out of corners and across lawns and against trees, bidding them vanish and make way for a new harvest later on."

Yet quite apart from all comparison, here is what literary historian David Hartwell described as among "the foundations of the contemporary horror genre" and a work of profound "moral complexity that helped to transform horror literature from antiquarian or metaphysical form into a contemporary and urban form with the gritty details of everyday realism." In that regard, he concludes, "From Ray Bradbury to Stephen King, a literary debt is owed to L. Ron Hubbard for *Fear.*"

One could cite many more: *Fear* is probably the singly most celebrated work to have emerged from the whole of this pulp kingdom. One could also say much more: beyond *Fear* stands a literal shelf of such fully unforgettable L. Ron Hubbard classics as *Typewriter in the Sky, Ole Doc Methuselah* and *The End Is Not Yet.* Then again, who can forget *To the Stars,*

The Shaping of Fear

Eventually, those surrounding LRH would tell several apocryphal tales regarding his authorship of *Fear:* how the work had virtually possessed him, how it had first been conceived over barbecued steaks on John Campbell's New Jersey lawn, how Ron had furiously rewritten the work on a midnight train from Connecticut. None of it is verifiable and the best description of how he came to author a tale of which so much would be said is found in his letters to friends from the third week in January 1940.

Knickerbocker Hotel
Jan. 18, 1940

I have been so upset about a story for the past few days that I have not written, not wanting to even touch this mill. However I finally got the plot of it licked and am doing research upon it.

The story will be named PHANTASMAGORIA and the theme is, "What happened to Dwight Brown on the day he cannot remember?" Twenty-four hours lost from a man's life. And if I handle it properly it will be something Dostoyevsky might have done. He strives to locate his deeds while missing everywhere but in the right place, for he fears to look there. He is surrounded, day by day, by more terror and apparitions as his solutions are gathered about him only to become hollow and half seen. He knows, deep down, that the day he recognizes his deeds of the day he cannot remember, on that day he shall die. And, having gone mad he has to choose between being mad forever and

being dead. And if you don't think that one was a tough one at which to arrive and now plot by incident...! And John Campbell all the while drumming new suggestions at me and insisting I use them......! And five conflicting stories to be woven into one.....!!!!!!!

Knickerbocker Hotel
Jan. 28, 1940

I tried, today, to start PHANTASMAGORIA, having fully outlined it last night. But for some reason I could not think connectedly enough or establish a sufficient mood. It is a pretty dolorous story and so I suppose I had better tell it very calmly and factually, without striving to dwell on mood.

I've been trying to coax up a certain tone for the story. And I think a nice, delicate style is best suited. Paint everything in sweetness and light and then begin to dampen it, not with the style, but with the events themselves. In other

"L. Ron Hubbard's Fear is one of the few books in the chiller genre which actually merits employment of the overworked adjective 'classic,' as in 'This is a classic tale of creeping, surreal menace and horror'... This is one of the really, really good ones."
—Stephen King

> *"L. Ron Hubbard has been, since the 40s, one of the five writers in the SF field who have served me as models and teachers. His stories, Fear in particular, directly influenced all my work..."*
> —*Ray Faraday Nelson*

words lead the reader in all unsuspecting and then dump the works on his head. Show very little true sympathy and do not at all try to make the facts worse than they are but rather make light of them. Oh hell! This is such a hard story! But I can see a sleepy college town with spring and elms and yawning students and a man just back from an ethnological expedition, called to take over from a professor who has become ill. A man suited to quiet solitude with a certain still idealism about him, who has come back to his home and his wife and is trying anxiously to fit into the picture which he so long ago left. If told almost dispassionately the thing ought to be good. In other words, I'll just write it. For I can't work up a gruesome mood. Ah, for a few days out of my adolescence! The character must take it all mildly, that's the easiest way. How I hate to make anyone "emote"!

L. Ron Hubbard's immortal *Fear:* originally published in July 1940 and riveting readers ever since. Moreover, this is the one that so captivated fellow authors of the realm, beginning with Ray Bradbury, who unabashedly declared, "*Fear* deeply influenced me."

LEFT: The seven *Astounding Science Fiction* installments of L. Ron Hubbard's *Ole Doc Methuselah*   **RIGHT:** The republished adventures of the Soldier of Light and his gypsum-eating, book-reading, four-armed servant known as Hippocrates

rightfully described as both the seminal story on Einstein's time-dilation effect and an altogether timeless statement on the loneliness of command? It is additionally remembered for what may well be the most unforgettable line in all science fiction:

"Space is deep, Man is small and Time is his relentless enemy."

But the time has now come to hear of these days from Ron himself. Dating from 1969, and originally offered in response to requests from a commemorative review, comes the retrospective "By L. Ron Hubbard." To what Ron recounts in the way of incidental events from those golden years, let us understand that his pseudonymous Kurt von Rachen was to finally author several memorable tales for *Astounding* and *Unknown,* including such appropriately

swashbuckling science fiction dramas as *The Idealist, The Mutineers* and *The Rebels.* Let us further understand that his mention of Willy Ley among Campbell, Asimov and Heinlein is especially meaningful; for, if finally a minor author, Ley played no insignificant part in that popularization of the Space Age and is properly remembered as among the earliest proponents of rocket propulsion. Also significant is Ron's mention of Leo Margulies, then editorial director of *Thrilling Wonder Stories* and among the few to carry that pulp tradition into the 1950s.

In referencing "way stops" in Hollywood, Ron is speaking of his ten-week stint on the Columbia Pictures lot, where he adapted his *Murder at Pirate Castle* to the screen as *The Secret of Treasure Island*—a fifteen-episode serial loosely inspired from adventures in the

"To the Stars is just as timely, just as awe-inspiring, just as profoundly moving as it was in 1950. Anyone who doubts the sheer creative and visionary genius of L. Ron Hubbard need just read this novel."
—The Barnes & Noble Review

To the Stars: L. Ron Hubbard's masterful epic of an outward-bound voyage across limitless spans of suspended time. This was the tale that helped inspire an American scientific community to set forth on a space race that all but eclipsed the arms race.

REMINGTON NOISELESS: Perhaps the most memorable of all those typewriters in the service of LRH is the Remington Noiseless. Originally purchased in 1949, here was the machine upon which he wrote the work for which he is best remembered: history's all-time bestselling self-help book, *Dianetics: The Modern Science of Mental Health.*

Right
Author, adventurer L. Ron Hubbard, in Washington, DC, 1941

Caribbean and breaking all box office records of the day. It was also through those typically productive ten weeks Ron contributed to / doctored such big-screen serials as *The Mysterious Pilot, The Great Adventures of Wild Bill Hickok* and (in conjunction with Norvell Page) *The Spider Returns.*

In citing the "petty squabbles," Ron is probably referencing the eventual feud between Campbell and A. J. Burks—apparently over money, and ultimately ending with the blackballing of Burks from the whole of science fiction. (If nothing else, recalled British science fiction author John Brunner, "John [Campbell] was a man who knew how to hold a grudge.") In either case, Ron is perhaps too kind: the squabbles were not always petty, and he was finally the only author from the great

pulp mainstream to emerge unscathed from Campbell's reign as science fiction czar.

By the same token, however, the friendship was real and many an LRH letter tells of dinners at the Campbell home in the wastes of New Jersey and lengthy lunches over plates of "horrible ham" garnished with slices of pineapple. Campbell was additionally among the first to sense what Dianetics represented as the means by which we might venture into that greatest unknown of all, the universe of the self. Then, too, it was Campbell who, inspired by later LRH research, began calling for stories not set in a distant future, but a prehistoric past—which, in turn, has arguably led to all we now celebrate as a new Golden Age of Science Fiction with tales from galaxies far away and a long, long time ago. ∎

Despite the fact that only 10 percent of his total body of fiction is composed of science fiction and fantasy, L. Ron Hubbard helped to create what is still considered the great, classic "Golden Age of Science Fiction"

By L. Ron Hubbar

"BY L. RON HUBBARD"

by L. RON HUBBARD

I GUESS I MUST HAVE written the line "By L. Ron Hubbard" many thousands of times between 1930 and 1950.

And every time I wrote it I had a sense of starting something pleasing, something exciting and, it worked out, something that would sell. Ninety-three and one-half percent of everything I wrote was accepted first draft, first submission.

I wrote adventure, detective stories, air stories, science fiction, fantasy, technical articles, you name it.

Production was about 100,000 words a month most months, done on an electric typewriter, working an average of three hours a day, three days a week.

Arthur J. Burks, Ed Bodin, Bob Heinlein, John Campbell, Willy Ley, Isaac Asimov, these and the rest of the greats were my friends.

I shuttled between New York and Hollywood with way stops at a hideous rainy ranch in Puget Sound.

When I took time off, I went on expeditions to freshen up the old viewpoint.

I had one main problem, and that was running out of magazines to write for.

So I added about five pen names for stories to be "by."

One issue of one magazine was totally filled with my stories, once. All by different names.

It came about this way. Old-timers had editor problems. Editors were also readers. They got tired of one's stories but mainly got tired of the high prices they had to pay per word to a real pro.

So now and then an editor would cut you off his list for a while.

Once when this happened, I got even. I went back home and wrote a story, *The Squad That Never Came Back* and signed it "Kurt von Rachen." Then I had my agent Ed Bodin, take it in to dear old Leo Margulies (bless him) as something by a "new" writer.

Ed was scared stiff. "But if he finds out—"

I pushed him hard. It was a gag on Leo. So Ed did it.

Day or two later, Ed called me in a panic. "They love it. But they want to know what this guy looks like."

So I said, "He's a huge brute of a man. Tough. Black hair, beard. His idea of a party is to rent the floor of a hotel, get everybody drunk and smash the place to bits. A tough character."

So Ed hung up and all seemed well. Then, next day, he called again in even more of a panic. "They want to know where he is! They want to see him! And sign a contract!"

So I said, "He's in the Argentine. He's wanted for murder in Georgia!"

So Ed hung up. And all went through smoothly.

Now it's not illegal to use a pen name. But to play such a joke on an old friend like Leo was bad.

So I went over to Leo's office to tell him for laughs.

Unfortunately, Leo met me with a manuscript in his hand.

He said, "You old-time pros think you are all there is! Look at this. A story brand-new, fresh. New writer. Got it all over you."

And the manuscript he was holding was *The Squad That Never Came Back* by "Kurt von Rachen."

I let it go.

I used the name, among others, for some years. But that isn't all there is to the story.

After the war, years later I was riding down in an elevator in Leo's building. A brand-new fresh writer had stepped in with me.

"I just sold three stories," he said.

I was glad for him. Most pros are for new young ones that are trying.

"Yeah," he said, "and this sure is a WILD town," meaning New York.

"Last night I was at a party. Guy rented a whole floor of a hotel, got everybody drunk, smashed the place up—"

I started, blinked. Could it be?

"What was his name?" I inquired breathlessly.

"Kurt von Rachen" he said. And left me standing there forgetting to get out.

———————

The dear old days. The good old days. The exciting, hard-working, screaming rush old days.

This name, that name. They go by in a rush.

Only six hundred writers total wrote the full story output of America. And only two hundred of them were the hard core professionals.

———————

I got into science fiction and fantasy because F. Orlin Tremaine, at the orders of the managing director of Street and Smith, brought me over and ordered John W. Campbell, Jr., then editor of *Astounding Science Fiction,* to buy whatever I wrote. To freshen the mag, up its circulation, to put in real people and real plots instead of ant men.

I wrote adventure, detective stories,

air stories, science fiction, fantasy,

technical articles, you name it.

Production was about 100,000 words

a month most months, done on an

electric typewriter, working an average

of three hours a day, three days a week.

I had one main problem, and that was

running out of magazines to write for.

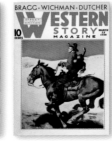

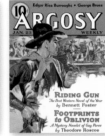

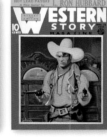

John, although we became dear friends later, didn't like this a bit. He was very fond of his ant men and machines that repaired machines and real people—well, now!

So I wrote my first science fiction. It was called *The Dangerous Dimension*.

After a while John came around and started *Unknown,* mainly I think to publish my fantasy novels.

As I notice, it folded when I stopped writing for it because of the war.

Ah, the old names, L. Sprague de Camp, Fletcher Pratt, Robert Bloch, Ed Hamilton, Frank Belknap Long, dear old Edd Cartier and his fantastic beautiful illustrations, names still going, names forgotten.

All for the "*by* line."

The petty squabbles, the friendly enmities.

I look back now and love them all.

We were quite a crew.

We made and popularized the space age.

We got the show on the road.

And the other day I heard they have a personnel down in the War Department who reads everything we ever wrote, trying to see if there's any hint or invention they've missed.

Well, all those years I was also working on mental technology. The last advance had been with Freud in 1894. Because I knew that someday Man would need it if he ever got into space.

And so I stepped off the bandwagon in 1950 and let them carry on.

They've gone on splendidly, those old writers. They've come up to a stature more like Gods than men.

And I love them all and all my fans and wish them well and well again. *ʅ*

The Kingdom of the Pulps wherein L. Ron Hubbard reigned for nearly twenty years. As even a cursory glance of magazine titles suggests, his output spanned every genre—adventure, mystery, western, science fiction, fantasy and even the occasional romance. Moreover, he produced in prodigious volume, factually totaling more than fifteen million words between 1929 and 1941.

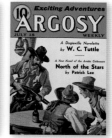

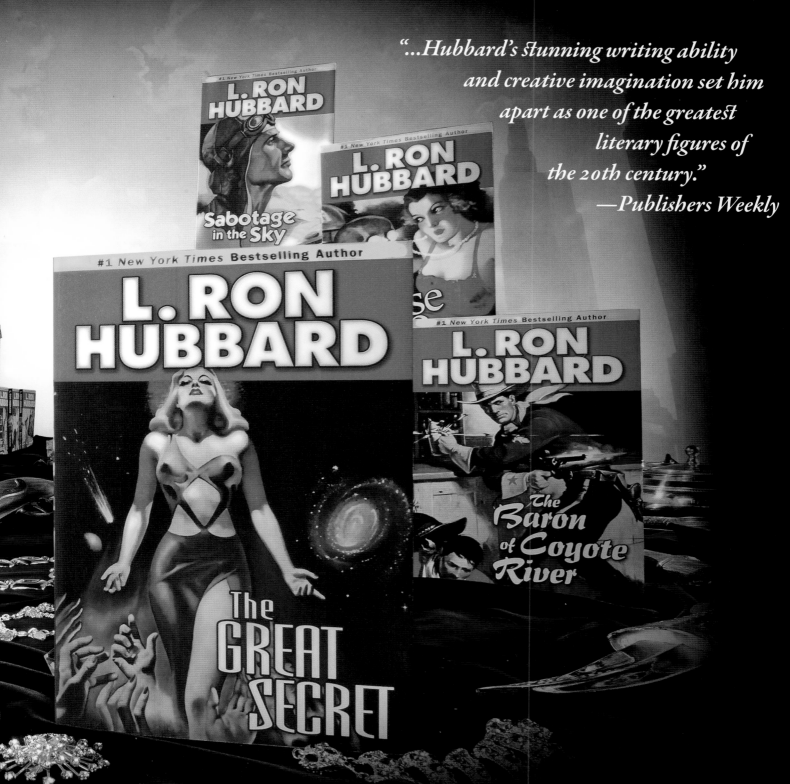

"...Hubbard's stunning writing ability and creative imagination set him apart as one of the greatest literary figures of the 20th century."
—Publishers Weekly

Stories from the Golden Age: comprising the mother lode of classic pulp fiction are more than 150 L. Ron Hubbard tales in eighty volumes and from every corner of the Great Pulp Kingdom. Westerns, mysteries, adventure, horror, science fiction, fantasy and even romance on the purple sage—here is both the definitive pulp collection and defining statement on what is aptly described as the "enduring allure of the pulps."

Here, too, is an entirely new dimension in "literary listening," with *Stories from the Golden Age* on audiobook. Born from an interplay of more than seventy performers recording in a single studio, here is an audiobook to exemplify what critics describe as that "special synergy not heard since the heyday of old time radio." Then again, here is what connoisseurs of the form describe as a complete "theatre of the mind" wherein listeners are awash in atmospheric sounds—from babbling brooks to bone-crunching blows, from whistling bullets to hooting howls. In consequence, and uniquely so, comes an audiobook to all but immerse the listener in a story.

Critical Acclaim

While the works of L. Ron Hubbard have always enjoyed critical acclaim, excerpts reprinted here reflect reviews from the whole spectrum of today's book and audiobook publications—thus underscoring the classic stature of an LRH tale and the enduring allure of the pulps.

"Hubbard was a first-rate pulp writer... He could go up against any of these giants [Hammett, Max Brand, H. P. Lovecraft, Edgar Rice Burroughs, Louis L'Amour]. And while most pulpsters worked in multiple genres, I don't know of any who covered the full spectrum of pulp categories more ambitiously than Hubbard."

—*Locus Magazine*

"Each of these outstanding audio books are two hour productions characterized by talented multi-cast performances, which are enhanced with impressive special effects and thematic music. Flawless technical recordings, each and every one of these very special audio books provides the listener with a true 'theatre of the mind' experience and is enthusiastically recommended for personal and community library audio book collections."

—*Midwest Book Review*

AudioFile ◁▷

"Who could have guessed that pulp fiction would make a comeback, finding new life in the form of delightfully over-the-top audio theater performances? Someone at Galaxy Audio obviously knew, because 150 stories later, the 'Golden Age Stories' have been made enduring all over again."

—*AudioFile Magazine*

"...rife with action and adventure and laced with melodramatic overtones....these full-cast, sound effects-laden productions will engage listeners of all ages, particularly fans of old-time radio, Westerns, genre fiction, action and adventure, and full-cast performances."

—Library Journal

PublishersWeekly

"Hubbard's classic pulp fiction tale was originally published in 1943 but shows no signs of age. With the tremendous attention to detail and production, audiences will find themselves captivated from beginning to end."

—Publishers Weekly

"If proof were needed that L. Ron Hubbard could handle the Western with the flair of a Louis L'Amour or Zane Grey, this book [Six-Gun Caballero] is it."

—True West Magazine

CALIFORNIA
CHRONICLE

"With his knowledge of the world and its people, and his ability to write in any style and genre, L. Ron Hubbard rapidly achieved prominence as a writer of action, adventure, western, mystery and suspense.

"Such was the respect of his fellow writers, including Raymond Chandler, Dashiell Hammett and Edgar Rice Burroughs, that he was only twenty-five when they elected him president of the New York Chapter of the American Fiction Guild."

—California Chronicle

Booklist

"...pulp fiction at its most entertaining."—*Booklist*

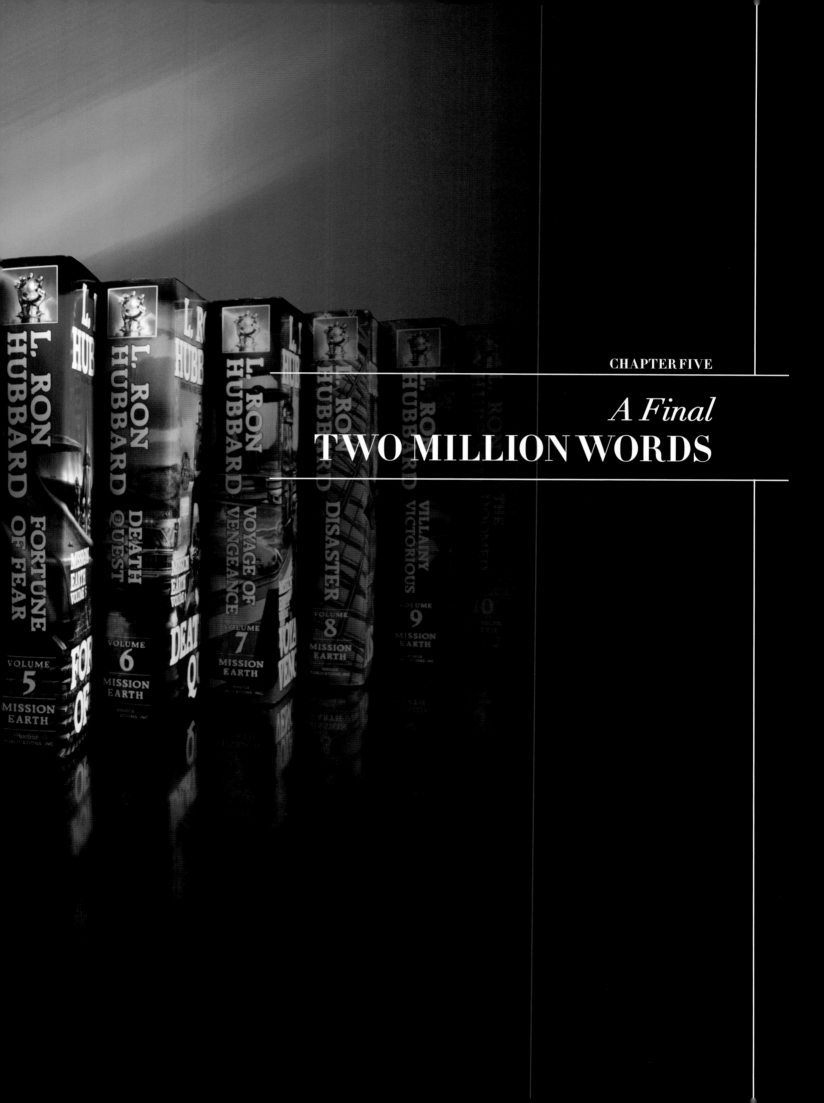

CHAPTER FIVE

A Final
TWO MILLION WORDS

A Final
Two Million
Words

H AVING DEVOTED THREE DECADES TO THE ADVANCEMENT
of Dianetics and Scientology beyond 1950, it was not until
the 1980s we find L. Ron Hubbard returning to the business
of popular literature. In the interim, the last of the pulps had quietly died
and the majority of those who had filled the rough-cut pages had slipped
into relative obscurity. (Although what with eventual film adaptation,
the likes of the Shadow, the Phantom and Doc Savage would continue
to dwell in popular imagination.) One might further argue that much of
what still endears us to the pulps, including the stylized power of seasoned
professionals with several million words to their credit, was also lost. Hence,
descriptions of the modern novel as a "screenplay with the 'he saids' left in,"
i.e., narratively flat and prosaic. Hence, too, the quite unprecedented fervor
following word of L. Ron Hubbard's return to the field, and the actual
newspaper headlines: "Writer Resumes Career with Masterful Epic." ▪

L. Ron Hubbard as millions of fans came to know him, as this was the
author's photograph on the dust jackets of his final science fiction epics,
Battlefield Earth and the *Mission Earth* series

The Writing of Battlefield Earth

THAT EPIC—AND THE TERM IS FULLY accurate—was *Battlefield Earth: A Saga of the Year 3000*. The work is nothing short of massive: "428,750 words long plus intro," as Ron finally calculated from the running tally with which he marked his daily progress. (Rather in awe, more than one critic would remark upon Ron's use of a then fairly rare word processor. In fact, however, he employed two Underwood manual typewriters—one to hammer out his several thousand words a day, while the other underwent repair. Every two or three weeks, he switched and proceeded to wear the alternate machine into a sorry state of disrepair.) Moreover, he was further to generate some seven hundred pages of handwritten notes, which further provide us some sense of how he approached the work.

The story, as meticulously detailed in those preliminary notes, tells of an Earth so fully devastated after a thousand years of Psychlo rule, barely thirty-five thousand human beings remain. Yet among those surviving humans is the wonderfully courageous Jonnie Goodboy Tyler. If he emerges from what is effectively a tribal community among the Rocky Mountains, he nonetheless proves more than a match for the inestimably cruel and technologically advanced Psychlos. Thus, the primary theme as reiterated in various ways through preliminary notes: the indomitable spirit of Man prevailing over those who mistakenly regard him as an animal.

One finds the whole of the Psychlo history among those preliminary notes, including chronicles of interplanetary conquest, a discourse on galactic diplomacy and much concerning the tooth-and-claw mores of the rampaging Psychlos. The implication here: Although John W. Campbell, Jr., would speak of the LRH story as rolling out in a single creative burst, *Battlefield Earth* was plainly a work of very careful design and all the more impressive for the mere eight months of writing. Both setting and structure were firmly established before word one, while additional notes detailed technological advancements as extrapolated from a most impressive grasp of time-space theory. Also found among those initial notes is much of what provides the thematic continuity, with delineated chapter motifs and character sketches.

Then, too, we find much pertaining to what is plainly satirical.

Left First edition *Battlefield Earth*, 1982

The more than seven hundred pages of preliminary notes from the authorship of *Battlefield Earth*. The work was written over an eight-month period in 1980 and originally entitled "Man: The Endangered Species."

> *"Battlefield Earth has everything: suspense, pathos, politics, war, humor, diplomacy and intergalactic finance... Hubbard keeps things moving so irresistibly...and the 800 pages go by quickly."*
> —*Publishers Weekly*

Transcending even the power of the Psychlos is a race of intergalactic bankers (literal descendants of sharks) with a pressing lien on the entirety of Earth, including existing resources, future proceeds from mineral exploitation and even the destiny of future populations. If utterly unconcerned as to the fate of those on the balance sheets, the indifference is not malicious. Merely, "This is all just routine. Ordinary banking business."

The greater whole is precisely what critics declared: "an intergalactic adventure with the imagery and impact of *Star Wars* and a plot that sets it apart as a masterpiece." It was also rightly declared a blockbuster of phenomenal scope—riding one national bestseller list after another for a full year, then topping international lists—and a genuine *event* in publishing history. "It caught everyone by surprise when L. Ron Hubbard returned to writing," remarked an insider from the book trade. "The closest equivalent would have been the Dodgers coming home to Brooklyn." Then again, with initial sales of more than two million copies, one inevitably heard much talk of the book as a cultural catalyst in itself. *Battlefield Earth* has inspired an undying devotion among fans of the genre and is regularly ranked among the six

most memorable stories in the whole of science fiction, along with Frank Herbert's *Dune* and Robert Heinlein's *Stranger in a Strange Land*. The work has further become the basis of study in some forty institutions—appropriately including both George Washington and Harvard universities, where LRH himself had lectured so many years earlier.

Finally, and of most immediate significance, there is all the novel came to represent as a legitimate trendsetter. The first work of science fiction in more than twenty years to attract a truly substantial mainstream readership (Heinlein's aforementioned *Stranger in a Strange Land* was the last), *Battlefield Earth* is legitimately credited with inspiring a resurgence for the whole of speculative fiction. In point of fact: Within four years of *Battlefield Earth*'s publication, a once-neglected speculative fiction—primarily fodder for the paperback original or specialty publisher—was suddenly accounting for a full 10 percent of all fiction sales. Hence, the eventual descriptions of *Battlefield Earth* as "landmark" and "an epic which will be talked about for years to come."

The following LRH causerie has been hailed as a legitimate classic in its own right—specifically "a delineating essay on

> *"Good old-fashioned space opera (Buck Rogers stuff) makes a solid comeback in L. Ron Hubbard's Battlefield Earth... If you think they don't write 'em anymore like they used to, take heart—here's 800 pages from one of the originals."*
>
> *—New York Newsday*

science fiction as 'the herald of possibility' and fantasy as 'postulating no limits at all.'" To what has thus far been said of Ron's place in those wonderful realms of possibility, we might add one more pertinent word: In describing himself as initially diffident and, actually, "quite ignorant" of science fiction, Ron is touching upon yet another significant point of science fiction history. What originally fueled the field was not, as is so frequently argued, a John Campbell vision of brave new technological wonders penned by a stable of techno-authors from MIT and Caltech. No, what fueled science fiction was the same stuff fueling all great fiction—which is to say, all we have examined through "this business of writing." ■

Taken from Battlefield Earth
A Saga of the Year 3000

AN INTRODUCTION TO SCIENCE FICTION

by L. RON HUBBARD

RECENTLY THERE CAME A period when I had little to do. This was novel in a life so crammed with busy years, and I decided to amuse myself by writing a novel that was *pure* science fiction.

In the hard-driven times between 1930 and 1950, I was a professional writer not simply because it was my job, but because I wanted to finance more serious researches. In those days there were few agencies pouring out large grants to independent workers. Despite what you might hear about Roosevelt "relief," those were depression years. One succeeded or one starved. One became a topliner or a gutter bum. One had to work very hard at his craft or have no craft at all. It was a very challenging time for anyone who lived through it.

First paperback edition, 1985

I have heard it said, as an intended slur, "He was a science fiction writer," and have heard it said of many. It brought me to realize that few people understand the role science fiction has played in the lives of Earth's whole population.

I have just read several standard books that attempt to define "science fiction" and to trace its history. There are many experts in this field, many controversial opinions. Science fiction is favored with the most closely knit reading public that may exist, possibly the most dedicated of any genre. Devotees are called "fans," and the word has a special prestigious meaning in science fiction.

Few professional writers, even those in science fiction, have written very much on the character of "sf." They are usually too busy turning out the work itself to expound on what they have written. But there are many experts on this subject among both critics and fans, and they have a lot of worthwhile things to say.

However, many false impressions exist, both of the genre and of its writers. So when one states that he set out to write a work of *pure* science fiction, he had better state what definition he is using.

It will probably be best to return to the day in 1938 when I first entered this field, the day I met John W. Campbell, Jr., a day in the very dawn of what has come to be known as The Golden Age of science fiction. I was quite ignorant of the field and regarded it, in fact, a bit diffidently. I was not there of my own choice. I had been summoned to the vast old building on Seventh Avenue in dusty, dirty, old New York by the very top brass of Street and Smith publishing company—an executive named Black and another, F. Orlin Tremaine. Ordered there with me was another writer, Arthur J. Burks. In those days when the top brass of a publishing company—particularly one as old and prestigious as Street and Smith—"invited" a writer to visit, it was like being commanded to appear before the king or receiving a court summons. You arrived, you sat there obediently, and you spoke when you were spoken to.

We were both, Arthur J. Burks and I, top-line professionals in other writing fields. By the actual tabulation of A.B. Dick, which set advertising rates for publishing firms, either of our names appearing on a magazine cover would send the circulation rate skyrocketing, something like modern TV ratings.

"Street and Smith was unhappy because its magazine was mainly publishing stories about machines and machinery. As publishers, its executives knew you had to have people in stories."

The top brass came quickly to the point. They had recently started or acquired a magazine called *Astounding Science Fiction*. Other magazines were published by other houses, but Street and Smith was unhappy because its magazine was mainly publishing stories about machines and machinery. As publishers, its executives knew you had to have *people* in stories. They had called us in because, aside from our A.B. Dick rating as writers, we could write about *real people*. They knew we were busy and had other commitments. But would we be so kind as to write science fiction? We indicated we would.

They called in John W. Campbell, Jr., the editor of the magazine. He found himself looking at two adventure-story writers, and though adventure writers might be the aristocrats of the whole field and might have vast followings of their own, they were *not* science fiction writers. He resisted. In the first place, calling in topliners would ruin his story budget due to their word rates. And in the second place, he had his own ideas of what science fiction was.

Campbell, who dominated the whole field of sf as its virtual czar until his death in 1971, was a huge man who had majored in physics at Massachusetts Institute of Technology and graduated from Duke University with a Bachelor of Sciences degree. His idea of getting a story was to have some professor or scientist write it and then doctor it up and publish it. Perhaps that is a bit unkind, but it really was what he was doing. To fill his pages even he, who had considerable skill as a writer, was writing stories for the magazine.

The top brass had to directly order Campbell to buy and to publish what we wrote for him. He was going to get *people* into his stories and get something going besides *machines*.

I cannot tell you how many other writers were called in. I do not know. In all justice, it may have been Campbell himself who found them later on. But do not get the impression that Campbell was anything less than a master and a genius in his own right. Any of the stable of writers he collected during this Golden Age will tell you that. Campbell could listen. He could improve things. He could dream up little plot twists that were masterpieces. He well deserved the title that he gained and kept as the top editor and the dominant force that made science fiction as respectable as it became. *Star Wars,* the all-time box office record movie to date (exceeded only by its sequel), would never have happened if science fiction had not become as respectable as Campbell made it. More than that—Campbell played no small part in driving this society into the space age.

You had to actually work with Campbell to know where he was trying to go, what his idea was of this thing called "science fiction." I cannot give you any quotations from him; I can just tell you what I felt he was trying to do. In time we became friends. Over lunches and in his office and at his home on weekends—where his wife Doña kept things smooth—talk was always of stories but also of science. To say that Campbell considered science fiction as "prophecy" is an oversimplification. He had very exact ideas about it.

Only about a tenth of my stories were written for the fields of science fiction and fantasy. I was what they called a high-production writer, and these fields were just not big enough to take everything I could write. I gained my original reputation in other writing fields during the eight years before the Street and Smith interview.

> *"Only about a tenth of my stories were written for the fields of science fiction and fantasy. I was what they called a high-production writer, and these fields were just not big enough to take everything I could write. I gained my original reputation in other writing fields..."*

Campbell, without saying too much about it, considered the bulk of the stories I gave him to be not science fiction but fantasy, an altogether different thing. Some of my stories he eagerly published as science fiction—among them *Final Blackout.* Many more, actually. I had, myself, somewhat of a science background, had done some pioneer work in rockets and liquid gases, but I was studying the branches of man's past knowledge at that time to see whether he had ever come up with anything valid. This, and a love of the ancient tales now called *The Arabian Nights,* led me to write quite a bit of fantasy. To handle this fantasy material, Campbell introduced another magazine, *Unknown.* As long as I was writing novels for it, it continued. But the war came and I and others went, and I think *Unknown* only lasted about forty months. Such novels were a bit hard to come by. And they were not really Campbell's strength.

So anyone seeking to say that science fiction is a branch of fantasy or an extension of it is unfortunately colliding with a time-honored professional usage of terms. This is an age of mixed genres. I hear different forms of music mixed together like soup. I see so many different styles of dance tangled together into one "dance" that I wonder whether the choreographers really know the different genres of dance anymore. There is abroad today the concept that only *conflict* produces new things. Perhaps the philosopher Hegel introduced that, but he also said that war was necessary for the mental health of the people and a lot of other nonsense. If all new ideas have to spring from the conflict between old ones, one must deny that virgin ideas can be conceived.

So what would *pure* science fiction be?

It has been surmised that science fiction must come from an age where science exists. At the risk of raising dispute and outcry—which I have risked all my life and received but not been bothered by, and have gone on and done my job anyway—I wish to point out some things:

Science fiction does NOT come after the fact of a scientific discovery or development. It is the herald of possibility. It is the plea that someone should work on the future. Yet it is not prophecy. It is the dream that precedes the dawn when the inventor or scientist awakens and goes to his books or his lab saying, "I wonder whether I could make that dream come true in the world of real science."

You can go back to Lucian, second century A.D., or to Johannes Kepler (1571–1630)—who founded modern dynamical astronomy and who also wrote *Somnium,* an imaginary space flight to the moon—or to Mary Shelley and her Frankenstein, or to Poe or Verne or Wells and ponder whether this was really science fiction. Let us take an example: a man invents an eggbeater. A writer later writes a story about an eggbeater. He has *not,* thereby, written science fiction. Let us continue the example: a man writes a story about some metal that, when twiddled, beats an egg, but no such tool has ever before existed in fact. He has now written science fiction.

> *"Science fiction does* NOT *come after the fact of a scientific discovery or development. It is the herald of possibility. It is the plea that someone should work on the future."*

Somebody else, a week or a hundred years later, reads the story and says, "Well, well. Maybe it could be done." And makes an eggbeater. But whether or not it was possible that twiddling two pieces of metal would beat eggs, or whether or not anybody ever did it afterward, the man still has written science fiction.

How do you look at this word "fiction"? It is a sort of homograph. In this case it means two different things. A professor of literature knows it means "a literary work whose content is produced by the imagination and is not necessarily based on fact; the category of literature comprising works of this kind, including novels, short stories and plays." It is derived from the Latin *fictio,* a making, a fashioning, from *fictus,* past participle of *fingere,* to touch, form, mold.

But when we join the word to "science" and get "science fiction," the word "fiction" acquires two meanings in the same use: 1) the science used in the story is at least partly fictional; and 2) any *story* is fiction. The *American Heritage Dictionary of the English Language* defines science fiction as "fiction in which scientific developments and discoveries form an element of plot or background; especially a work of fiction based on prediction of future scientific possibilities."

So, by dictionary definition and a lot of discussions with Campbell and fellow writers of that time, science fiction has to do with the material universe and sciences; these can include economics, sociology, medicine, and suchlike, all of which have a material base.

Then what is fantasy?

Well, believe me, if it were simply the application of vivid imagination, then a lot of economists and government people and such would be fully qualified authors! Applying the word "imaginative" to fantasy would be like calling an entire library "some words." Too simplistic, too general a term.

In these modern times many of the ingredients that make up "fantasy" as a type of fiction have vanished from the stage. You hardly even find them in encyclopedias anymore. These subjects were spiritualism, mythology, magic, divination, the supernatural and many other fields of that type. None of them had anything really to do with the real universe. This does not necessarily mean that they never had any validity or that they will not again arise; it merely means that man, currently, has sunk into a materialistic binge.

The bulk of these subjects consists of false data, but there probably never will come a time when *all* such phenomena are explained. The primary reason such a vast body of knowledge dropped from view is that material science has been undergoing a long series of successes. But I do notice that every time modern science thinks it is down to the nitty-gritty of it all, it runs into (and sometimes adopts) such things as the Egyptian myths that man came from mud, or something like that. But the only point I am trying to make here is that there is a whole body of phenomena that we cannot classify as "material." They are the nonmaterial, nonuniverse subjects. And no matter how false many of the old ideas were, they still existed; who knows but what there might not be some validity in some bits of them. One would have to study these subjects to have a complete comprehension of all the knowledge and beliefs possible. I am not opening the door to someone's saying I believe in all these things: I am only saying that there is another realm besides dedicated—and even simple-minded—materialism.

"Then what is fantasy? Well, believe me, if it were simply the application of vivid imagination, then a lot of economists and government people and such would be fully qualified authors!"

"Fantasy," so far as literature is concerned, is defined in the dictionary as "literary or dramatic fiction characterized by highly fanciful or supernatural elements." Even that is a bit limited as a definition.

So fantasy could be called any fiction that takes up elements such as spiritualism, mythology, magic, divination, the supernatural and so on. *The Arabian Nights* was a gathering together of the tales of many, many countries and civilizations—not just of Arabia as many believe. Its actual title was *A Thousand and One Nights of Entertainment*. It abounds with examples of fantasy fiction.

When you mix science fiction with fantasy you do not have a pure genre. The two are, to a professional, separate genres. I notice today there is a tendency to mingle them and then excuse the result by calling it "imaginative fiction." Actually they don't mix well: science fiction, to be credible, has to be based on some degree of plausibility; fantasy gives you no limits at all. Writing science fiction demands care on the part of the author; writing fantasy is as easy as strolling in the park. (In fantasy, a guy has no sword in his hand; bang, there's a magic sword in his hand.) This doesn't say one is better than the other. They are simply very different genres from a professional viewpoint.

But there is more to this: science fiction, particularly in its Golden Age, had a mission. I cannot, of course, speak for my friends of that period. But from Campbell and from "shooting the breeze" with other writers of the time, one got the very solid impression that they were doing a heavy job of beating the drum to get man to the stars.

At the beginning of that time, science fiction was regarded as a sort of awful stepchild in the world of literature. But worse than that, science itself was not getting the attention or the grants or the government expenditures it should have received. There has to be a *lot* of public interest and demand before politicians shell out the financing necessary to get a subject whizzing.

Campbell's crew of writers were pretty stellar. They included very top-line names. They improved the literary quality of the genre. And they began the boom of its broader popularity.

A year or so after The Golden Age began, I recall going into a major university's science department. I wanted some data on cytology for my own serious researches. I was given a courteous reception and was being given the references when I noticed that the room had been gradually filling up. And not with students but with professors and deans. It had been whispered around the offices who was in the biology department, and the next thing I knew, I was shaking a lot of hands held out below beaming faces. And what did they want to know: What did I think of this story or that? And had I seen this or that writer lately? And how was Campbell?

They had a literature! *Science fiction!* And they were proud of it!

For a while, before and after World War II, I was in rather steady association with the new era of scientists, the boys who built the bomb, who were beginning to get the feel of rockets. They were all science fiction buffs. And many of the hottest scientists around were also writing science fiction on the side.

> "...science fiction, to be credible, has to be based on some degree of plausibility; fantasy gives you no limits at all."

In 1945 I attended a meeting of old scientist and science fiction friends. The meeting was at the home of my dear friend, the incomparable Bob Heinlein. And do you know what was their agenda? How to get man into space fast enough so that he would be distracted from further wars on Earth. And they were the lads who had the government ear and authority to do it! We are coming close to doing it. The scientists got man into space and they even had the Russians cooperating for a while.

One can't go on living a naive life believing that everything happens by accident, that events simply follow events, that there is a natural order of things and that everything will come out right somehow. That isn't science. That's fate, kismet, and we're back in the world of fantasy. No, things do get planned. The Golden Age of science fiction that began with Campbell and *Astounding Science Fiction* gathered enough public interest and readership to help push man into space. Today, you hear top scientists talking the way we used to talk in bull sessions so long ago.

Campbell did what he set out to do. So long as he had his first wife and others around him to remind him that science was for *people,* that it was no use to just send machines out for the sake of machines, that there was no point in going into space unless the mission had something to do with people, too, he kept winning. For he was a very brilliant man and a great and very patient editor. After he lost his first wife, Doña, in 1949—she married George O. Smith—and after he no longer had a sounding board who made him keep people in stories, and when he no longer had his old original writing crew around, he let his magazine slip back, and when it finally became named *Analog,* his reign was over. But The Golden Age had kicked it all into high gear. So Campbell won after all.

When I started out to write this novel, I wanted to write *pure* science fiction. And not in the old tradition. Writing forms and styles have changed, so I had to bring myself up to date and modernize the styles and patterns. To show that science fiction is not science fiction because of a particular kind of plot, this novel contains practically every type of story there is—detective, spy, adventure, western, love, air war, you name it. All except fantasy; there is none of that. The term "science" also includes economics and sociology and medicine where these are related to material things. So they're in here, too.

In writing for magazines, the editors (because of magazine format) force one to write to exact lengths. I was always able to do that—it is a kind of knack. But this time I decided not to cut everything out and to just roll her as she rolled, so long as the pace kept up. So I may have wound up writing the biggest sf novel ever in terms of length. The experts—and there are lots of them to do so—can verify whether this is so.

Some of my readers may wonder that I did not include my own serious subjects in this book. It was with no thought of dismissal of them. It was just that I put on my professional writer's hat. I also did not want to give anybody the idea I was doing a press relations job for my other serious works.

"The Golden Age of science fiction that began with Campbell and Astounding Science Fiction gathered enough public interest and readership to help push man into space."

There are those who will look at this book and say, "See? We told you he is just a science fiction writer!" Well, as one of the crew of writers that helped start man to the stars, I'm very proud of also being known as a science fiction writer. You have satellites out there, man has walked on the moon, you have probes going to the planets, don't you? Somebody had to dream the dream, and a lot of somebodies like those great writers of The Golden Age and later had to get an awful lot of people interested in it to make it true.

I hope you enjoy this novel. It is the only one I ever wrote just to amuse myself. It also celebrates my golden wedding with the muse. Fifty years a professional—1930–1980.

And as an old pro I assure you that it is *pure* science fiction. No fantasy. Right on the rails of the genre. Science is for people. And so is science fiction.

Ready?

Stand by.

Blast off!

"Think of the Star Wars sagas, and Raiders of the Lost Ark, mix in the triumph of Rocky I, Rocky II and Rocky III and you have captured the exuberance, style and glory of Battlefield Earth."
—Baltimore Evening Sun

"Without a doubt, L. Ron Hubbard is one of the most prolific and influential writers of the twentieth century."
—Stephen V. Whaley, PhD
Professor of English and Foreign Languages

The perennially bestselling *Battlefield Earth:* it has been translated into scores of languages and published in dozens of nations. It is without a doubt the most broadly acclaimed single-volume science fiction novel in the history of the genre.

Battlefield Earth for the new millennium: science fiction's classic epic of the twentieth century becomes an enduring classic for this twenty-first century. The cover-painting depicting Jonnie and Chrissie in visceral confrontation with the villainous Psychlo, Terl, is science fiction history in and of itself. For here is the fully realized, but never before published, cover by Sci-fi and Fantasy grand master, Frank Frazetta. Moreover, just as Frazetta long loved the tales of L. Ron Hubbard, so Ron long cherished the work of Frazetta. Consequently, here is the king of science fiction's Golden Age at long last paired with the king of mythic illustration.

Battlefield Earth audiobook: featuring some seventy performers representing 198 characters to ultimately make for nearly fifty hours of dramatic listening, the *Battlefield Earth* audiobook signals an unprecedented advance in the medium. It also signals a new dimension in audiobook production. To be sure, all was scrupulously directed in alignment with the author's notes on characterization, scene description and ambiance.

Science fiction does *not* come after the fact of a scientific discovery or development. It is the herald of possibility. It is the plea that someone should work on the future. Yet it is not prophecy. It is the dream that precedes the dawn when the inventor or scientist awakens and goes to his books or his lab saying, "I wonder whether I could make that dream come true in the world of real science."

—L. Ron Hubbard

13

The awards and recognitions presented to L. Ron Hubbard's *Battlefield Earth*. Included in the array is an unprecedented Saturn Award from the Academy of Science Fiction, Fantasy and Horror Films. Although typically reserved for dramatic works of art, this was a Saturn bestowed on what was bluntly described as L. Ron Hubbard's "masterpiece novel." Also on display are the sixty-eight national and international bestseller lists *Battlefield Earth* rode for 368 weeks.

The Magnum Opus: Mission Earth

ATTLEFIELD EARTH WAS NOT, however—as many a critic initially declared—the LRH *magnum opus*. Rather, that distinction is more generally afforded to the next of the final LRH works, the ten-volume, 1.2-million-word *Mission Earth* series. How he managed those 1.2 million words in what amounted to the space of eight months is yet another of those legendary literary feats in line with the perfect dictated sentences of the later Henry James or the virtually flawless handwritten manuscripts of the later Charles Dickens. In either case, the LRH rate of production alone is astonishing, actually surpassing his fabled speed in the heyday of pulps, and even more impressive considering those rotating Underwood manuals—one in the shop for repair, while he rapidly wore down the other and then switched.

Again, a mass of preliminary notes reveals an intricate plan behind all that seems so freely wrought—every chapter carefully outlined, every character neatly sketched. The whole is a wonderfully crafted tale of a suave and swashbuckling Fleet combat engineer from the planet Voltar who must battle a nefarious intelligence chief to save an unsuspecting Earth and thwart the subversion of Voltar itself. The bulk of the narrative represents an after-the-fact

confession from former Coordinated Information Apparatus (CIA) executive Soltan Gris, and otherwise employs a uniquely villainous viewpoint. The intrepid combat engineer, Jettero Heller, has been implanted with a video-relayer allowing Gris to see and hear all our hero experiences. What ensues is a perfectly wry and ironic assessment of a well-intentioned and capable hero—as when this Soltan Gris insists we view Heller as a hopeless innocent among savagely clever CIA operatives...even as Heller effortlessly outwits them all.

"I loved *Mission Earth*," declared Ray Faraday Nelson of the genre's new wave. "The CIA will hate it." He was undoubtedly correct, and particularly in light of later charges that Agency personnel had been financing Central American operations with profits from the heroin trade—all as more or less portrayed in the pages of *Mission Earth*. Similarly, there is all *Mission Earth* has to say concerning drug enforcement officials on the take—more or less in line with later scandals involving Mexican enforcement agencies—and all else the series lampoons as regards Earth-raping multinationals, death-dealing bureaucracies,

Left First edition of the *Mission Earth* "dekalogy"

In addition to the 1.2-million-word *Mission Earth* manuscript, LRH compiled more than 1,500 pages of handwritten notes wherein he sketched every chapter, every character and a wealth of relevant technical information

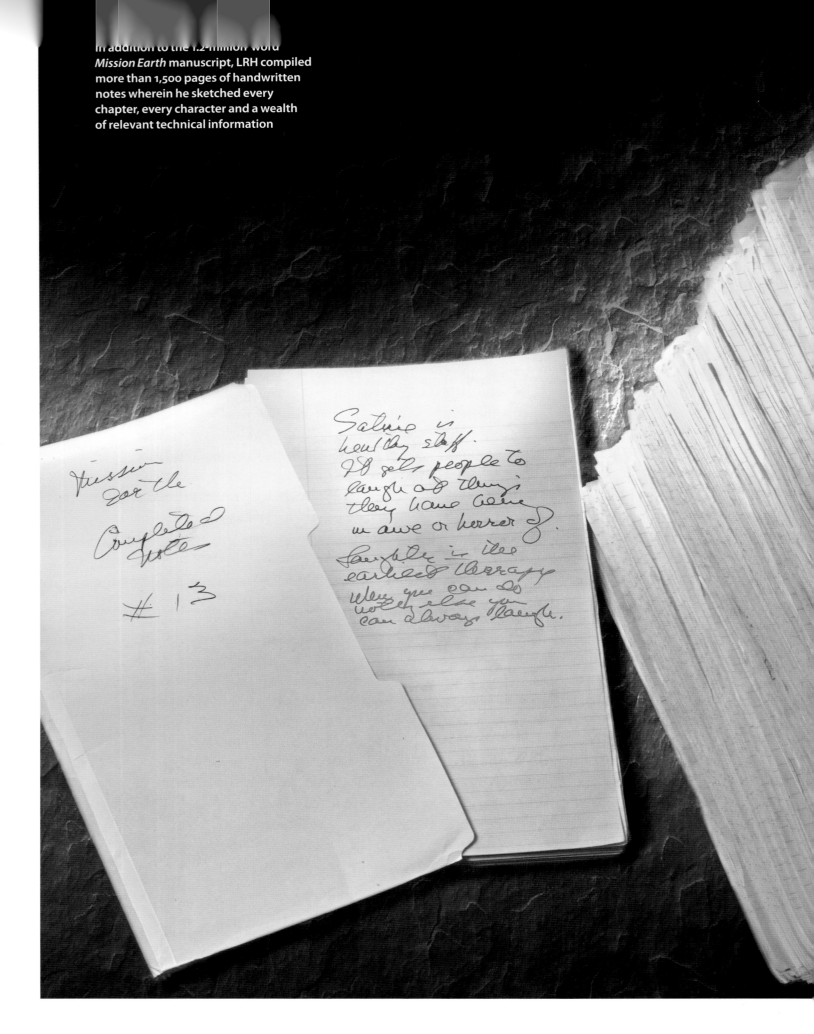

conniving media, casual murder and rampant immorality. Or as yet another critic described it, "in a biting commentary on exactly who is doing what on today's Earth."

The statement is supremely apt, and actually even more so given what the shape of society as we embark into this new millennium. For example, much of Heller's trials involve his efforts to salvage Earth from wanton pollution at the hands of a John Delbert Rockecenter and the Seven Brothers, i.e., the Seven Sisters. In the process, Heller stumbles upon an alien plot to subvert Voltarian society with several thousand tons of Turkish opium. (Although physiologically superior in certain respects, Voltarians are nonetheless subject to the same dark temptations as the earthling.) The result: an utterly pandemic drug-abuse crisis, much like what we suffer today. There is likewise much regarding the patently illegal methods of law enforcement agencies (as in a Federal Bureau of Investigation now known to have wiretapped the telephones of United States Congressional representatives) and the employment of a J. Walter Madison to keep the reading public fully uninformed—as in the J. Walter Thompson public relations conglomerate representing highly dubious medical, pharmaceutical and petroleum interests, and latterly charged with helping incite the first Persian Gulf War.

Rather in awe of the 430,000-word *Battlefield Earth,* more than one reviewer would remark upon Ron's use of a then fairly rare word processor. In fact, however, he employed these two conveniently portable Underwood manual typewriters, specially selected for high-speed keyboard action. While he hammered out several thousand words a day on one, the other underwent complete refurbishing inasmuch as he had hammered it into complete disrepair. Thus, just as one machine expired, its newly rebuilt twin would replace it in round-robin fashion.

> *"I loved Mission Earth. The CIA will hate it. Hubbard has produced a real knee-slapper...he's laughing at the sacred cow of the eighties, the so-called intelligence community... Few writers have had the knack of making a serious philosophical point without ever stopping to preach, without ever slowing the action for an instant."*
> *—Ray Faraday Nelson*

Finally, there is also much on the psychiatric and psychological encouragement of sexual perversion as a means of population control—all under a banner of "Mental Stealth" and all perfectly in line with the smorgasbord of sexual perversion now advertised everywhere under that ever-popular euphemism "The Alternative Lifestyle."

and resolvable. It's simply a question of cutting through that J. Walter Madison double talk and the psychobabble from a world association of "Mental Stealth" and getting to the source of the problem. Although as Jettero Heller so painfully discovers, "The way this planet is organized, apparently, is that if you try to do anything to help it, some special-interest

> *"SF and fantasy hold out the prospect of possibility and in possibility you have choice and in choice you have freedom and there you have touched on the basic nature of every person."—L. Ron Hubbard*

The point—and this from a secretary / research assistant charged with collecting the small mountain of background literature—*Mission Earth* is a work of definitive satire and expressly intended "for the raising of social consciousness." If the world portrayed is the height of hypocrisy—where the most saintly are, in fact, the most outlandishly criminal, where political and corporate corruption is the order of the day and populations are regarded as sheep for the slaughter—nothing is accidental, nothing just a byproduct of human genetics as psychiatry would have us believe. Rather, there are explicit reasons for all that plagues this planet, and those reasons are both identifiable

group jumps all over you." As something of a footnote here, it might further be mentioned that much of what the series satirically addresses, LRH himself very seriously addressed as both the Founder of Scientology and founder of the world's most singularly effective programs for drug rehabilitation, criminal reform and moral regeneration. In other words, as a genuine opponent of those forces which underlie criminality, drug abuse and immorality, here is an author who knows of what he writes.

What such insight ultimately made for is a work of truly phenomenal and enduring popularity. As noted, each consecutive volume of the *Mission Earth* dekalogy successively rose to international bestseller lists until those lists were all but filled with *Mission Earth*. At one point, readers found no less than seven *Mission Earth* volumes among the ten bestselling hardcover books, prompting author and professor of journalism James Gunn to declare, "I don't know anything in publishing history to compare with it." As further noted, the series is now routinely described as a legitimate classic, repeatedly drawing comparison to the works of Jonathan Swift, and so prompting Golden Age author-editor Damon Knight to summarize the LRH impact as absolutely unequivocal: "He cut a swath across the science-fantasy world the likes of which has never been seen." Finally there is all *Mission Earth* has come to represent "as a milestone work of mainstream fiction," to cite yet another critic, and all else the series represents in terms of what its author described as a "plea that someone should work on the future." ∎

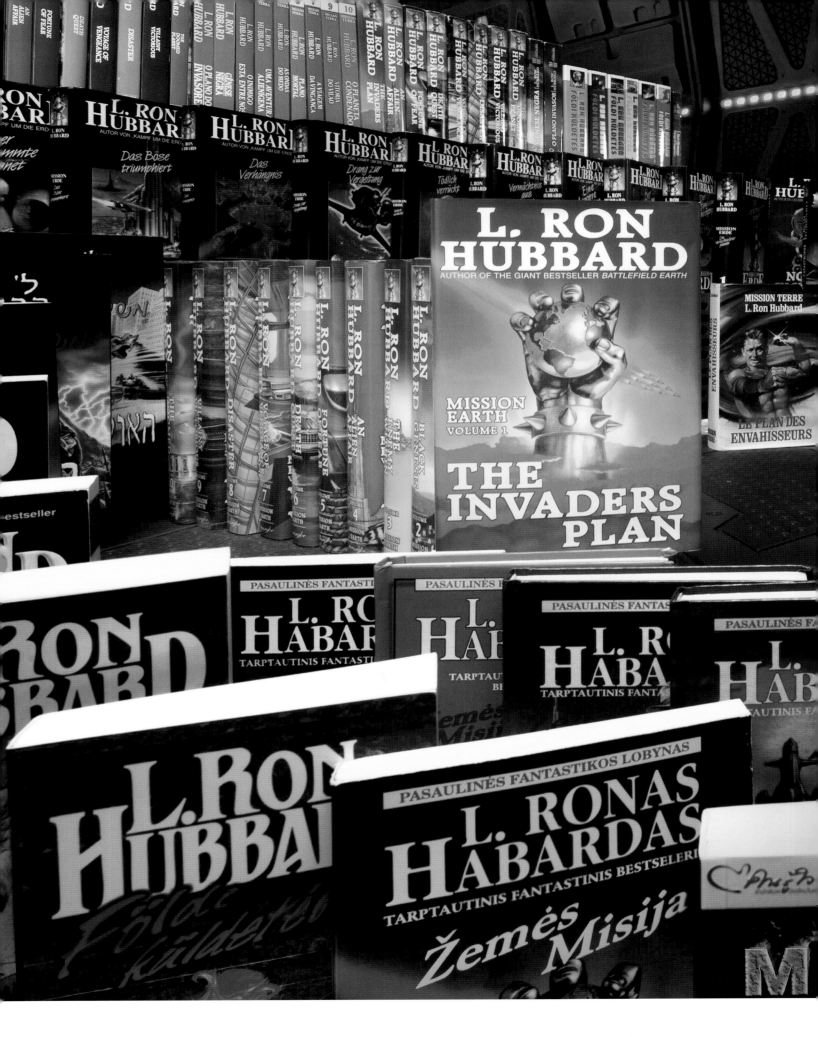

We do not collect trendy authors, nor do we collect minor authors. In the field of American literature, for instance, we select with care only those American or Californian authors who we determine are important contributors to the state, to the country and to the world. L. Ron Hubbard is perhaps the quintessential western author, and his works fit perfectly in our collection."
—Thomas V. Lange, *The Huntington Library*

The international array of *Mission Earth* editions: just as the tale of Jettero Heller and company spans a myriad of nations and cultures, so, too, the appeal. To be sure, there is scarcely a land on Earth where readers have not yet thrilled to Heller's valiant mission to save this beleaguered planet.

Mission Earth for the new millennium: just as the world of which L. Ron Hubbard wrote in the late twentieth century is all the more imperiled in this twenty-first century, so the rapier wit of *Mission Earth* is all the more pointed. Also for the new millennium comes the *Mission Earth* audiobook. The longest and most ambitious audiobook project in history, here are 123 hours of unabridged, multicast recording. In full, 278 performers dramatize nearly a thousand roles—from alien invaders to mafia dons. Here, too, is an all-original musical score incorporating an array of L. Ron Hubbard lyrics. The result is an audiobook that all but envelops listeners in the rollicking world of *Mission Earth* and indeed makes for a listening experience like nothing in history.

A publishing phenomenon unto itself, all ten volumes of the *Mission Earth* series topped international bestseller lists. In reply came a veritable parade of international awards, including a coveted *Publishers Weekly* award to honor significant publishing events. Also included is a Cosmos 2000 Award on behalf of French readers and another again on behalf of Italian fans.

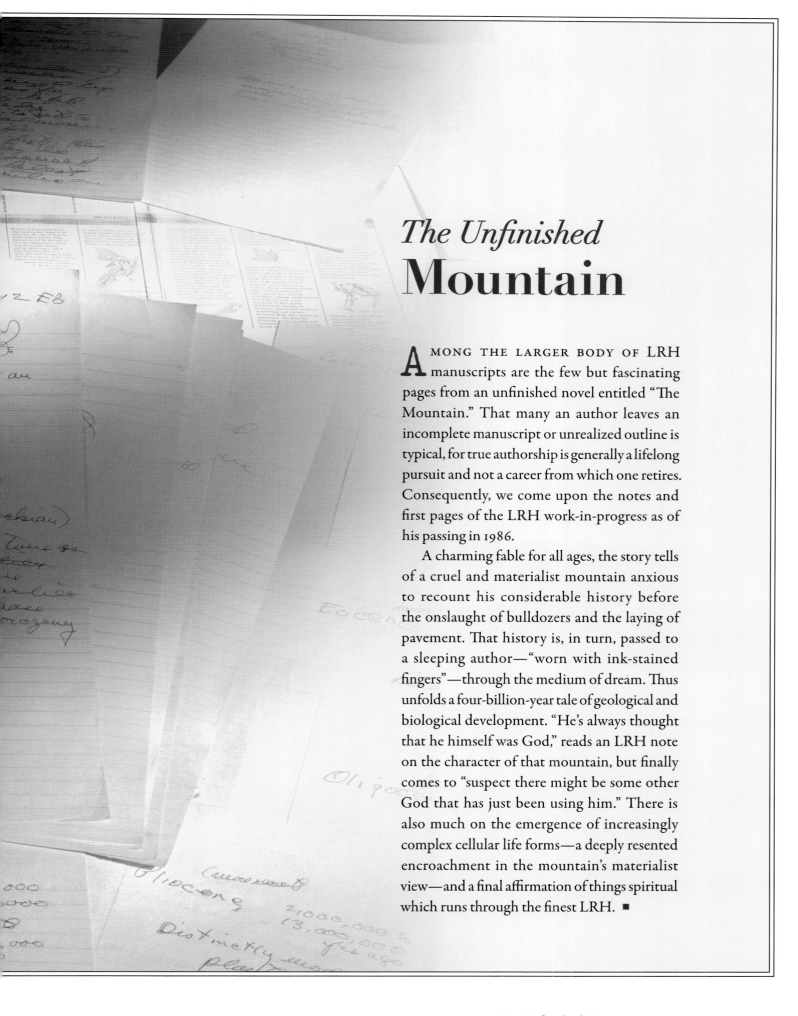

The Unfinished
Mountain

AMONG THE LARGER BODY OF LRH manuscripts are the few but fascinating pages from an unfinished novel entitled "The Mountain." That many an author leaves an incomplete manuscript or unrealized outline is typical, for true authorship is generally a lifelong pursuit and not a career from which one retires. Consequently, we come upon the notes and first pages of the LRH work-in-progress as of his passing in 1986.

A charming fable for all ages, the story tells of a cruel and materialist mountain anxious to recount his considerable history before the onslaught of bulldozers and the laying of pavement. That history is, in turn, passed to a sleeping author—"worn with ink-stained fingers"—through the medium of dream. Thus unfolds a four-billion-year tale of geological and biological development. "He's always thought that he himself was God," reads an LRH note on the character of that mountain, but finally comes to "suspect there might be some other God that has just been using him." There is also much on the emergence of increasingly complex cellular life forms—a deeply resented encroachment in the mountain's materialist view—and a final affirmation of things spiritual which runs through the finest LRH. ■

Original Story by
L. Ron Hubbard

ADDITIONALLY AMONG THE FINAL works of L. Ron Hubbard are two original screenplays for full-length feature films. That he would revisit scriptwriting in the early 1980s, just as he returned to his novels, is altogether apt; for it was an abiding passion and well beyond his 1937 stint in Hollywood adapting his own work for the screen, he continued scriptwriting and script-doctoring. In point of fact, by early 1940, he was regularly reworking scenes for Clark Gable and later still for Boris Karloff.

But with his scripts from the 1980s comes a story quite unique in literary circles. Moreover, it is a story that returns us to another abiding L. Ron Hubbard passion. Namely: his continuing efforts to help younger authors find their literary feet and which came to fruition with his Writers of the Future Contest for the discovery and nurturing of new talent. Thus it was Ron directed the stories on which his final screenplays were based be "bequeathed" to up and coming authors from his Writers of the Future stable; and in that way, he gave those authors a golden opportunity to effectively *co-author* a novel with L. Ron Hubbard.

The first, entitled *Ai! Pedrito!* is a set piece of mistaken identity. The story was inspired by a series of actual incidents beginning in the winter of 1932 when Ron tells of entering a Cuban embassy and there encountering a stranger who cries out: *"Ai! Pedrito! Cómo está?"* When he indeed pleads mistaken identity, the stranger replies with what amounts to a wink and nod: *"Oh, that's all right, Pedrito. I won't tell anybody you're here."*

Next and just as suggestively, he writes of meeting three mining engineers in the Puerto Rican hinterland who similarly greet him with an exuberant, *"Ai! Pedrito! Cómo está?"* Then comes the proverbial stranger in a bar with a pistol in his pocket—"and if I hadn't kicked him in the shins, I would have been a dead man"—followed by the Panamanian beauty who indignantly snubs him with a glance. Whereupon he can only conclude he has crossed the path of a perfect look-alike, if not an honest-to-goodness *Doppelgänger,* known as Pedrito Miraflores.

What ensues is like a shadowy figure glimpsed from a distance before slowly coming into focus. Not surprisingly, this Pedrito Miraflores is a scoundrel of the first order. He is a prodigal son of a wealthy Brazilian clan and wanted by authorities in half-a-dozen nations. He is fleeing fathers of at least as many jilted lovers and latterly links with a Nazi network extending through France to Latin America. But after simmering

Ai! Pedrito!: an original story by L. Ron Hubbard, novelized by Kevin J. Anderson, first edition, 1998

for some fifty years, the tale of Pedrito Miraflores becomes *Ai! Pedrito! When Intelligence Goes Wrong*.

As the subtitle suggests, it is a tale of intelligence run amok. The storyline specifically follows a cadre of Soviets attempting to substitute Pedrito for his dead-ringer, look-alike in a United States Naval Missile Security Group. That the character of Pedrito—a hard-drinking, fast-living womanizer—is diametrically opposite his straight-laced double naturally adds to the mix. But the net result is far from buffoonery. On the contrary, it is all too sadly representative of spy–counter-spy shenanigans ripping Latin America to pieces through the 1980s. (Witness CIA support of Nicaraguan counterrevolutionaries, replete with a drugs-for-guns arrangement and Agency links to a cocaine pipeline running through Los Angeles.)

That *Ai! Pedrito!* proved an immediate *New York Times* bestseller confirms the fact it was indeed a golden opportunity for co-author Kevin J. Anderson. To be sure, Anderson subsequently enjoyed a meteoric career as a collaborative author with dozens of bestselling titles to his credit.

The second original story by L. Ron Hubbard "bequeathed" for novelization by another is *A Very Strange Trip*. It is a tale indicative of sheer literary range; for if readers were previously treated to emotionally charged science fiction with L. Ron Hubbard's *To the Stars,* science fiction *adventure* with L. Ron Hubbard's

A Very Strange Trip: an original story by L. Ron Hubbard, novelized by Dave Wolverton, first edition, 1999

Battlefield Earth and science fiction *satire* with his *Mission Earth* series, then here is unabashed science fiction *comedy.*

The plotline follows a none-too-bright Private Everett Dumphee as he transports a top-secret device from the United States Army's Trenton Arsenal in New Jersey to an Experimental Weapon's Battalion in Denver, Colorado. Unbeknownst to Dumphee, his cargo is a none-too-dependable time machine that tends to activate whenever his All Terrain Vehicle hits a significant bump in the road. In consequence comes what critics described as the "ultimate off-road adventure." To wit: Dumphee traverses not only a landscape but also a timescape and it ultimately transports him to a late Jurassic world where he hunts *Tyrannosaurus rex.* The work is not, however, without its serious side inasmuch as Dumphee is not a slapstick clown. He is a victim of the army, of technology, of cultures. Hence what Ron describes as a "hint of haunting tragedy" at every comedic turn.

That *A Very Strange Trip* was yet another L. Ron Hubbard title to hit bestseller lists is still another reason to qualify the work as a golden opportunity for co-author Dave Wolverton. Indeed, Wolverton subsequently authored dozens of award-winning novels and numerous *New York Times* bestsellers. That the work was further deemed a science fiction landmark for the fact it took the genre out of the "serious drab" and into playful comedy makes it an appropriate final tribute to an L. Ron Hubbard critics now described as a literary god. ∎

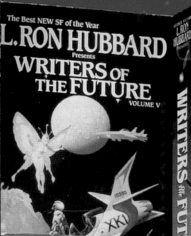
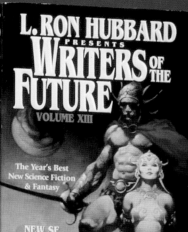

CHAPTER SIX

L. Ron Hubbard's

WRITERS OF THE FUTURE

Finalists and winners of the L. Ron Hubbard
Writers of the Future Contest are
published in annual anthologies. For
many winners this provides the catalyst
for a professional writing career.

L. Ron Hubbard's
Writers of the Future

G IVEN THE TRADITIONALLY DIFFICULT PATH FROM FIRST manuscript to published novel—and particularly so in an era when publishers tend to devote the lion's share of advertising budgets to but a few household names—L. Ron Hubbard, "initiated a means for new and budding writers to have a chance for their creative efforts to be seen and acknowledged." That means was his Writers of the Future Contest. Established in 1983, expressly for the aspiring author, Writers of the Future has subsequently become the most respected and significant forum for new talent in the whole of the fantasy and science fiction realms.

Accordingly, the roster of judges past and present includes some of the most celebrated names in the genre: Robert Silverberg, Frank Herbert, Jerry Pournelle, Andre Norton, Anne McCaffrey and—longtime LRH friends from that fabled Golden Age—Jack Williamson and C. L. Moore. Also counted among early supporters of the contest were A. E. van Vogt and Ray Bradbury (the latter being an especially touching tribute in light of his epic tale of literary perseverance, *Fahrenheit 451*). In consequence, L. Ron Hubbard's Writers of the Future Contest now stands alongside the Hugo and Nebula as the third in a triad of the genre's most celebrated acknowledgments for literary excellence. Moreover, and just for good measure, Writers of the Future winners have subsequently earned well over fifty literary awards, very much including scores of Hugo and Nebula Awards.

Quite in addition to cash awards, winning entries are annually published in the *L. Ron Hubbard Presents Writers of the Future* anthology. In a word, it is the bestselling new fiction anthology of its kind. Original republication orders set new records and the text is now a measure of things to come in speculative fiction circles world over. Hence, a *Publishers Weekly* description of the text as a perennial "glimpse of tomorrow's stars" and a "must-have for the genre reader."

The L. Ron Hubbard Golden Pen Award bestowed to grand prize winners of L. Ron Hubbard's Writers of the Future Contest

Needless to say, the anthology also serves as that all-important springboard into professional ranks. In point of fact, authors first appearing in *L. Ron Hubbard Presents Writers of the Future* have subsequently authored hundreds of novels and thousands of short stories, including some of the most recognizable titles on science fiction and fantasy shelves. Then, too, more than a few of them are *New York Times* bestselling authors, not to mention internationally acclaimed; while even more to the greater point: a full third of those taking honors have since professionally published, which is, frankly, unparalleled in literary circles.

To that same end—literary professionalism— the Writers of the Future program additionally includes a celebrated Writing Workshop. It is conducted by distinguished judges and specifically directs students to the very articles published herein. Thus, for example, just as Ron wrote of conceiving a tale from an everyday object in "Magic Out of a Hat," students of his workshop are challenged to emulate the same, i.e., conceive a story based on some randomly selected everyday object. As another word on results, one workshop participant tells of collecting 105 rejection slips before entering the program—after which he promptly placed a first novel with a first-rate New York publisher.

Likewise bespeaking of practical results are the numerous high schools and universities now hosting Writers of the Future Workshops—very much including George Washington University, where Ron himself lectured so many years ago.

Similarly in keeping with the greater tradition in which Ron wrote is the companion contest to Writers of the Future: L. Ron Hubbard's Illustrators of the Future Contest. It follows from the fact science fiction and fantasy long depended upon illustrations to bring improbable worlds to life. It also follows from Ron's own long and close association with illustrators—the legendary Edd Cartier, for example, who originally provided illustrations for his *Ole Doc Methuselah* series, that veritable king of illustrators, Frank Frazetta and the venerable Frank Kelly Freas, who spoke of a "creative synergy" between every tale and the art that illustrates it. In that same spirit, the Illustrators of the Future Contest pairs artists with authors to illustrate the L. Ron Hubbard anthology, and many an illustrious career has followed. To be sure, and just as with Writers of the Future, those emerging from the Illustrators

contest have left a prestigious mark all over graphic novels, coffee-table books, jacket covers and Academy Award-winning films.

Finally, and in recognition of what the contests represent to all who work for the future, award ceremonies have enjoyed participation from some of the world's most distinguished scientists. Nobel laureate Dr. Sheldon Glashow, for example, served as panelist for award ceremonies at the United Nations, while astronaut Story Musgrave (of Hubble repair fame) served in the same capacity at the National Aeronautics and Space Administration in Houston. The point, as Dr. Musgrave himself so aptly phrased it:

"You, the science fiction writers and illustrators, led us to the space program starting over one hundred years before we ended up in space.

"Your fiction and what you do is indeed a literature of human hope.

"So what you are doing with the Writers and Illustrators of the Future—the people who are getting their start—in the spirit and mentorship of bringing people along the line and the vision of Mr. Hubbard to create these awards is another way that he has become immortal." ■

Top The legendary Frank Kelly Freas and Ray Bradbury at the inaugural Illustrators of the Future Contest, 1988. Mr. Freas was the first coordinating judge of the Illustrators contest while Mr. Bradbury counted himself an L. Ron Hubbard fan for more than forty years.

Bottom left King of Fantasy Illustrators, Frank Frazetta. Not only did he lend his considerable talent to L. Ron Hubbard's *Battlefield Earth,* he also served on the panel of judges for Illustrators of the Future.

Bottom right Edd Cartier, forever immortalized as illustrator of L. Ron Hubbard's *Ole Doc Methuselah* series and another judge of the first Illustrators of the Future Contests.

The Judges

ANNE McCAFFREY
A Hugo and Nebula Award winner as well as a Grand Master of Science Fiction Writers of America, she is best known for her Dragonriders of Pern series

"A very generous legacy from L. Ron Hubbard—a fine, fine fiction writer—for the writers of the future."

ROBERT SILVERBERG
Multiple Hugo and Nebula Award-winning author, also a Grand Master of Science Fiction Writers of America

"What a wonderful idea—one of science fiction's all-time giants opening the way for a new generation of exciting talent! For these brilliant stories, and the careers that will grow from them, we all stand indebted to L. Ron Hubbard."

FRANK HERBERT
Creator and author of the world-renowned Dune series

"I'm very happy to be able to lend my help to the Writers of the Future program. From time to time, though, people have come up to me and asked why I want to 'create competition' by helping newcomers. Talking about 'competition' in that way is nonsense! The more good writers there are, the more good readers there will be. We'll all benefit—writers and readers alike!"

TIM POWERS
World Fantasy Award winner, author of Last Call and On Stranger Tides (basis for the fourth installment of the Pirates of the Caribbean adventure)

"Certainly L. Ron Hubbard's accomplishments span many fields, but I'm most mindful of the work he did to help new writers. No writer has ever done more to help the talented but unpublished newcomer acquire skills and gain recognition than L. Ron Hubbard."

ORSON SCOTT CARD
Multiple Hugo, Nebula Award winner and author of the novels Ender's Game, Ender's Shadow and Speaker for the Dead

"The Writers of the Future simply is the best way to launch a career. It's one of the forces that keep science fiction alive."

KEVIN J. ANDERSON

Author of numerous national and international bestsellers, including The Saga of Seven Suns and several books in the Dune saga co-authored with Brian Herbert. He also novelized the L. Ron Hubbard screenplay Ai! Pedrito!

"When looking over past volumes of Writers of the Future, it becomes apparent how great an impact L. Ron Hubbard and this contest have had on the entire field of science fiction."

LARRY NIVEN

Renowned for his Known Space science fiction series of which Ringworld is the most acclaimed. He also co-authored, with fellow judge Dr. Jerry Pournelle, The Mote in God's Eye, Lucifer's Hammer and Footfall

"I wish the Writers of the Future Contest had been a part of my early life. It's a wonderful opportunity, a powerful boost for a new writer: not just the money, but publication in an anthology that has garnered much prestige over the decades."

SEAN WILLIAMS

Australia's bestselling science fiction author and a #1 New York Times bestseller

"The Writers of the Future program is just one of many endeavors L. Ron Hubbard founded. It has had a profound effect on my life, bringing me into contact with peers around the world, guiding me along the path to being a professional writer, and instilling in me the same keen sense of *paying forward* that lies at the heart of this extraordinary bequest."

DAVE WOLVERTON

Author of the bestselling fantasy series The Runelords and Of Mice and Magic. He also novelized the L. Ron Hubbard screenplay A Very Strange Trip

"The Writers and Illustrators of the Future Contests have become an invaluable institution in the field, discovering important new talent, and both contests are still growing. No other program offers the unique combination of high-paying prize money, payment for publication, workshops with blue-ribbon professionals for the winners, along with continued promotion long after the contest. We owe a debt of gratitude to L. Ron Hubbard, who recognized the need for such an institution and who, in 1983, created and launched the program."

Author Services, Inc.

IN 1986, TO MEET A CONTINUING DEMAND for the works of L. Ron Hubbard, the LRH literary agency of Author Services, Inc., commenced a schedule for the republication of all early LRH fiction and all remaining unpublished works. *Fear* and *Final Blackout*, among the first to see reprint, promptly soared to bestseller lists in a telling restatement of popularity from fifty years earlier, as did *Buckskin Brigades* and *To the Stars*.

But what amounts to the mother lode of the L. Ron Hubbard literary legacy and the catalyst of a Pulp Fiction Renaissance is what Author Services dubbed *Stories from the Golden Age*. Featuring original artwork and comprising more than eighty volumes, here are 150 classic tales positively shimmering with pulp magic. In consequence comes what is indeed a rebirth of pulp fiction with an international fan base now including fervent readers all over Africa, Asia and Arabia. Also in consequence comes a worldview and retrospective view of an author *Publishers Weekly* described as "one of the greatest literary figures of the century." While if only to cap it with an appropriate flourish, with *Stories from the Golden Age*, L. Ron Hubbard additionally earns three Guinness World Records as *Most Published Author, Most Translated Author* and *Author with Most Audio Books*.

There is substantially more; for under Author Services stewardship comes a collection of L. Ron Hubbard audiobooks that have likewise earned an unprecedented place in the annals of twenty-first century publishing. To be sure, here were the first audiobook presentations to feature a total "sonic-landscape" enveloping listeners in a total literary environment—replete with howling wind, cracking whips, gunshots and cries of vengeance, as the case may be. Here, too, were the first audiobooks to feature scores of actors in a multicast reading that captures the synergy of a live reading. In short, here were the first audiobooks to effectively replicate Golden Age of Radio presentations of the 1930s.

Similarly, evoking the Golden Age of Radio are Author Services theatrical readings of L. Ron Hubbard tales. Frequently featuring original performers from the audiobook cast, live readings likewise inspire an international following from as far afield as Malaysia, Curaçao and Copenhagen.

Author Services, Inc., on Hollywood Boulevard: exclusively devoted to the works of L. Ron Hubbard, it is here pulp fiction was reborn as a twenty-first century literary phenomenon

Top "Poe, Sir Walter Scott and Mark Twain ended their lives dead broke. That was because they did not retain Author Services, Inc."—signed L. Ron Hubbard and gracing the wall of Author Services Reception.

Bottom Writers of the Future Hall: the shelves of which are lined with hundreds of novels, novelettes and short-story collections authored by contest winners and esteemed judges. Also prominently displayed are award-winning illustrations from the Illustrators contest and the numerous recognitions presented to contest administrators. Similarly holding a place of prominence is the coveted Golden Pen Award as bestowed quarterly and annually to those who indeed become Writers of the Future.

Right The L. Ron Hubbard Library at Author Services, Inc., presenting the full body of L. Ron Hubbard's literary legacy. On the shelves are well over two hundred titles from almost every conceivable genre. Moreover, here are titles published and distributed in nearly a hundred lands and translated into dozens of languages.

The point here: What was once described as a "Great American Pulp Movement" is no longer a solely American phenomena. Hence, the L. Ron Hubbard tales in languages as varied as Chinese Mandarin, Malay, Thai and Dutch. Hence, a body of pulp fiction that is once again synonymous with *popular* fiction. And hence, an author who indeed has taught us what this business of writing is finally all about. ■

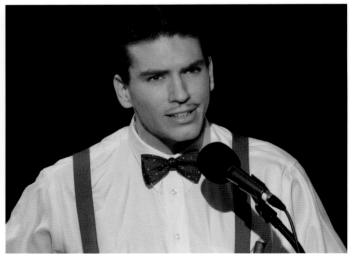

The international acclaim for L. Ron Hubbard's literary achievements and contributions to the field of the arts through the Writers and Illustrators of the Future Contests is evident in the hundreds of recognitions and awards bestowed. Included in this parade of diverse accolades are the United Nations Society of Writers Award, the Dubai Culture and Arts Authority Award and the Charlie Award from the Hollywood Arts Council and which, in fact, marked the inauguration of an entirely new award category: Literary Arts as presented in recognition of L. Ron Hubbard's Writers of the Future Contest.

A Closing Note

"Learn to write when you would rather sleep. Learn to exercise this gift of language when no conscious portion of your wits can vibrate anything but worry. Learn to write so, my son, and you can call yourself a writer."

L. RON HUBBARD

And so he did for over half a century, through which he authored more than three hundred novels, novelettes and short stories and *for* which he will never be forgotten.

We may further now call him a *consummate* writer who loved nothing more than to "tie into a yarn," as he described it and leave the paper "charred by the blast of its composition."

Then again, we can call him a *writer's writer* of whom it was said he delighted in "giving the other fellow a lift," which is saying a lot, inasmuch as he was also an "all-time giant in an age of prodigious storytelling and an author whose influence can only be measured in centuries."

But most of all, he was a writer who indeed exercised that gift of language until—and this, too, as he described it—the prose would "ripple and flow as composition should." Whereupon it would transport readers "to not only far lands but to far times or times which don't exist at all."

At which point, we can call him a writer in the most expansive sense of the word and mark it down in the history of world literature that a universal love for his stories has now placed the works of L. Ron Hubbard in the hands of hundreds of millions of readers.

APPENDIX

GLOSSARY

A

abashed: feeling embarrassed or ashamed. Used figuratively. Page 69.

A.B. Dick: a company founded in 1884 by Albert Blake Dick (1856–1934). Originally a lumber company, the firm became a manufacturer of copy machines after Dick licensed patents from Thomas Edison and coined the word *mimeograph*. The A.B. Dick company has continued in the field of publishing and photography. Page 150.

abounds: contains something in large numbers or amounts. Page 153.

accolades: awards, honors or expressions of high praise or great regard for someone. Page 198.

advance: a sum of money paid before it is due. Hence *"advance-against-royalties"* means money paid by a magazine before any royalties would be due to the author of a story, for example, so that the author receives income while awaiting publication. *See also* **royalties.** Page 5.

Adventure: an American pulp magazine founded in 1910. One of the pulps produced by Popular Publications, the magazine featured adventure and fiction stories. Page 58.

afforded: given or applied to. Page 163.

air book: a pulp magazine featuring stories about aviation. Page 85.

Alaska: a state of the United States in northwestern North America, separated from the other mainland states by part of Canada. Page 63.

alchemy: a magical power, from the literal meaning of *alchemy,* an early form of chemistry practiced in the Middle Ages, which sought to discover a substance that would change metals (such as lead) into gold and that would prolong life. Page 63.

allegory: a description of something using objects, characters, events, etc., as symbols to represent ideas (such as truth, death, etc.) having a deeper, often spiritual, meaning. Page 5.

all over (someone), got it: is superior to (someone else). Page 124.

All Terrain Vehicle: a motor vehicle designed for use on rough, uneven or sandy ground or roads. (*Terrain* means ground or a piece of land seen in terms of its surface features.) Page 181.

allure: powerful attraction or fascination. Page 135.

aloft: in the higher part of a ship, as the mast or the rigging. Page 63.

along about: somewhere near the stated or implied point in time. Page 87.

alp to climb, an: literally, a high mountain to climb. Used figuratively to mean a difficult task to accomplish. Page 45.

ambiance: the quality or character given to a sound recording by the space in which the sound occurs. Page 159.

American Fiction Guild: a national organization of magazine fiction writers and novelists in the United States in the 1930s. L. Ron Hubbard was the president of the New York chapter in 1936. (A *guild* is an organization of persons with related interests, goals, etc., especially one formed for mutual aid or protection.) Page 2.

amok, run: behave in an out-of-control way. Page 180.

ancillary: that serves as an aid; assisting. Page 51.

Anderson, Kevin J.: (1962–) bestselling American author of more than one hundred books. He is best known for his Dune novels (co-authored with Brian Herbert), his *Saga of Seven Suns* series and his numerous novels based on *The X-Files,* Batman, Superman and *Star Wars.* Anderson has also been a Writers of the Future judge since 1996. Page 191.

animistic: of or pertaining to *animism,* the belief that individual spirits inhabit every material form of reality (for example, plants and stones) as well as natural phenomena such as thunderstorms and earthquakes, often including belief in the continued existence of individual disembodied spirits capable of exercising a helpful or evil influence. Page 112.

another matter: a situation that is likely to be judged differently; something different entirely. Page 78.

antiquarian: relating to (the study of) old times or old things. Page 113.

anything for it, wasn't: a variation of *there was nothing for it* or *there was nothing for it but to,* meaning that there was no other course of action open (except that of). The phrase usually precedes a statement of what that course of action ended up being. Page 56.

Anytown, USA: any real or fictional community regarded as a typical small town in the United States. Page 11.

apocalyptic: warning about or predicting a disastrous future or outcome. Page 4.

apocryphal: of doubtful authenticity. Page 15.

Arabian Nights, The: or *A Thousand and One Nights,* a collection of stories from Persia, Arabia, India and Egypt, compiled over hundreds of years. They include the stories of Aladdin and Ali Baba and have become particularly popular in Western countries. Page 110.

arcane: understood by few; mysterious. Page 108.

Argentine, the: a reference to *Argentina,* the second-largest nation in South America, occupying most of the southern tip of South America. Its official name is Argentine Republic. Page 124.

Argosy: an American fiction magazine published by the Frank A. Munsey Company, first produced in the late 1800s. Containing science fiction, fantasy and other genres, *Argosy* featured some of the best adventure writers of the twentieth century. (The word *argosy* originally meant a large merchant ship and figuratively came to mean a rich, plentiful store or supply of something.) Page 51.

arms race: competition between unfriendly countries to achieve superiority in quantity and quality of military arms. Page 109.

arsenal: a place for the making, repairing and storing of weapons, ammunition and other military equipment and supplies, especially such a place operated and maintained by the government. Page 181.

ascension: the act of *ascending,* moving upwards in degree, level or status. Page 36.

Asimov, Isaac: (1920–1992) Russian-born American writer, renowned for his science fiction and for his popular works in all branches of science. His first science fiction novel was published in 1950 and he went on to author more than four hundred books for young and adult readers. Asimov's best-known science fiction works include *I, Robot* (1950) and *The Foundation Trilogy* (1951–1953), to which he wrote a sequel thirty years later, *Foundation's Edge.* Page 116.

Astoria: a biography of American merchant John Jacob Astor (1763–1848), written by Washington Irving. Astoria is a city in northwestern Oregon, founded in 1811 by John Jacob Astor, who planned Astoria as a key trading post in the beaver fur trade. The post was taken over by British interests but eventually returned to US control when the boundary between the US and Canada was settled (1846). Page 58.

Astor, John Jacob: (1763–1848) American merchant and fur trader. Astor was born near Heidelberg, Germany, and immigrated to the United States in 1783. Entering the fur trade, he set up the American Fur Company in an effort to combat British interests and established trading posts, including one at Astoria (now in Oregon). Page 59.

Astounding (Science Fiction): a pulp magazine founded in 1930 as *Astounding Stories of Super Science,* which featured adventure stories and, later, science fiction. In March 1933 *ASF* ceased publication. However, shortly after this the title was bought by Street & Smith Publishing, which restored it to its monthly schedule, changing the name to *Astounding Stories.* The magazine became a going concern and in 1937 Street & Smith appointed a young writer, John W. Campbell, Jr. (1910–1971), as its editor and changed its name to *Astounding Science Fiction.* Page 107.

Atlanta: a city in and the capital of Georgia, a state in the southeastern United States. Page 116.

Atlas: a large range of mountains extending 1,500 miles (2,400 kilometers) through three countries of northwestern Africa (Morocco, Algeria and Tunisia). Page 76.

AudioFile Magazine: a magazine focusing on reviews of audiobooks, along with interviews with authors and readers. Published since 1992, the magazine appears in print and online. Page 136.

B

babbling: murmuring or bubbling, from the sound that water makes as it flows along. Page 135.

background: the scene, description or the like that forms a setting for the main characters and events in a story. Page 57.

bade: told to do something. Page 70.

bad egg(s): a worthless, untrustworthy person; a crook. Page 70.

bait (someone): annoy someone, as with constant nagging about something. Page 25.

Baltimore: a city of northern Maryland, an eastern state of the United States. Page 156.

barflies: a slang term for people who spend large amounts of time in bars. Page 63.

Barnes & Noble: a US bookselling company, one of the largest in the country, founded in 1917. Page 117.

Bedford Jones, H.: (1887–1949) Canadian historical adventure, fantasy and science fiction writer. Page 59.

belaying pin: a short, removable wooden or metal pin fitted in a hole in the rail of a boat and used for securing a rope. Page 78.

beleaguered: troubled or threatened persistently with difficulties. Page 72.

bellicosely: in a way that is inclined or eager to fight or aggressively hostile; belligerently. Page 44.

belly-wash: any barely drinkable liquid or beverage, as inferior soda, beer, coffee or soup. Used figuratively. Page 29.

belt, hitting below the: not in accord with the principles of fairness and decency. Originally said of a blow in boxing that landed below the opponent's waist and so was illegal. Page 25.

belt, under (one's): done, experienced or acquired something that will be of benefit to one in the future. Page 58.

bequeathed: handed down; passed on. Page 179.

bespeaking: giving evidence of. Page 188.

bewailing: expressing great sadness about; uttering cries of sorrow over. Page 63.

bidding: commanding or ordering (someone or something) to do something, carry out an action, etc. Page 113.

Big Five: the five publishing companies: Popular, Standard, Munsey, Dell, Street & Smith. Page 90.

bilge-green: a reference to the unpleasant color of water on a ship that collects by seeping into the *bilge,* the flat bottom part of a ship. Page 93.

binge: a period of excessive indulgence in something. Page 153.

blackballing: rejecting socially; excluding, by general consent, from society, friendship, conversation, privileges, etc. From an old custom in some English social clubs whose members would vote on allowing others to enter the club. A candidate receiving white or red balls in a ballot box was admitted, but membership was refused to someone receiving a single black ball, which signified a negative vote. Page 118.

Blackfeet: a group of Native North American peoples including the Blackfeet of Montana and several tribes now living in Canada. The group controlled areas that were fought over by fur traders in the 1800s. Page 51.

Black Mask: one of the best-known and admired pulp fiction magazines. Originally an all-around publication that included detective, westerns and aviation stories, *Black Mask* later focused on detective fiction, publishing stories by top writers in the field. Page 74.

black-tie: requiring that guests wear semiformal clothing, especially that men wear black bow ties with tuxedos or dinner jackets. Page 35.

bless 'em: a contraction of *bless them,* an expression used to show approval and support for something. Page 84.

blithely: in a cheerful, carefree or casual manner. Page 18.

Bloch, Robert: Robert Albert Bloch (1917–1994), American writer of crime, horror and science fiction stories, best known as the author of the thriller novel *Psycho,* which was later adapted into the film (1960), directed by Alfred Hitchcock (1899–1980). Page 111.

blood brother: either one of two men or boys who have sworn mutual loyalty and friendship, typically by a ritual or ceremony involving a superficial cut in the skin and the mingling (mixing) of each other's blood. Page 51.

bloody thunderer: from the phrase *blood and thunder,* an adventure tale characterized by bloodshed, violence and uproar. Page 64.

Bloomfield: Howard Bloomfield, editor of the pulp magazine *Adventure.* Page 61.

blow: a violent windstorm or hurricane. Page 69.

blows, came to: started fighting physically as the result of an argument. Page 15.

blue, in the: in the sky. Page 44.

blue-ribbon: specially chosen for high standing; first-rate. From *blue ribbon,* the highest distinction or first prize in a particular field. Page 191.

B.O.: an informal term for body odor. Such catchy abbreviations of the early 1900s, designed to sell personal-hygiene products, were also accompanied by advertising slogans like "Even your best friends won't tell you." Page 75.

Bodin, Ed: a literary agent, located in New York City, who represented L. Ron Hubbard during much of the 1930s. Page 15.

Boeing: a United States aircraft company founded in 1916 that became one of the world's largest manufacturers of military and commercial aircraft. Named after its founder, William E. Boeing (1881–1956). Page 56.

book for advertising: factual information about a person, such as an autobiographical essay, in which a writer presents his background, accomplishments and the like. Page 26.

Booklist: a book review magazine published by the American Library Association since 1905. *Booklist* covers recommended books and audiovisual materials for all ages and in a wide variety of genres. Page 137.

book of knowledge: a reference to an illustrated children's encyclopedia, first published in the early 1900s. Page 94.

bound: traveling toward a particular place, as in *"New Orleans bound."* Page 72.

boxer stalling for the bell: someone waiting for something one knows is coming. In boxing, a bell is sounded at the end of each one of the periods, each three minutes in length, that the boxing match is divided into. Page 80.

"Boy Stood on the Burning Deck, The": a reference to the poem "Casabianca" by English poet Felicia Dorothea Hemans (1793–1835). The poem tells the story of the deaths of French naval captain Louis de Casabianca, commander of the flagship *L'Orient,* and his ten-year-old son Giacomo during the Battle of the Nile (1798). The boy had been put on watch by his father, but the ship caught fire and the captain was mortally wounded. Though others of the crew fled, the boy remained, standing heroically in an effort to help his father until the ship exploded. Page 58.

brace studded: (of a cartridge belt) covered with *braces,* devices that hold cartridges for a machine gun firmly in place on the belt. Page 73.

Bradbury, Ray: (1920–) award-winning American writer of science fiction, fantasy and other genres. Notable among his more than six hundred short stories, novels, poems, children's books and screenplays are *The Martian Chronicles* (1950), *Fahrenheit 451* (1953) and his screenplay for the 1956 film *Moby Dick.* Page 113.

braid: a band or cord on a uniform that shows the rank of the wearer. Page 72.

branding: the action of putting on a *brand,* a recognized symbol or character burned onto cattle to indicate ownership. Page 56.

Brand, Max: (1892–1944) best-known pen name of American novelist and poet Frederick Faust, who wrote more than five hundred novels, mostly westerns. Page 9.

Brass Keys to Murder: an LRH story first published (under the pen name Michael Keith) in *Five-Novels Monthly* in April 1935. A Navy lieutenant, accused of murder, risks his life to find the real killer and discovers the motive: the brass keys. Page 80.

breeze, shooting the: engaging in light or casual conversation; chitchatting. Page 153.

brethren: fellow members. *Brethren* is an earlier plural form of brother. Page 44.

brigade(s): in the Canadian and US fur trade, a convoy of canoes, sleds, wagons or pack animals used to supply trappers during the eighteenth and nineteenth centuries. Page 50.

British Secret Service: the branch of the British Government that conducts secret investigations, especially investigations into the military strength of other nations. Page 9.

broadside: a strongly worded critical attack, from the literal sense of the firing of all the guns from one side of a warship. Page 70.

broker: a person who is paid to act as an agent for others—for example, in negotiating contracts or buying and selling goods and services. Hence *button broker,* one who negotiates contracts or buys and sells buttons, such as used in the manufacture of clothing. Page 15.

brooding: preoccupied with depressing or painful memories or thoughts; worried or troubled. Page 36.

Brooklyn: an administrative district of New York City, lying across the East River from Manhattan. As one of the nation's leading seaports, Brooklyn has numerous shipbuilding and ship-repair yards. Page 146.

Browning: a manufacturer of automatic weapons, including automatic rifles, pistols and machine guns. American arms designer John Moses Browning (1855–1926) produced more gun innovations than any other American inventor and Browning guns were widely used by the United States and many other countries during the twentieth century. Page 18.

Bruce, George: (1898–1974) American writer and airplane pilot. His stories and screenplays concentrate on action and adventure. Page 93.

Brunner, John: John Kilian Houston Brunner (1934–1995), British science fiction author whose works are noted for their literary innovation. His novels and short stories have won many awards, including the Hugo for his 1968 novel *Stand on Zanzibar,* about overpopulation. Brunner is credited with coining the term *worm* in his 1975 novel *The Shockwave Rider,* in which he describes software that reproduces itself across a computer network. Page 118.

Buck Rogers: a science fiction comic strip, originally appearing in 1929, that tells the adventures of a twentieth-century American Air Force officer (Buck Rogers) who awakens after being caught in suspended animation for five centuries. With the help of superscientific equipment and futuristic weapons, Buck travels through space fighting the forces of evil. Page 147.

Buckskin Brigades: a novel by L. Ron Hubbard, published (1937) by The Macaulay Publishing Company and hailed as a first-ever authentic description of Native North American people and way of life. Set in the early 1800s, the story centers on the Blackfeet Indians, a powerful Native American nation threatened by the fur trade and by white men intent on trapping beaver for the fur, a valuable commodity in Europe. The trappers build forts and organize brigades (convoys of canoes, sleds, wagons or pack animals used to supply trappers), all without regard for either the Indians or the environment. Page 50.

buffoonery: the silly or foolish practices or actions of a *buffoon,* a person who amuses others by tricks, jokes, odd gestures, etc. Page 180.

bugaboo: a recurring or persistent problem. Also a source of concern or anxiety. Page 91.

bull sessions: informal discussions or conversations among a small group. Page 154.

bunion(s): a painful swelling of the big toe, often caused by walking with poorly fitted shoes, that can be painful to someone traveling on foot. Page 56.

Burks, Arthur J.: (1898–1974) American writer whose enormous output for the pulps included aviation, detective, adventure and horror stories. Page 10.

burned up: angry about something. Page 83.

Burroughs, Edgar Rice: (1875–1950) American writer best known for creating the character Tarzan in his novel *Tarzan of the Apes,* which appeared in 1914. Burroughs also wrote science fiction novels. Along with his twenty-six Tarzan stories, he wrote a total of more than seventy books. Page 136.

button, on (one's): on the point of the chin. Page 79.

buzzword: an informal term for a word, phrase or concept that has become popular. From *buzz,* something being talked about excitedly; a rumor. Page 112.

C

cadre: a group of activists in a communist or other revolutionary organization. Page 180.

California Chronicle: an online news service covering news and feature articles, primarily for the state of California. Page 137.

calk: a spiked plate attached to the bottom of a boot or shoe to prevent slipping. Page 78.

Caltech: California Institute of Technology, a private university and research institute founded in 1891 in Pasadena, California, with divisions in chemical engineering, biology, physics, mathematics, astronomy and others. Page 147.

came around: gave in and changed actions or opinions to what another has proposed. Page 127.

Campbell, Jr., John W.: (1910–1971) American editor and writer who began writing science fiction while at college. In 1937 Campbell was appointed editor of the magazine *Astounding Stories,* later titled *Astounding Science Fiction* and then *Analog.* Under his editorship *Astounding* became a major influence in the development of science fiction and published stories by some of the most important writers of that time. Page 100.

canal-boat out: remove or pull out as if by means of a *canal boat,* a freight-carrying boat, usually long and narrow, used on canals. A *canal* is an artificial waterway built for shipping, recreation or the like, and which may take in parts of natural rivers along its course. Page 57.

canary: a small, yellow singing bird native to the Canary Islands. Canaries feed on small seeds and are a popular household pet, having been bred for their song for hundreds of years. Page 23.

canons: general rules or principles by which something is judged. Page 49.

capped: followed with something better; surpassed. Page 59.

Card, Orson Scott: (1951–) American author of science fiction, fantasy, poetry, plays and scripts. His speculative fiction novels have earned him numerous awards including the Nebula and Hugo. Card is a professor of literature and writing and has authored two books on writing. He has also been a Writers of the Future judge since 1994 and served as an instructor at the first Writers of the Future Workshop in 1986. Page 190.

careworn: worn out; damaged from overuse; showing the effects of wear. Page 55.

carrack: a large Mediterranean trading ship in use from the fourteenth through the sixteenth centuries. A carrack usually had two masts with two square sails on each mast. Page 110.

carriage: the rotating and sliding paper holder on a typewriter. Page 10.

Cartier, Edd: Edward Daniel Cartier (1914–2008), American pulp magazine illustrator. From the 1930s to the 1950s, his work regularly appeared in many of the foremost pulp magazines. During the 1990s his lifelong accomplishments were recognized with special awards from fan and professional associations and he further contributed his artistic expertise as a judge of the Illustrators of the Future Contest, starting in its inaugural year. Page 127.

catalyst: something that stimulates a reaction, development or change. Page 146.

causerie: a short piece of writing in a conversational style. Page 146.

Centre Street: the address of New York City's police headquarters from the early 1900s until the 1970s. Page 24.

C.G. base: an abbreviation for *Coast Guard base.* A *base* is a center of operations, as of a military, naval or other activity; headquarters. *See also* **Coast Guard.** Page 69.

Chandler, Raymond: (1888–1959) American author of crime and detective stories, mostly set in Los Angeles during the 1930s and 1940s. Page 3.

charred: slightly burned. Page 201.

chart room: a compartment in a ship, in which the charts (navigational maps), navigating instruments, etc., are kept. Page 79.

check, right as a: completely right; totally correct. A reference to a *check* or *checkmark,* a symbol indicating approval or that something is correct. Page 59.

cherub: an angel depicted as a chubby-faced child with wings, sometimes simply as a child's head above a pair of wings. Page 35.

chief petty officer: a senior over *petty officers,* low-ranking officers just above sailors. Page 70.

chimera(s): a fire-breathing monster of Greek mythology with a lion's head, a goat's body and a serpent's tail. Used figuratively, the term refers to an unreal creature of the imagination, a wild fancy or an unfounded conception. Page 44.

CIA: 1. an abbreviation for *Coordinated Information Apparatus* (an agency on the planet Voltar in LRH's *Mission Earth*), a play on *CIA,* the Central Intelligence Agency of the US Government. Page 163.
2. the Central Intelligence Agency, a United States Government agency created in 1947. The stated purpose of the CIA is to gather information (intelligence) and conduct secret operations to protect the country's national security. Page 163.

claptrap: important-sounding nonsense; insincere or empty language. Page 4.

clearing: an open space in a forest. Page 73.

Coast Guard: the branch of the armed forces that is responsible for coastal defense, protection of life and property at sea, and enforcement of customs, immigration and navigation laws. Page 69.

cockpit: (formerly) a space below the waterline in a warship, occupied by the quarters of the junior officers and used as a dressing station for those wounded in action. Page 58.

Colorado, El: in Spanish, *el* means the, and *colorado* means red. Hence *El Colorado,* used here as a nickname meaning *the redhead,* the person with red hair. Page 59.

Colossus: a person of enormous size, from the giant statue some 120 feet (37 meters) tall at the entrance to the harbor of the Greek island of Rhodes. Built around 280 B.C., the statue was destroyed by an earthquake in the early 200s B.C. Page 79.

Columbia Pictures: a motion picture studio established in Hollywood, California, during the 1920s, becoming one of the largest US film companies. Page 116.

Columbus: Christopher Columbus (1451–1506), Italian explorer who sailed across the Atlantic Ocean in search of a westward sea route to Asia and was responsible for the European discovery of America in 1492. Page 110.

cómo está?: a Spanish phrase meaning "How are you?" Page 179.

conceit: an imaginative idea, especially one that is fanciful or unusual in some way. Page 113.

Congressional Record: the record of the proceedings of the United States Congress, with a transcript of the discussion, published daily by the government while Congress is in session. Page 78.

Congressional representative: a person who is a member of the United States Congress, lawmaking body of the government, specifically of the part of Congress called the House of Representatives. The other body within Congress is the Senate. Page 165.

conjugate: state systematically the forms of verbs to show the various uses. For example, in English, conjugating the verb *to be* includes stating these forms: *I was, he was, you were, they were.* Page 110.

conniving: cooperating secretly (with someone or something), especially in wrongdoing; scheming in an underhanded way. Page 165.

connoisseur: someone who has specialist knowledge of or training in a particular field of the arts or who is considered to have excellent taste and appreciation in such a field. Page 135.

continuity: the fact of staying the same, of being consistent throughout; the quality of remaining consistent or uninterrupted throughout. Page 143.

contract writer: a writer employed under a contract (for a publishing house, motion picture company or the like) to write stories, screenplays, etc. Page 75.

converse: opposite or contrary. Page 61.

copious: large in quantity or number; abundant. Page 24.

cosmology: a particular description or system of how the universe is structured, the forces that created it and the like. Page 112.

Cossack: a member of a group of cavalry warriors in Ukraine and Russia with traditions of fierce independence. From a Turkish word *(kazak)* meaning free, independent person, adventurer. Page 96.

counterrevolutionaries, Nicaraguan: people of Nicaragua, a country in Central America, who fought against the government of Nicaragua during the 1980s. A revolution in Nicaragua in 1979 brought to power a new government that the US accused of being communist. Opposing this government were groups of Nicaraguan rebels, called *counterrevolutionaries.* During much of the 1980s, the counterrevolutionaries (who were supported by the US) fought against the government for control of the country. This civil war continued until 1990, when new elections brought the counterrevolutionaries to power. *See also* **drugs-for-guns.** Page 180.

coup d'état: a sudden and decisive action. (From French, literally, stroke concerning the state, used in reference to a sudden overthrow of a government and seizure of political power, especially in a violent way and by the military.) Page 58.

C.P.O.: an abbreviation for *Chief Petty Officer,* a low-ranking officer in the US Navy or Coast Guard. Page 70.

Crane, Stephen: (1871–1900) American author and journalist, best known for his novel *The Red Badge of Courage* (1895). Page 3.

creeps, the: a sensation of horror, fear, disgust, etc., suggestive of the feeling caused by something crawling over the skin. Page 89.

cribbing: stealing someone's ideas or work; plagiarizing. Page 57.

cue was for laughter, the: the statement acted like a cue (something said or done that provides the stimulus or direction to somebody) that prompted one to laugh. Page 45.

Cussler, Clive: Clive Eric Cussler (1931–), American adventure novelist, underwater explorer and member of the Explorers Club, more than seventeen of whose novels have reached the *New York Times* bestseller list. His writings also include nonfiction on marine (ocean) history, an interest that contributed to his founding of a maritime exploration organization that has discovered over sixty historically significant underwater wrecks. Page 113.

cut a swath: attracted notice or accomplished much. From the literal meaning of *swath,* an area or amount of grass or grain cut in one sweep of a scythe (a farming tool with a long, curved blade fastened to a handle) or in one passage of a mower or other machine. Page 169.

cut (one's) teeth: learn how to do something and gain experience from it. Page 74.

cytology: the study of cells, their formation, structure and function. Page 154.

czar: any person exercising great authority or power in a particular field. Page 118.

D

Daffy Dill: the pulp character Joe "Daffy" Dill, a newspaper reporter who was constantly landing in difficult situations. Created by American writer Richard Sale, the Daffy Dill stories appeared in *Detective Fiction Weekly,* where they were among the magazine's most popular features. Page 10.

day, of the: of the time period referred to or under consideration. Page 3.

Dead Men Kill: an LRH story first published in *Thrilling Detective* magazine in July 1934. A detective investigating a series of murders finds himself battling corpses that carry the smell of damp earth and undertakers. Page 9.

dead-ringer: characteristic of a *dead ringer* (also *ringer*), one who closely resembles another. From *dead,* meaning complete or absolute, and the phrase *rings a bell,* reminds one of something. Page 180.

Death Flyer: an LRH story first published in *Mystery Novels Magazine* in April 1936. The Death Flyer tears through the blackness, a ghost train with Jim Bellamy aboard, trying to save the life of a girl who died in its wreckage ten years before. Page 36.

de Camp, L. Sprague: (1907–2000) American writer who produced works of fantasy, nonfiction, fiction and science fiction during a sixty-year literary career. Page 127.

defendant teeth: false teeth that are characterized as being *on trial,* that is, accused in a court of law, a pun on the quoted advertisement for *"False Teeth, 60 Day Trial,"* where *trial* means a test of something in order to determine performance, qualities or suitability. Page 86.

deference to, in: out of respect or courtesy to somebody. Page 73.

definitive: having a fixed and final form; providing a solution or final answer; satisfying all requirements. Page 68.

Defoe, Daniel: (1660?–1731) English novelist, journalist and social thinker who produced some five hundred books and pamphlets during the course of his career. His first and most famous novel, *The Life and Strange Surprizing Adventures of Robinson Crusoe, of York, Mariner,* appeared in 1719. Page 51.

dekalogy: a group of ten related volumes, from Greek *deka-,* ten, and *-logy,* a collection or group of writings. Page 163.

Dell: Dell Publishing Company, one of the major pulp magazine publishing companies during the early twentieth century; later, a major publisher of paperback books. Page 57.

denouement: the final resolution of the intricacies of a plot, as of a drama or novel. Page 4.

Dent, Lester: (1904–1959) American pulp fiction writer best known as the author of a series of stories on Doc Savage, a superhuman scientist and adventurer. Page 11.

Denver: the capital and largest city of Colorado. Founded in the mid-1800s by gold prospectors, the city has become the distribution, manufacturing and transportation center for the Rocky Mountain region of the United States. Page 181.

department letters: letters, anecdotes or the like supplied by writers to an editor of a magazine for inclusion in a *department,* a specialized column or section appearing regularly in a magazine, such as one providing a forum for writers to discuss their background, an experience leading to the writing of a particular story, etc. Page 26.

Department of Commerce: a department of the United States Government established in 1903 with the purpose to promote domestic and foreign trade and to advance, serve and promote the nation's economic development and technological advancement. The Civil Aeronautics Administration, which was in the Department of Commerce, issued pilot licenses to aviators. (During the mid-twentieth century, the Civil Aeronautics Administration was reorganized as the Federal Aviation Administration in the Department of Transportation.) Page 56.

detective sergeant: an officer of the police force (with the rank of *sergeant,* a roughly mid-level rank) whose function is to obtain information and evidence, as of offenses against the law. Page 24.

diametrically: used to emphasize that a difference or contrast is as great as it can be; completely. Page 180.

Dianetics: Dianetics is a forerunner and substudy of Scientology. Dianetics means "through the mind" or "through the soul" (from Greek *dia,* through, and *nous,* mind or soul). It is a system of coordinated axioms which resolve problems concerning human behavior and psychosomatic illnesses. It combines a workable technique and a thoroughly validated method for increasing sanity, by erasing unwanted sensations and unpleasant emotions. Page 1.

Dickens, Charles: (1812–1870) prolific English novelist of the mid-nineteenth century whose books are noted for picturesque and extravagant characters in the lower economic strata of England. Page 163.

diffident: restrained or reserved in manner, conduct, etc. Page 147.

Digest: *Writer's Digest,* a monthly American magazine published since 1920 that provides information, "how-to" instruction and encouragement for those who enjoy writing. The magazine includes advice from well-known, bestselling authors, tips for improving manuscripts and where and how to sell one's fiction, nonfiction, poetry, etc. Page 99.

digs: an informal term for living quarters. Page 36.

discourse: 1. express oneself orally; communicate one's thoughts in a continuous way; talk. Page 44. 2. a formal written treatment of a subject. Page 143.

disgorged: spilled out, likened to something being poured out of something. Page 72.

dispassionately: in a manner free from emotion or bias; calmly; impartially. Page 115.

dissemble: give a false or misleading appearance to something. Page 43.

ditch (someone): a slang expression meaning get rid of, as in no longer continuing to employ someone. Page 25.

divination: the methods or practice of attempting to foretell the future or discover the unknown through omens or supernatural powers. Page 153.

divine fire: liveliness of imagination or poetic inspiration viewed as coming from a holy source. Page 57.

Doc Savage: a fictional character in pulp magazines starting in the 1930s. As portrayed in some one hundred and eighty stories, most of which were written by American author Lester Dent (1904–1959), Doc Savage was a physician, scientist and adventurer with near-superhuman abilities, trained to fight the forces of evil. Page 3.

Dodgers: the name of a professional American baseball team formed in 1890. Beginning their career in Brooklyn, New York, the Dodgers moved to Los Angeles, California, in 1958. Page 146.

dog-eared: old and worn; showing signs of wear and tear. Page 36.

dogging: worrying or hounding; causing continual worry. Page 59.

dolorous: very sorrowful or sad; mournful. Page 114.

dons, mafia: heads of organized crime families in the *mafia,* a secret Italian organization allegedly engaged in smuggling, trafficking in narcotics and other criminal activities in Italy and elsewhere. Page 173.

Don't Rush Me: an LRH story first published in *Argosy* in July 1936. The trench he is ordered to dig is never dug—yet Sergeant "Don't Rush Me" Marshall has to defend it from the enemy. Page 61.

do (one's) stuff: perform (one's) duty, function or skill; do what is required or expected. *Stuff* is any unspecified kind of matter and is used here figuratively to mean (one's) actions, movements, duties, functions, etc. Page 57.

dope: an informal term for information, data or news. Page 57.

Doppelgänger: a ghost that is identical to a living person. A German term meaning, literally, double goer. Page 179.

Dostoyevsky: Feodor Mikhailovich Dostoyevsky (1821–1881), Russian writer and thinker, whose psychologically intense works probed the motivations and moral justifications for his characters' actions. Page 112.

double talk: verbal expression intended to be, or which may be, interpreted in more than one sense; deliberately ambiguous or imprecise language. Page 168.

drab: something having a dull or lifeless appearance or character. Page 181.

drifter, lonesome: in a western story, a lonely man who moves about, taking jobs here and there, without remaining long in any one place. Page 49.

drugs-for-guns: an illegal trade involving shipping and selling drugs, then using the funds to purchase guns, especially in reference to 1980s CIA support of Nicaraguan rebels. Reports of the shipping and sale of illegal drugs have been linked to the subsequent use of the drug profits for purchase of arms, the guns being shipped to rebels for use in their attacks on the Nicaraguan government. Page 180.

drugstore: a store selling medicines and a variety of other goods, including magazines, cigarettes, cosmetics, etc., and sometimes serving soft drinks and light meals. Page 65.

Dubai: a city in and capital of the state of Dubai, a part of the United Arab Emirates (UAE), an *emirate* being a region headed by an emir (prince). Located on the southern coast of the Persian Gulf, the UAE is composed of Dubai and six other emirates. Each emirate has control of its internal affairs, while the UAE handles foreign relations and defense for the entire country. Page 198.

Duke University: a private, coeducational institution in Durham, North Carolina, with schools of arts and sciences, business, theology, engineering, environment, law, medicine and nursing. Page 107.

Dune: a bestselling science fiction novel by American author Frank Herbert (1920–1986). Published in 1965, *Dune* is the story of forces battling for control in a complex society some eight thousand years in the future. It explores the themes of politics, religion and environmental science. Page 146.

dungarees: work pants made from strong material, usually blue denim. Page 72.

Dunkirk: a major seaport on the north coast of France. Due to its strategic location, Dunkirk was the scene of heavy bombing attacks both in World War I (1914–1918) and in the early days of World War II (1939–1945) until captured by the Germans (May 1940). Page 109.

dust off: finish (something) off. Page 79.

dynamical astronomy: *dynamical* refers to energy and forces that produce motion. *Astronomy* is the scientific study of the universe, especially of the motions, positions, sizes, composition and behavior of celestial (of the sky or outer space) objects. Thus *dynamical astronomy* is that branch of astronomy that deals with the laws of motion as regards planets, moons and stars. It includes the discovery that the Earth and other planets travel around the Sun in oval-shaped orbits. Page 152.

E

ear, had (someone's or something's): trusted as one to listen to, accept information from or the like. Page 154.

eclipsed: made less outstanding or important by comparison; surpassed. Page 117.

eczema: a noncontagious skin disorder of unknown cause, characterized by inflammation, itching and the formation of scales (any thin, flaky or platelike layer or piece, as of dry skin). Page 82.

Egtvedt: C. L. Egtvedt (1892–1975), president of Boeing Aircraft Company (1933–1939). Page 56.

Ekaterinburg: a city on the eastern slope of the Ural Mountains, a major industrial center and a station on the Trans-Siberian Railroad. Emperor Nicholas II and his family were held captive in the city by the Communists after the Russian Revolution and were killed there in 1918. Page 97.

El Colorado: in Spanish, *el* means the, and *colorado* means red. Hence *El Colorado,* used here as a nickname meaning *the redhead,* the person with red hair. Page 59.

electric icebox: an earlier name for a refrigerator operated by electricity. Page 85.

Elkton marrying parson: a humorous reference to a busy minister performing marriages in Elkton, Maryland. During the early 1900s, marriages in Maryland (a state in the eastern United States) were performed with little formality and few legal requirements, resulting in many couples traveling to Elkton, near the state border, from other areas to get married. During a peak year (1936), more than eleven thousand marriage licenses were issued, which would have required "Elkton marrying parsons" to work hard every day performing marriage ceremonies. Page 78.

Embarcadero: a waterfront section in San Francisco, from *embarcadero,* an American-Spanish term meaning a wharf or landing place. Page 63.

emote: show or express emotion. Page 115.

Empire State (Building): a skyscraper completed in 1931 in New York City, New York, USA. For many years it was the tallest building in the world, standing 1,250 feet (381 meters) high with 102 stories. (*Empire State* is a name for New York State.) Page 75.

Encinitas: a coastal town in Southern California, established in the late 1800s. Page 10.

enclave: a small, distinct area or group enclosed within a larger one. Page 35.

endears: attracts (someone) to (something); makes (someone) have a greater regard or affection for (something). Page 141.

End Is Not Yet, The: an LRH story first published in *Astounding Science Fiction* magazine as a three-part series, appearing in the August, September and October 1947 issues. The setting is a dangerous postatomic world, where a conspiracy to provoke a nuclear war is defeated by a coalition of scientists. Page 113.

enigmatic: difficult to interpret, understand or explain. Page 75.

enmity: the feelings characteristic of an enemy; hostility. Page 24.

epic: a work of literature, such as a long novel, especially one portraying heroic deeds or historical traditions and often covering an extended period of time. Page 58.

epitome of, the: something that is a perfect example (of a quality or type). Page 45.

Ernst, Paul: (1899–1985) American author of science fiction short stories, fantasy, thrillers and horror. Ernst wrote for science fiction, fantasy and hero magazines throughout the 1930s. Page 35.

escapism: diversion of the mind to purely imaginative activity or entertainment to escape from reality. Page 3.

ethnological: of or having to do with *ethnology,* the science that analyzes cultures, especially in regard to their historical development and the similarities and dissimilarities between them. Page 112.

ethnologist: someone trained and specializing in ethnology. *See also* **ethnological.** Page 112.

euphemism: a polite, tactful or less explicit term used to avoid the direct naming of an offensive reality. Page 168.

existential: involving or concerned with human existence, as for example by describing circumstances, problems, questions or the like that relate to human existence. Page 2.

Existentialist: one who is involved in or puts forth the ideas of *existentialism,* a philosophical and literary movement influential during the early and mid-1900s. Existentialism emphasizes that each person is alone in a world without meaning or purpose. Individuals are therefore free to choose how to live their lives and are responsible for their own decisions and actions. Page 10.

expatriate: a person who has left his homeland to live or work in another country, usually for a long period of time. Page 36.

expound: present and explain (a theory or idea) systematically; set forth, point by point; state in detail. Page 149.

extraordinaire: outstanding in a particular capacity. Page 15.

eye to, with an: with a view to; with the object or intention of. Page 23.

F

Fall of the House of Usher, The: a well-known short story written in 1839 by American author Edgar Allan Poe (1809–1849). A horror mystery set in a lonely desolate mansion, the story describes the degeneration and decay of the Usher house and family. Page 81.

fanned: literally, directed a current of air upon, with or as if with a fan, to increase the strength of a fire. Used figuratively to mean stir up or increase activity, emotions, etc. Page 44.

fastens (upon): focuses attention; concentrates. Page 75.

fatuous: marked by lack of intelligence and rational consideration, or foolish, complacent disregard of reality. Page 43.

fedora: a man's soft felt hat with the crown creased lengthwise and a somewhat curved brim. Page 51.

feline: characteristic of animals of the cat family; used figuratively to mean catlike in the ability to accomplish goals by being clever. Page 27.

fervor: powerful, intense emotion, feeling, expression or enthusiasm (toward or about something). Page 141.

finger worn to the second joint: figuratively, as though the fingers have been used so much (in striking the keys of a keyboard) that it is as if they have worn down to the second joint. Page 10.

first crack out: at the first opportunity; before anything else; immediately, from *get a crack at,* an expression that refers to someone getting a shot at an animal, as in hunting. *Crack* here means an opportunity or attempt. Page 57.

fish patrol: government officials responsible for guarding the fishing and enforcing fishing laws in San Francisco Bay. Page 65.

Fitzgerald: F. Scott Fitzgerald (1896–1940), American writer, whose novels and short stories describe the social changes occurring during the 1920s. He is best known for his novels *The Great Gatsby* (1925) and *Tender Is the Night* (1934). Page 3.

Five-Novels Monthly: a pulp magazine published from 1928 until the late 1940s. The monthly schedule was continued until 1943, when paper shortages during World War II (1939–1945) forced it to a quarterly schedule and a resultant name change to *Five Novels* magazine. Page 15.

fodder: something regarded as material for a specific use. Page 146.

fold, the professional: a group or community with the shared aims and values of professional writers. Page 11.

force majeure: a French phrase meaning major force. Page 107.

Ford: a reference to the *Ford Motor Company,* a United States automobile manufacturer founded in 1903 by American industrialist Henry Ford (1863–1947). Also, an automobile made by the Ford Motor Company. Page 18.

foredeck: the front part of the main deck of a ship. Page 72.

Forensic Medicine: a periodical concerned with *forensic medicine,* the application of the principles and practice of all branches of medicine to legal proceedings in a court of law. The term *forensic* means connected with or used in such courts or proceedings. Forensic medicine's most frequent use is in clarifying doubtful questions in the investigation of sudden deaths or deaths from unnatural causes, such as drowning, strangulation, shooting and poisoning. The knowledge of medicine is used to establish the cause of such deaths and determine if they were due to accident, suicide or murder. Page 58.

foreshadow: a technique said to be used by some writers, as in short stories, novels or the like, to give the reader hints or suggestions about coming action. It is used to develop expectancy in a reader by giving clues as to what is about to happen. *Foreshadow* literally means a shadow cast before an object. Page 4.

"frame" yarn: also *frame story,* a story serving as a type of framework, or underlying structure, within which another story or several other stories are told. Page 94.

Franzawi: an Arabic word for Frenchman. Page 76.

fray, into the: into the fight or struggle. Page 79.

Frazetta, Frank: (1928–2010) renowned American artist. A child prodigy who began attending art school at the age of eight, Frazetta's work appeared on movie posters as well as the covers of numerous adventure, science fiction and fantasy books and magazines, including many editions of the *L. Ron Hubbard Presents Writers of the Future* series. Beginning in 1988, Frazetta also served as a judge on the Illustrators of the Future Contest. Page 188.

Freas, Frank Kelly: (1922–2005) acclaimed American artist and illustrator. Beginning in the early 1950s, Freas' art appeared on covers and in interiors of science fiction and fantasy books and magazines, as well as in other materials, such as record albums and advertising, earning him some eleven Hugo Awards. In 1988 Freas became the long-running Coordinating Judge of L. Ron Hubbard's Illustrators of the Future Contest. Page 188.

French Foreign Legion: a unit of the French army, one of the most famous fighting forces in the world. Formed in 1831, the Foreign Legion consists of eight thousand men who apply for duty and are generally accepted regardless of background or occupation and must come from a country other than France. Page 36.

fresco: a painting done in watercolor on wet plaster on a wall or ceiling, in which the colors penetrate the plaster and become fixed as it dries. Page 35.

G

Gable, Clark: (1901–1960) American motion picture actor. During the 1930s and early 1940s, Gable was the most successful leading man in Hollywood films. He served as a pilot during World War II (1939–1945). He is best known for his portrayal of Rhett Butler in the film *Gone With the Wind* (1939). Page 10.

gag paragraphs: short, humorous descriptions, jokes, stories or the like, often only a few paragraphs long. A *paragraph* is a section of a piece of writing, usually consisting of several sentences dealing with a single subject. The first sentence of a paragraph starts on a new line. Page 18.

Gajda: Radola Gajda (1892–1948), Czech military commander and politician, born Rudolf Geidl, who fought with the Czech Legions during the latter part of World War I (1914–1918). A supporter of fascism during the 1920s and 1930s, Gajda was elected to the Czech parliament. During World War II (1939–1945), he was involved in resistance efforts against Germany. Page 96.

gallery: a collection of photographs or portraits of criminals. Page 24.

Gardner, Erle Stanley: (1889–1970) American author and lawyer who wrote nearly one hundred detective and mystery novels. Drawing on his legal experience, Gardner created accurate courtroom scenes and brilliant legal maneuvers in his stories, particularly in those involving his best-known character, the lawyer-detective Perry Mason. Page 74.

garnish: make something fancy or striking. From the literal meaning, add something to food that provides flavor, decorative color or the like. Page 43.

garrulous: talking or tending to talk much or freely. Page 63.

genre(s): a category of artistic composition, as in music or literature, marked by a distinctive style, form or content. Page 1.

geography: the range or extent of the natural features of a place or region. Hence, *"had walked some geography,"* had traveled around in and over the natural features of various areas and regions. Page 20.

George Washington University: a private university, founded in 1821, in the city of Washington, DC. Named after the first president of the United States, George Washington (1732–1799), it maintains various schools of education, including the School of Engineering and Applied Science and the Columbian College of Arts and Sciences. The university has a long history of supporting research in physics and other technical fields. Page 2.

Georgia: a state in the southeastern United States, on the Atlantic Ocean. Page 124.

get off in high: literally, start moving in *high gear,* the top gear of a vehicle, allowing the greatest speed. Used figuratively to mean getting started on any project at a fast rate of speed. Page 81.

gibe: an insulting or mocking remark. Page 38.

Gibson, Walter: Walter Brown Gibson (1897–1985), American author and stage magician. Best known as the creator of the pulp fiction character the Shadow (writing some two hundred and eighty stories in the series), Gibson also wrote more than one hundred books on magic, mysteries and psychic phenomena. Page 11.

Gide, André: (1869–1951) French novelist and playwright whose writings were devoted to examining the problems of individual freedom and responsibility. In addition to his numerous works of fiction and criticism, he also made distinguished translations of works by Shakespeare and other English authors. Page 10.

Glashow, Sheldon: Sheldon Lee Glashow (1932–), American physicist and winner of the 1979 Nobel Prize in physics for his work on the nature and behavior of elementary particles (the basic constituents of which matter and energy are composed). Page 188.

goods, proven: things promised to be worthwhile or valuable and that have been demonstrated beyond a doubt to be so. From the literal idea of *goods,* things produced, as items for sale. Page 81.

Gothic: a type of fiction emphasizing mystery, horror and the supernatural. Gothic novels rose to popularity in the early 1800s, with settings that included medieval castles, ghost-haunted rooms, underground passages and secret stairways. The influence and popularity of Gothic fiction has continued with novels of mystery, fantasy and the supernatural. Page 11.

got it all over (someone): is superior to (someone else). Page 124.

granddaddy: used to denote something that is the first or oldest of its kind or the one being longest in existence. Literally, *granddaddy* is an informal term for one's grandfather. Page 85.

grand master: someone who is at the highest level of ability or achievement in a particular field. Page 159.

grand old man: literally, a highly respected, usually elderly, man who has been a major or the most important figure in a specific field for many years. Used figuratively for any long-standing and well-known item, in this case, a pulp magazine. Page 85.

Great Depression: a drastic decline in the world economy starting in the United States, resulting in mass unemployment and widespread poverty that lasted from 1929 until 1939. Page 2.

green seas: solid waves of water coming aboard a ship, so called from the green color of a mass or sheet of water that is too large to be broken up into small drops of spray. Page 72.

Greenwich Village: a residential section of Manhattan (the economic center of New York City), inhabited by artists, writers and students. Page 35.

greyhound: a fast ship likened to the tall, slim fast-running dog with a smooth coat, narrow head and long legs, widely used for racing. Page 70.

Grey, Zane: (1875–1939) American author, one of the most popular writers of novels about the Wild West. In his career he wrote more than fifty books, involving careful research and authentic details about Western life. Page 137.

grist for (one's) mill: something that is to one's advantage or profit. *Grist* is grain that is to be ground up. Page 49.

grizzled soul: a person of a particular type—in this case, someone with hair that is gray or streaked with gray. Page 70.

groove, down the: along a channel or particular course. Page 59.

ground, to the: entirely; completely. Page 23.

guarded: careful to not reveal one's position, purpose or the like; cautious. Page 15.

Guinness World Records: a collection of world records, both of human achievements as well as of the natural world, which is published as an annual reference book. Page 193.

Gulf: the Gulf of Mexico, an arm of the Atlantic Ocean, bordered on the north by the United States, on the east by Cuba and on the south and west by Mexico. Page 70.

Gunn, James: James Edwin Gunn (1923–), American science fiction writer, editor and anthologist, who has also served as an officer in several science fiction associations. Page 169.

gutter bum: a homeless person, one with an impoverished and degraded existence or way of life. Page 149.

gypsum: a widespread colorless, white or yellowish mineral used in the manufacture of various plaster products. Page 116.

H

hack: a writer producing dull, unoriginal work. Page 17.

hailed: praised or approved with enthusiasm. Page 146.

Haiti: a country occupying the western third of the island of Hispaniola (island lying southeast of Cuba and west of Puerto Rico) in the northern Caribbean. Page 9.

half-bake: a person lacking in judgment, intelligence or common sense. Page 44.

half, not: not at all. Page 76.

Hamilton, Ed: Edmond Moore Hamilton (1904–1977), American science fiction writer. His short stories appeared in pulp magazines of the 1920s and 1930s and he also authored science fiction novels. Page 127.

Hammett, Dashiell: (1894–1961) highly influential American author of detective novels. Drawing on his years of work as a private detective, Hammett began writing in the early 1920s. With his realistic writing style, he created enduringly popular characters and plots, with a number of his best-known works, such as *The Maltese Falcon* (1930), later adapted for film. Page 3.

hangs a story, thereby: in that connection or relation there is something to tell. Page 93.

hapless: unlucky or unfortunate. Page 36.

hard-line: following a hard or firm policy or course of action, as in one's profession, and not softening or weakening the policy or course of action for other considerations. Page 10.

hard put, be: have considerable difficulty or trouble. Page 72.

Harper's: a monthly magazine published in New York City, well known for its original articles on science, literature, politics and the arts. Page 23.

harrowing: extremely distressing. Page 74.

harry: annoy or be a nuisance to by constant demands or annoyances. Page 25.

Hartwell, David: David G. Hartwell (1941–), American editor, literary historian and critic, whose annual anthologies of science fiction and fantasy have won numerous awards. Page 113.

Harvard University: the oldest and one of the foremost universities in the United States (founded 1636), located in Cambridge, Massachusetts, a state in the northeastern US on the Atlantic coast. Page 38.

hat: slang for the title and work of a job or position; taken from the fact that in many professions, such as railroading, the type of hat worn is the badge of the job. Page 155.

hauls (one) back on (one's) haunches: pulls (one) back suddenly, causing (one) to come to a complete stop, likened to a horse that is given a forceful pull on the reins, such that the animal's forelegs come off the ground and it ends up almost sitting on the hindquarters (haunches). Page 76.

hawser: a large rope used for towing or mooring a ship. Page 79.

head off, working (one's): working very hard at something. Page 20.

Hegel: Georg Wilhelm Friedrich Hegel (1770–1831), German philosopher. His philosophy held, in part, that every idea or event led to its opposite. These opposites, being in conflict with each other, were supposed to ultimately resolve into an "absolute" in which all opposites are one. Page 151.

Heinlein, Robert: (1907–1988) American author considered one of the most important writers of science fiction. Emerging during science fiction's Golden Age (1939–1949), Heinlein went on to write many novels, including the classic *Stranger in a Strange Land* (1961). He won four Hugo Awards and was presented with the first Grand Master Nebula Award for lifetime achievement in science fiction. Page 4.

Helena: city and capital of Montana, a state in the northwestern United States bordering on Canada. Page 9.

hell on wheels: extremely demanding; aggressive or wild. Page 58.

hell's bells: a slang expression indicating impatience, anger, emphasis, etc. Page 87.

Hemingway: Ernest Hemingway (1899–1961), American novelist and short-story writer, a number of whose stories addressed social issues, as in *For Whom the Bell Tolls* (1940) about the Spanish Civil War. Many of Hemingway's works are regarded as classics of American literature. Page 3.

Henry, Alexander: (1739–1824) fur trader who traveled through parts of what are now Canada and the northern United States and, in partnership with other traders, helped to set up the fur-trading company called the North West Company. Henry left a valuable journal of his travels and adventures. Page 59.

herald: a person or thing that comes before to announce or give an indication of what follows. Page 147.

Herbert, Frank: (1920–1986) acclaimed American science fiction author. While beginning his writing career in the 1950s, he is best known for his bestselling novel *Dune* (1965) and subsequent books in the *Dune Chronicles,* a series that sparked a major motion picture and television series. Herbert also served as a judge in the Writers of the Future Contest. Page 146.

He Walked to War: an LRH story first published in *Adventure* magazine in October 1935. Tired of walking, E. Z. Go transfers to another Marine post to become an airplane gunner, only to find himself walking, this time through the Nicaraguan forests. Page 61.

heyday: the stage or period of greatest vigor, strength, success, etc. Page 35.

hied: went with speed; hastened. Page 70.

high, get off in: literally, start moving in *high gear,* the top gear of a vehicle, allowing the greatest speed. Used figuratively to mean getting started on any project at a fast rate of speed. Page 81.

hinterland: an area far from big cities and towns. Page 179.

hobo: a poor, homeless person, who travels from place to place trying to find work. Page 109.

hold out: offer something, as if by extending the hand toward someone. Page 168.

Hollywood Arts Council: an organization established to support and promote the arts in Hollywood, California, stemming from "the belief that the arts revitalize people as well as communities." Page 198.

homogenous: made up of the same kind of elements or being similar in nature. Page 21.

homograph: a word that is spelled in the same way as one or more other words but is different in meaning—for example, the verb *project* and the noun *project.* Page 152.

hope to tell you, I: I would like to say (that something happened just as has been stated). Page 72.

house: a company that publishes books, pamphlets, etc. Page 20.

household name: someone that most people know about. Page 185.

Houston: a city and port in southeastern Texas, a state in the southwestern United States. NASA's Johnson Space Center in Houston has been headquarters for manned spacecraft projects since the early 1960s. The center is named for Lyndon B. Johnson (1908–1973), thirty-sixth president of the United States. *See also* **National Aeronautics and Space Administration.** Page 188.

hovel: a small, dirty or poorly built house. Page 65.

Hudson's Bay Company: a fur-trading company originally established by English merchants in 1670 for the purpose of trade and settlement in the Hudson Bay region in northeast Canada. Page 59.

Hugo: an award for science fiction writing (Hugo Award), initiated in 1953 by the World Science Fiction Society. It is named for influential science fiction editor, writer and inventor Hugo Gernsback (1884–1967), who is credited with starting modern science fiction by founding the first magazine dedicated to this literary field, *Amazing Stories,* in 1926. Page 185.

hull: the main body of a large vehicle such as an airplane or a tank. Page 72.

Huntington Library: one of the largest research libraries in the United States with more than six million books, manuscripts, maps and other documents in the fields of British and American history and literature, located in San Marino, a city near Los Angeles, California. Page 171.

I

IBM: *International Business Machines Corporation,* one of the largest manufacturers of business machines during the early and mid-1900s and, later, a manufacturer of the first large-scale computers. Page 51.

icebox, electric: an earlier name for a refrigerator operated by electricity. Page 85.

iconic: characteristic of a person regarded as an *icon,* someone widely admired and often regarded as a symbol of a movement, field of activity or the like. Page 196.

Idealist, The: an LRH story first published in *Astounding Science Fiction* (under the pen name Kurt von Rachen) in July 1940. The first story of the *Kilkenny Cats* series, *The Idealist* is set in the year 2893, when the world is controlled by a dictator. Two groups antagonistic to the government—and to each other—are sent to colonize another planet, the government's hope being that they will kill each other off. But some aboard have other plans. *See also **Kilkenny Cats** series.* Page 116.

idiom: the way of using a particular language that comes naturally to its native speakers and involves both knowledge of its grammar and familiarity with its usage. Page 52.

inaugurated: introduced into use; formally begun. Page 113.

incident: a distinct piece of action, or an episode, as in a story or play. Page 114.

indomitable: that cannot be subdued or overcome, such as persons, will, courage or spirit; unconquerable. Page 143.

inestimably: too large or great to be measured or estimated. Page 143.

Inquisitorial: having the nature of an *inquisition,* a harsh or very searching investigation. Used figuratively for anything that seems to demand answers in an intense, searching way. Page 44.

Inside Passage: a natural protected waterway in northwestern North America, 950 miles (1,500 kilometers) long. It extends along the coast from Seattle, Washington, USA, past British Columbia, Canada, to the southern area of Alaska. The passage is made up of a series of channels running between the mainland and a string of islands on the west that protect the passage from Pacific Ocean storms. Page 64.

intrepid: bold and fearless. Page 163.

iron-bound: unchanging. From the literal meaning, wrapped (bound) in iron bands. Page 24.

Irving, Washington: (1783–1859) American writer and one of the first whose works received recognition in Europe as well as in the United States. Besides his well-known stories *Rip Van Winkle* and *The Legend of Sleepy Hollow,* Irving also wrote stories of his travels in the American West and in Europe as well as historical works on figures such as George Washington and Christopher Columbus. Page 58.

J

James, Henry: (1843–1916) American writer who produced twenty novels and more than one hundred short stories. The theme of many of his works focuses on the contrasts between Americans and Europeans. He also wrote literary criticism, biography and travel essays. Page 3.

jane: a slang term for a girl or woman. Page 87.

jibe(d): conform or agree with something or with another; be in harmony or accord with. Page 59.

jilted: abruptly refused (by a lover) without warning. Page 179.

Jurassic: the period of the Earth's history during which dinosaurs flourished and birds and mammals first appeared, extending from 210 million years to 140 million years ago. Page 181.

K

Karloff, Boris: (1887–1969) British actor, born William Henry Pratt. Beginning his acting career in silent movies, he became best known for his roles in horror films, from the classic 1931 *Frankenstein* to horror films spanning the next three decades. On stage he appeared in comedy and as Captain Hook in the fantasy *Peter Pan* and he also performed in television and on radio. Page 179.

Kepler, Johannes: (1571–1630) German astronomer and mathematician, noted for formulating and verifying laws of planetary motion, such as that every planet follows an oval-shaped path. He also contributed to the science of optics, showing how lenses work. Page 152.

***Kilkenny Cats* series:** a series of five LRH stories first published in *Astounding Science Fiction* (under the pen name Kurt von Rachen) between July 1940 and February 1942. The term *Kilkenny cats,* which refers to a pair of cats that legend says fought each other until only their tails remained, is used figuratively for any opponents who fight until they destroy each other. Page 124.

King's Letter Boys: in the British navy, the nickname for midshipmen (junior officers in training) during the seventeenth and eighteenth centuries. Young boys of good families were sent to sea with a *letter of service,* a document from the king advising the ship captain to see to the boy's instruction in seafaring, with a view to his eventually becoming a naval officer after specified training and passing an examination. Page 58.

King, Stephen: (1947–) award-winning American novelist and short-story writer and one of the world's bestselling authors. Renowned for his tales of horror, fantasy and the supernatural, King has produced many stories and books that have been made into films. Page 4.

kismet: a Turkish word for fate or destiny. Page 154.

Klondike: a sparsely populated region (and river) located in northwest Canada, just east of Alaska, the site of a gold rush in the late 1800s. (A *rush* is an eager rushing of numbers of persons to some region that is being occupied or exploited, especially because of a new mine.) Page 62.

Knight, Damon: Damon Francis Knight (1922–2002), American science fiction author, editor and critic. His stories appeared in pulp magazines during the 1940s. Later, he wrote numerous critical reviews and served as an editor for many important science fiction works. Page 169.

knock the stuffing out of: give a merciless beating to; defeat thoroughly. Page 79.

kopeks: in Russian currency, a small amount of money. A hundred kopeks make up a *ruble,* which is the standard unit of currency in Russia. Page 97.

L

L: an *elevated* railway, a railway supported on pillars above street level. Page 81.

ladle out: carry, move or present something one section or part at a time, from the literal idea of a *ladle,* a long-handled spoon with a deep bowl, used to serve soup or other liquids. Page 80.

L'Amour, Louis: Louis Dearborn L'Amour (1908–1988), a popular American author whose many novels have been admired for their accurate portrayals of the historical periods he wrote about, which range from the Middle Ages in Europe to the frontier days in America. Page 136.

lampoon: mock or ridicule in a *lampoon,* a work of literature, art or the like, ridiculing severely the character or behavior of a person, society, etc. Page 163.

land lay, how the: the position or arrangement of parts, as of the features of a landscape. Page 57.

last word: something regarded as the best or most advanced of its kind. Page 61.

latterly: at a subsequent time; later. Page 165.

lay away: to put something away so as to save it. Page 43.

leading light: someone who influences or sets an example to others. Page 1.

lean years: a time period that is not productive or profitable. Page 27.

legionnaire: a member of the *French Foreign Legion,* a unit of the French army consisting of volunteers of other nationalities. The legion was formed in 1831 and headquartered in Algeria (a country in northern Africa) until it was relocated to France in the early 1960s. Page 52.

Letter Boys, King's: in the British navy, the nickname for midshipmen (junior officers in training) during the seventeenth and eighteenth centuries. Young boys of good families were sent to sea with a *letter of service,* a document from the king advising the ship captain to see to the boy's instruction in seafaring, with a view to his eventually becoming a naval officer after specified training and passing an examination. Page 58.

Lewis and Clark: Meriwether Lewis (1774–1809) and William Clark (1770–1838), the first explorers to travel across the northwestern United States, from the Mississippi River across the Rocky Mountains to the Pacific coast and back (1804–1806). Page 59.

Lewis, Sinclair: (1885–1951) American novelist, noted for the primary theme of his works, such as the novel *Babbitt* (1922), of the monotony, emotional frustration and lack of spiritual and intellectual values in American middle-class life. Page 82.

Ley, Willy: (1906–1969) German-born writer and space advocate who helped popularize rocketry and spaceflight in Germany and the United States. Page 116.

Library Journal: a periodical for the library field, published since 1876. Along with news and features of interest to librarians, the book review section of the *Library Journal* covers thousands of books and audiovisual materials each year. Page 137.

license, writer's: intentional deviation from rule, convention or fact, as for the sake of literary or artistic effect. Page 26.

lid: a slang term for a cap or hat. Page 93.

lien: the legal right to keep or sell somebody else's property as security for a debt. Page 146.

light love: a romantic story characterized as being *light,* not profound or serious. Page 24.

light of, make: treat as unimportant. Page 115.

line, in every and any: in any and every area of interest, activity, pursuit or study; an area that is one's specialty or profession. *Line* here is used to mean a course of conduct; action or procedure; an area of activity. Page 24.

line, out of: other than the usual or expected. Page 18.

lion's share: the largest part or portion. Page 185.

literati: persons of scholarly or literary attainments; intellectuals. Page 65.

liver bile: a yellowish-green digestive fluid that helps the body digest fats. Bile is produced in the *liver,* an organ in the body that stores and filters blood and takes part in many other functions. Page 86.

loaded dice: in gambling, dice which have been made heavier on one side by cutting a hole and inserting a substance and plugging the hole back up again. The purpose is to make the dice land on selected sides so as to cause someone to win or to lose a game. Page 93.

Locus Magazine: an award-winning monthly magazine, founded in 1968, that reports on the science fiction and fantasy writing industry. *Locus* covers news on the science fiction scene around the world, along with book reviews and listings of new books and magazines. Page 136.

loins, girded up (one's): summoned up one's inner resources in preparation for action, alluding to the phrase in the Bible, meaning to secure one's clothing with a belt so as to allow freer action to the body. *Girded* means fastened or secured with a belt or band, and *loins* means the region of the hips and lower abdomen. Page 58.

London, Jack: (1876–1916) American author, journalist, political activist and one of the most widely read American authors, with works translated into numerous languages. His adventures in gold mining and his sea voyages served as material for many of his more than fifty books. Page 62.

Long, Frank Belknap: (1901–1994) American writer of horror, fantasy and science fiction stories. His works have won numerous awards throughout his career and he also is the recipient of several lifetime achievement awards. Page 127.

lore: accumulated facts, traditions or beliefs about a particular subject. Page 61.

Louisiana: a state in the southern United States on the Gulf of Mexico. Page 70.

Lovecraft, H. P.: Howard Phillips Lovecraft (1890–1937), American author of fantasy and horror stories. With fiction first published in the early 1920s, Lovecraft became known for his fascination with dark forces in settings that sometimes seem realistic and other times seem dreamlike. Page 136.

lowbrow: of or pertaining to a person who does not have strong or advanced intellectual interests or who lacks intellectual sophistication. Page 3.

Lucian: (A.D. 120?–180?) Greek writer who satirized superstitious beliefs and false philosophical doctrines. In *True History* he described a journey to the Moon and adventures within the belly of a huge sea monster. Page 152.

lumberjack: a person whose job is to cut down trees for use in building, etc., or to transport trees that have been cut down. (Also called a *lumberman.*) Page 51.

M

Macaulay: The Macaulay Publishing Company, a publishing firm that was founded in the early 1900s, located in New York City. Page 59.

mafia dons: heads of organized crime families in the *mafia,* a secret Italian organization allegedly engaged in smuggling, trafficking in narcotics and other criminal activities in Italy and elsewhere. Page 173.

magic lamp: an allusion to a magic lamp in the story "Aladdin and the Wonderful Lamp," one of the best-known stories in *The Arabian Nights,* a collection of tales from Persia, Arabia, India and Egypt about magical adventures, genies and love, dating from the tenth century A.D. Aladdin, the hero, retrieves a wonderful lamp from a cave and discovers that, by rubbing it, a powerful genie appears who grants him every wish. Page 55.

magnum opus: a large or important literary work. A Latin expression, the term literally means great work. Page 163.

mahogany, across the: from one side to the other (as in paying for or being served food or drink in a saloon) of a counter made of *mahogany,* a strong, hard, reddish-brown wood that can be polished to a high gloss, used extensively for making fine furniture. Page 63.

majored in: specialized as a student in a particular subject. Page 150.

make light of: treat as unimportant. Page 115.

Malaysia: a country in Southeast Asia. It consists of two geographical regions divided by the South China Sea. Page 81.

Mandarin: the standard literary and official form of the Chinese language. Page 196.

Marquiss, Walter: American writer for pulp magazines during the 1930s. Page 93.

Massachusetts Institute of Technology: an American university of engineering, science and technology, located in Cambridge, Massachusetts, and founded in the 1860s. Emphasizing basic research in such fields as engineering, social and physical sciences, the institute has more than seventy laboratories, with research facilities in communications science, earth and life sciences, energy, electronics, nuclear and space science, etc. Page 107.

mass-market: designed for sale to as wide a range of people as possible, rather than to a particular group in society. Page 5.

Masters of Sleep, The: an LRH story first published in *Fantastic Adventures* magazine in October 1950. A sequel to *Slaves of Sleep* (1939), the story continues the adventures of Jan Palmer in his efforts to win control of both the sleep and waking worlds. Page 112.

matter, another: a situation that is likely to be judged differently; something different entirely. Page 78.

maudlin: tearfully or weakly emotional; foolishly sentimental. Page 2.

maunder: move, go or act in an aimless, confused manner. Page 44.

m'boy: a contraction of *my boy,* a familiar way of addressing someone, in this case used humorously for oneself. Page 69.

McCaffrey, Anne: (1926–2011) one of the most successful and popular science fiction and fantasy authors in the latter half of the twentieth century. Best known for her *Dragonriders of Pern* series, she became the first woman to win the Hugo and Nebula Awards. McCaffrey served as a judge of the Writers of the Future Contest beginning in 1985. Page 185.

McChesney, Florence: editor of the pulp magazine *Five-Novels Monthly.* Page 51.

McCoy, Horace: (1897–1955) American writer, best known for his novel *They Shoot Horses, Don't They?* (1935), which was later made into a film (1969). Hailed by French writers as an American existentialist novel, the story centers on a dance marathon (a contest of who can keep dancing the longest) that symbolizes the lack of purpose and meaning in life. *See also* **Existentialist.** Page 10.

medulla oblongata, swift sock to the: literally, a blow to the back of the head, used figuratively to refer to being presented forcefully and suddenly with information or data. (The *medulla oblongata* is the lowest part of the brain, continuous with the spinal cord and controlling involuntary vital bodily functions, such as those involved with the heart and lungs.) Page 78.

metaphysical: of or relating to *metaphysics. See* **metaphysics.** Page 112.

metaphysics: books and other writings dealing with the branch of philosophy concerned with the ultimate nature of existence or the nature of ultimate reality that is above or goes beyond the laws of nature or is more than the physical. Page 108.

meteoric: developing very fast and attracting a lot of attention. Page 180.

midshipmen: formerly, the boys or young men who formed the group from which naval officers were chosen. Page 58.

Midwest Book Review: an organization that publishes monthly book reviews in a series of publications that are available on-line for libraries and the general public. Established in 1976, Midwest Book Review is located in Wisconsin, a state in the north central United States. Page 136.

mien: a person's appearance, bearing or posture, especially facial expressions, as an indication of mood or character. Page 27.

miffed: offended or irritated. Page 70.

miles: by a great amount or by a long way, as in *"miles better."* Page 2.

mill: a typewriter, in reference to it as a machine for composing written copy, likened to a machine that performs certain operations on material in the process of manufacture. Used figuratively. Page 26.

millennium: a period of one thousand years. Page 159.

millrace: a strong current of water flowing in a narrow channel. Literally, a *millrace* is the current of water that drives a mill wheel. The water of the millrace falls against the paddles attached to the mill wheel, pushing the mill wheel around and around. This, in turn, drives machinery, such as large stone wheels used for grinding grain to make flour. Page 79.

MIT: an abbreviation for *Massachusetts Institute of Technology*. *See also* **Massachusetts Institute of Technology.** Page 147.

mobilization: the organization of people or resources to be ready for action in a military emergency, used here in reference to World War II (1939–1945). Page 110.

moderns, the: works of art (also those creating such works), viewed as representative of current styles, specifically those that depart from accepted or traditional styles. Page 43.

Moore, C. L.: Catherine L. Moore (1911–1987), an American writer of fantasy and science fiction novels and short stories. Her stories appeared in pulp magazines in the 1930s and in *Astounding Science Fiction* magazine throughout the 1940s. One of the first women to write in the genre, thus paving the way for many other female writers, Moore also was a judge for the Writers of the Future Contest from its first year. Page 185.

mother lode: a plentiful supply of something having great value, from the literal idea of a *mother lode,* the main deposit of gold in a particular region or district. Page 135.

Mr. Tidwell, Gunner: an LRH story first published in *Adventure* magazine in September 1936. Set during the Napoleonic Wars, the story follows the adventures of schoolmaster Tidwell, assigned to teach the young boys, future officers, aboard one of British Admiral Nelson's warships. His unforeseen involvement in a major naval battle makes for a compelling historical narrative. *See also* **Napoleonic Wars** and **Nelson.** Page 51.

mulch: cheat someone out of something, especially money. Page 93.

multinationals: large companies that operate or have investments in several countries. Page 163.

Munsey: the Frank A. Munsey Company, publisher of *Argosy* pulp magazine. Page 91.

muse: the spirit that is thought to inspire a poet or other artist; source of genius or inspiration. Originally, the muses were the nine sister-goddesses of Greek mythology, regarded as the inspirers of learning and the creative arts. Page 155.

Museum of Modern Art: a major art museum in New York City, founded in 1929 and holding one of the foremost collections of painting, sculpture, etc., from the late 1800s to the present. Page 35.

Musgrave, Story: Franklin Story Musgrave (1935–), United States astronaut, scientist, veteran of six space shuttle missions. It was during his fifth mission, in 1993, that Musgrave performed three space walks to repair the Hubble Space Telescope. Page 188.

Mutineers, The: an LRH story first published in *Astounding Science Fiction* (under the pen name Kurt von Rachen) in April 1941. *The Mutineers* continues the story of the *Kilkenny Cats* series, in which two rival forces are sent from Earth to colonize a planet and, hopes the government of Earth, kill each other off. *See also* **Kilkenny Cats** series. Page 116.

muzjik: a Russian peasant. Page 97.

mythic: having characteristics suitable to myth, especially by being fully imagined or by having qualities of fantasy. Page 110.

N

nail up (one's) scalp: indicate protest of what is viewed as an error, and demand and obtain correction. Page 80.

nap is a bit worn: literally, the surface of a fabric, made of small soft fibers sticking up slightly, is showing some signs of wear, as by becoming thin in places. Used figuratively to refer to any method, course of action or the like that is used so much as to no longer be attractive. Page 81.

Napoleonic Wars: a series of wars fought between France and a number of European nations from 1799 to 1815. In 1799 France came under the domination of French military leader Napoleon Bonaparte (1769–1821), who rose to power by force and declared himself emperor. He led military campaigns across Europe, conquering large territories, but was finally defeated (1815) by armies allied against him. Page 58.

National Aeronautics and Space Administration: the United States Government agency, established in 1958, that conducts and coordinates research on flight within and beyond Earth's atmosphere. The National Aeronautics and Space Administration (NASA) also oversees the development of launch vehicles and spacecraft. It was NASA's Apollo 11 spacecraft that became the first to land human beings on the Moon. Page 188.

Nazi: of or about the National Socialist German Workers' party, which in 1933, under Adolf Hitler, seized political control of the country, suppressing all opposition and establishing a dictatorship over all activities of the people. It promoted and enforced the belief that the German people were superior and that the Jews were inferior (and thus were to be eliminated). The party was officially abolished in 1945 at the conclusion of World War II (1939–1945). *Nazi* is from the first part of the German word for the name of the party, *Nati(onalsozialistische),* which is pronounced *nazi* in German. Page 179.

Nebula: one of the major prizes for science fiction literature (Nebula Award) initiated in 1965. The Nebula is given by the Science Fiction and Fantasy Writers of America for the best writing in the fields of science fiction and fantasy published in the United States during the previous year. Page 185.

nefarious: extremely wicked or villainous; criminal. Page 3.

Nelson: Horatio Nelson (1758–1805), England's greatest admiral and naval hero. His victory over the French at the Battle of the Nile (1798) forced Napoleon to withdraw from the Middle East, while his 1805 victory over the combined French and Spanish fleets broke France's naval power and established England's rule of the seas for the rest of the 1800s. Page 51.

Nelson, Ray Faraday: Radell "Ray" Faraday Nelson (1931–), American science fiction author and cartoonist. His literary career began in the Paris of the 1950s, where he met French and American poets and writers. Nelson's first novels and short stories began appearing in the 1960s and he has also collaborated on film scripts. Page 115.

neophyte: a young or inexperienced practitioner or student. Page 11.

netherworld: a figurative term for the world of organized crime or the people involved in it; literally, the underworld, hell. Page 3.

Newsday: a New York newspaper founded in 1940 and winner of numerous journalism awards. Primarily serving eastern portions of the New York City, New York, metropolitan area, *Newsday* maintains a broad readership throughout the entire city and ranks as one of the largest circulation newspapers in the United States. Page 147.

New York Times: a daily newspaper established in 1851 and published in New York City, New York. Its Sunday edition includes book reviews and the prestigious *New York Times* bestseller list. Page 1.

Nicaraguan counterrevolutionaries: people of Nicaragua, a country in Central America, who fought against the government of Nicaragua during the 1980s. A revolution in Nicaragua in 1979 brought to power a new government that the US accused of being communist. Opposing this government were groups of Nicaraguan rebels, called *counterrevolutionaries*. During much of the 1980s, the counterrevolutionaries (who were supported by the US) fought against the government for control of the country. This civil war continued until 1990, when new elections brought the counterrevolutionaries to power. *See also* **drugs-for-guns.** Page 180.

1984: a famous satirical novel by English author George Orwell (1903–1950), published in 1949. The novel is set in the future in a supposed "perfect society," but where freedom of thought and action have disappeared and the world is dominated by a few totalitarian states. The government maintains continual surveillance on its people, denying any privacy, with placards proclaiming "Big Brother [the all-powerful dictator of the state] Is Watching You." Page 109.

nitty-gritty: the basic and most important details of something. Page 153.

Niven, Larry: Laurence van Cott Niven (1938–), American science fiction author who began his professional speculative fiction writing career in 1964. He has authored and co-authored dozens of novels, including the Hugo and Nebula Award-winning *Ringworld* and (with Jerry Pournelle) the national bestsellers *The Mote in God's Eye*, *Lucifer's Hammer* and *Footfall*. Niven has been a Writers of the Future Contest judge since 1985. Page 191.

noosed for less: literally, hung for crimes that are less important. Used humorously to refer to actions that are considered to be in very bad taste. Page 83.

Norton, Andre: Alice Mary Norton (1912–2005), one of the most popular science fiction and fantasy authors, with more than three hundred titles during her long career, many of which were geared for young-adult readers. In 2006 a special award (Andre Norton Award) was instituted to recognize excellent fantasy and science fiction writing for this segment of the reading public. She acted as a Writers of the Future judge from 1988 until her death in 2005. Page 185.

Nor'Westers: the North West Company, a fur-trading company in northern North America from the 1780s until 1821, when it merged with its main rival, the Hudson's Bay Company (HBC). Page 59.

Notes from the Underground: a short novel by Russian writer and thinker Feodor Mikhailovich Dostoyevsky (1821–1881), published in 1864, in which the unnamed narrator, who describes himself as a sick and spiteful man, recalls incidents from his past and questions the reader's sense of morality as well as the foundations of rational thinking. Page 113.

not half: not at all. Page 76.

novelette(s): a brief novel. A *novel* is a work of fiction usually divided into chapters, often with a complex plot, in which the story develops through the action, speech and thoughts of its characters. Page 5.

number, the next: the next in series of any of the single (numbered) issues of a magazine or other periodical. Page 36.

O

off-road: having to do with travel off public roads, especially over rough ground. Page 181.

old money: a reference to the hobby of collecting coins, paper money, etc., from earlier times. Page 90.

Ole Doc Methuselah: science fiction stories by LRH about the adventures of the title character, a member of the elite Soldiers of Light organization dedicated to the preservation of Mankind, combating disease, corruption and the desperate perversities of human behavior along the intergalactic spaceways. Written under the pen name of Rene Lafayette, these stories appeared in *Astounding Science Fiction* between October 1947 and January 1950. Page 113.

Olympia: a city in the western part of the state of Washington and the capital of the state. It has a deep-water port and is a commercial and manufacturing center. Page 56.

one-pounder: a gun firing ammunition that weighs one pound (.45 kilogram). Page 70.

Orwell: George Orwell, pen name of Eric Arthur Blair (1903–1950), well-known English author who gained a reputation for his political shrewdness and his sharp satires. Writing both novels and essays, Orwell first achieved prominence in the 1940s for his two most well-known books, *Animal Farm* and *1984,* both of which reflect his lifelong distrust and disagreement with dictatorial government. Page 109.

oyster pirate: a reference to the teenage Jack London's adventures in San Francisco Bay, which he explored in his small sailboat, at times stealing oysters (edible shellfish grown commercially in oyster farms) and at other times working for the government *fish patrol,* officials guarding fishing and enforcing fishing laws in the bay. Page 65.

P
_____

Pacific Northwest: an area of the United States that includes the states of Washington, Oregon, Idaho and western Montana. Page 2.

Page, Norvell: (1904–1961) American pulp fiction writer, journalist and editor best known as the author of the majority of the adventures of the Spider, a crime fighter wanted by the law for executing his criminal antagonists. Page 51.

Painton, Fred: Frederick C. Painton, American writer of adventure, detective and war stories for pulp magazines during the 1930s. Page 93.

pallor: unusual or extreme paleness, as from fear, ill health or death. Page 96.

pandemic: general; universal. Page 165.

Panhandle: part of the state of Alaska that extends along the Pacific coast, south from the main part of the state. A *panhandle* is a narrow section of land shaped like the handle of a cooking pan, that extends away from the body of the state or territory it belongs to. Page 64.

passing: lasting only a short time; temporary. Page 9.

patently: obviously, plainly or clearly. Page 165.

pathos: the quality or power in an actual life experience or in literature, music, speech or other forms of expression, of evoking a feeling of pity or compassion. Page 146.

Pearl Pirate: an LRH story first published in *Thrilling Adventures* magazine in May 1934. The nautical tale of deceit and treachery, set in the pre–World War II southern Pacific Ocean, leaves a ship captain in possession of two vessels and a box of black pearls. Page 9.

perennial(ly): lasting for a long time; enduring or continually recurring. Page 4.

Perils of Pauline, The: a 1914 film serial that centered on danger and suspense-filled endings aimed at bringing the audience back to see the next in the series. Each story told of the heroine's

(Pauline's) evasions of her evil guardian and his attempts to take her life. It was one of the most popular serials of its time. Page 76.

Persian Gulf War: a war between Iraq and a number of countries organized mainly by the United States and the United Nations (UN). It occurred in 1991, prompted by Iraq's invasion of the tiny oil-rich nation of Kuwait, both countries situated at the northern end of the Persian Gulf. Page 165.

"Phantasmagoria": the LRH story published as *Fear* in *Unknown* magazine, July 1940. *Phantasmagoria* means a constantly shifting, complex succession of things seen or imagined (as in a dream or state of fever). Page 112.

Phantom: a pulp magazine character created during the 1930s. The hero of some 170 stories, the Phantom was portrayed as wealthy Richard Curtis Van Loan, who traded his life of ease for the thrilling adventures of a crime-solving detective and master of disguise, whom he called the Phantom. Page 3.

Pharaoh's chief poets: leading poets who would write for the *Pharaoh,* the title given to kings in ancient Egypt (the civilization that thrived in northeastern Africa from about 3000 to 30 B.C.). The origins of poetry go back many thousands of years and the art was practiced by the ancient Egyptians, hence used here to emphasize the length of time in question. Page 44.

Picasso: Pablo Picasso (1881–1973), Spanish painter and sculptor who was the leading figure in the development of modern abstract art (art that does not attempt to represent external, recognizable reality). Page 35.

piece, speak (one's): state one's opinions and views on a particular subject, event or situation. Page 91.

piles: an informal term for *hemorrhoids,* painful, swollen veins in the canal of the anus. Page 86.

pillbox: a small, low structure for machine guns that is usually made of concrete with overhead cover and forms part of a defensive position. A humorous use of *pillbox,* literally a small, shallow round box for holding pills. Page 77.

plea: an earnest and urgent request. Page 152.

plied: (of a boat or ship) sailed on, as in traveling between different ports. Page 64.

plot twist: an unexpected development of events, or a treatment, idea, etc., that differs from the usual, in the *plot,* the story or main sequence of events in a play, novel or film. Page 15.

Poe: Edgar Allan Poe (1809–1849), American short-story writer, poet and critic, widely recognized as one of the greatest American writers. His most popular tales are filled with an atmosphere of the strange and bizarre. Page 81.

Pohl, Frederik: (1919–) American science fiction writer and editor whose decades-long career has resulted in many achievements in the science fiction field. Not only has his editorship of science fiction magazines been recognized with several Hugo Awards, but his writings also have won both Hugo and Nebula Awards. Page 38.

police reporter: a newspaper reporter assigned to cover stories concerning crime and police activity. Page 20.

Popular Mechanics: a monthly American magazine founded in 1902 that contains articles on the latest developments in science and technology and examines new products and techniques in a variety of fields, such as aviation, automobiles and electronics. Page 58.

Popular (Publications): one of the largest publishers of pulp magazines, with titles covering western fiction, romance, detective and adventure. Page 91.

porkpie: a man's hat having a low, flat crown and a flexible brim. Page 35.

potence: also *potency,* power, authority or influence. Page 17.

Pournelle, Jerry: (1933–) American author, essayist and journalist. He has written numerous science fiction novels, including the national bestselling *The Mote in God's Eye, Lucifer's Hammer* and *Footfall.* Pournelle has edited many anthologies and written a range of nonfiction pieces for the speculative fiction media. A past president of the Science Fiction Writers of America, he has been a Writers of the Future judge since 1986. Page 185.

Powers, Tim: Timothy T. Powers (1952–) American fantasy and science fiction author whose novels have won numerous awards, including the World Fantasy Award. Powers has taught at renowned science fiction writing workshops, including the first Writers of the Future Workshop in 1986, as well as at Michigan State University. He has been a Writers of the Future Contest judge since 1993. Page 190.

Pratt, Fletcher: Murray Fletcher Pratt (1897–1956), American writer of science fiction, fantasy and naval history, particularly on the American Civil War. Page 127.

pray tell: please say or tell; *pray,* meaning please, is used in making a polite request (here used ironically). Page 43.

preempted: taken or used before someone else. Page 112.

premium: figuratively, a cost or price for something, from the literal meaning of *premium,* payment. Page 57.

prodigal son: a person who spends money from his parents in a wasteful manner. Page 179.

prodigious: extraordinary in size, amount, extent or degree. Page 201.

prolific: producing large quantities of something or with great frequency. Page 4.

proponent(s): a person who brings forward or advocates an action, a proposal, project or the like. Page 116.

prosaic: using or related to *prose,* the ordinary form of written or spoken language; also, ordinary or commonplace. Page 91.

prostate gland: a small organ in men, near the bladder, that produces a liquid in which sperm is carried. Page 87.

protagonist: the most important character in a novel, play, story or other literary work. Page 110.

prototypic: of or being a *prototype,* the original or model on which other things are based or formed. Page 110.

proven goods: things promised to be worthwhile or valuable and that have been demonstrated beyond a doubt to be so. From the literal idea of *goods,* things produced, as items for sale. Page 81.

provocative: serving to stimulate or excite the mind, thought or imagination. Page 13.

pseudonymous: of or being a *pseudonym* or *pen name,* a name other than an actual name that is used by an author in publications. Page 116.

psoriasis: a common disease in which areas of skin turn red and are covered with small dry pieces of skin. Page 89.

psychobabble: writing or talk that, using the language and concepts of psychology or psychiatry, is trite, superficial and deliberately confusing. Page 168.

Publishers Weekly: an international newsmagazine for the book publishing and bookselling industry, founded in the United States in 1872. It provides comprehensive news on the publishing industry, with data on bestsellers, statistics and annual reviews of several thousand books. It is subscribed to by bookstores, libraries, media, literary agents, publishers and others. Page 135.

puerile: silly or immature, especially in a childish way. Page 43.

Puerto Rican Mineralogical Expedition: also known as the *West Indies Mineralogical Expedition,* an expedition organized and conducted by L. Ron Hubbard during the early 1930s. The expedition also toured other Caribbean islands, while conducting its primary mission, the first complete mineralogical survey of Puerto Rico under United States jurisdiction. Page 9.

Puget Sound: a long, narrow bay of the Pacific Ocean on the coast of Washington, a state in the northwestern United States. Page 51.

pulpateer: a writer for the pulps, from the word *pulp* combined with the ending *-ateer,* a variation of *-eer,* a person who produces, handles or is otherwise significantly associated with (the pulps). Page 10.

pulp(s): a magazine printed on rough-surfaced paper made from wood pulp and devoted to adventure, science fiction, western stories, etc. Page 3.

purple sage: a region or area characterized by *purple sage,* a type of *sagebrush,* a bushy plant native to dry regions of the western United States that has fragrant, silvery leaves and clusters of purple flowers. Also, an allusion to the title of a famous early western novel, *Riders of the Purple Sage* by American author Zane Grey (1875–1939), in which a gunslinger in the Old West helps a woman protect her property. Page 135.

Q
_____

quarterly: a periodical that is published once every quarter of a year, a period of three months. Page 2.

quintessential: representing the most perfect example. Page 171.

R
_____

rails, on the: in the correct, normal or usual condition; functioning, working or acting correctly. The phrase alludes to a train that is running on its railway tracks and traveling correctly. Page 155.

raking: sweeping a length or area with gunfire. Page 110.

Rebels, The: an LRH story first published in *Astounding Science Fiction* (under the pen name Kurt von Rachen) in February 1942. A continuation of the story of the *Kilkenny Cats* series, *The Rebels* finds the hero faltering in his determination to overthrow the dictator of Earth, until he must overcome those who want to dispose of him. Page 116.

Red: a person who supports or advocates Communism; a Communist. Page 97.

reduced (to): presented in a simplified form. Page 19.

relief: goods or money given by a government agency to people because of need or poverty. Page 149.

relief maps: maps showing variations in land height, usually by means of lines or different colors. Page 110.

Remington: a typewriter manufactured by the Remington & Sons company of New York. Remington typewriters were first produced in the early 1870s. A manual typewriter requires no electricity to operate. Page 10.

renaissance: any revival, or period of marked improvement and new life, in art, literature, etc. Page 193.

replete: abundantly supplied or provided; filled. Page 36.

retrospective: 1. an article, essay or the like in which the author looks back over past situations, events, etc. Page 116.
2. marked by a looking back over past situations, events, etc. Page 193.

revel: take great pleasure in something. Page 66.

ride, take (one) for a buggy: help (one) out, as by pointing out the better way to do something, etc., a variation of *thanks for the buggy ride,* an expression of gratitude for having been helped in some way. A *buggy* is a carriage, usually pulled by one horse, and also a slang term for an automobile. Page 73.

right as a check: completely right; totally correct. A reference to a *check* or *checkmark,* a symbol indicating approval or that something is correct. Page 59.

ripped off: pulled something out or away from something else in a vigorous manner, as when typed sheets are removed quickly from a typewriter; produced something in a rush or with great speed. Page 18.

Riverside Drive: a famous street in New York City, overlooking the Hudson River. The street is known for its impressive buildings, monuments and fine parks, as well as being a fashionable residential area. Page 51.

Rocky Mountains: major mountain system of western North America, extending approximately 3,000 miles (4,800 kilometers) through the United States and Canada. The width of the system varies from 70 to 400 miles (110 to 650 kilometers) and the elevation from 5,000 feet (1,500 meters) to 14,433 feet (4,399 meters) at Mount Elbert, Colorado, the highest point in the Rockies. Page 143.

roller, comes out of the: is produced because a story, which can be sold, is typed on paper in a typewriter. The paper is then pulled out of the machine. A typewriter includes a hard rubber roll, or *roller,* against which the paper is held while typing is being done. Page 23.

roller, typewriter: a cylindrical roll of hard rubber in a typewriter, against which the paper is held while typing is being done. Page 75.

rolls: equipment consisting of rollers that mix and squeeze soap flakes to make bars of a hard soap that lathers better than other types of soap. Page 18.

roll (something): act, operate or function so as to produce something. Page 155.

Roosevelt: Franklin D. Roosevelt (1882–1945), thirty-second president of the United States (1933–1945). He was the only president elected four times. Roosevelt led the United States through the economic depression of the 1930s and through World War II (1939–1945). Page 82.

roster: any list, especially of names. Page 185.

rough-stock periodical: a magazine printed on paper (stock) that has a rough surface, usually making it less expensive than smooth-surfaced paper. Page 3.

round-robin: one after another; in sequence. Page 166.

Royal: a typewriter produced by the former Royal Typewriter Company, established in the early 1900s and located in New York City. The company was known for creating typewriters with key advances in typewriter technology. Page 109.

royalties: payments to an author, composer or inventor consisting of a percentage of the income from the individual's book, piece of music or invention. Page 5.

Rugby: a city located in a predominantly rural area of central England. The city itself has a wide range of industry, including the production of electrical equipment, and is well known as the site of Rugby School, a famous school for boys founded in 1567. Page 110.

rung, the lowest: the very bottom (lowest) level. A *rung* is any of the steps of a ladder and is used figuratively to suggest a state, level or position. Page 27.

rupture: a condition, also known as a *hernia,* in which part of an internal organ such as the intestine projects abnormally through the wall of the cavity that contains it. Ruptures often develop in an area of weakness following unusual stress or strain, as from the abrupt lifting of a heavy object. Page 84.

Ruski: a slang term for Russian or for a Russian person. Page 93.

Russia back into fighting shape: a reference to attempts to persuade Russia to resume fighting during World War I (1914–1918). In March 1918 Russia had signed a peace treaty with Germany and was no longer a participant in the war. Page 96.

S

sacred cow: an idea, institution, etc., unreasonably held to be exempt from questioning or criticism (with reference to the Hindus' respect for the cow as a holy animal). Page 168.

sage, purple: a region or area characterized by *purple sage,* a type of *sagebrush,* a bushy plant native to dry regions of the western United States that has fragrant, silvery leaves and clusters of purple flowers. Also, an allusion to the title of a famous early western novel, *Riders of the Purple Sage* by American author Zane Grey (1875–1939), in which a gunslinger in the Old West helps a woman protect her property. Page 135.

salacious: having or conveying undue or indecent interest in sexual matters. Page 82.

Sale, Richard: American writer for pulp magazines and films of the 1930s and creator of the pulp character Joe "Daffy" Dill, a newspaper reporter who was constantly landing in difficult situations. Sale's Daffy Dill stories appeared in *Detective Fiction Weekly,* where they were among the magazine's most popular features. Page 10.

salt(s): an informal term for an experienced sailor. Page 63.

San Diego: a city and seaport in southwestern California, the second-largest city in the state (after Los Angeles). Page 2.

Sartre, Jean-Paul: (1905–1980) French writer and philosopher whose works, such as the 1938 novel *Nausea,* contributed to the development of existential philosophy. Much of Sartre's work focuses on the challenge of creating meaning by acting responsibly in an indifferent world. Page 10.

Saturday Evening Post: a general magazine featuring text and photographs on a wide range of subjects, the *Saturday Evening Post* was published weekly from 1821 to 1969. It went out of business in 1969 but was revived as a monthly publication in 1970. Page 23.

sauce for the gander will also serve the goose, what's: what applies to one applies to both. (A *gander* is a male goose.) Page 92.

scalp, nail up (one's): indicate protest of what is viewed as an error, and demand and obtain correction. Page 80.

schooner: a sailing ship with sails set lengthwise (fore and aft) and having from two to as many as seven masts. Page 9.

Scientology: Scientology is the study and handling of the spirit in relationship to itself, universes and other life. The term Scientology is taken from the Latin *scio,* which means "knowing in the fullest sense of the word" and the Greek word *logos,* meaning "study of." In itself the word means literally "knowing how to know." Page 1.

Scott, Sir Walter: (1771–1832) Scottish novelist, poet and critic, one of the most prominent and influential figures in English literature, especially famous for his historical novels. In *Ivanhoe* he presented cultural conflicts in England of the early Middle Ages and in a popular series called the Waverly novels, which included *Rob Roy* and five other books, he portrayed key events in Scottish history. Page 194.

scrap: a struggle or fight. Page 79.

scrupulously: with methods that are rigorously precise and exact. Page 27.

Seattle: a city in west central Washington State in the northwestern US and a major seaport and commercial center. Page 56.

seconded: supported. From the definition of a *second,* an assistant to a contestant, as in a duel. Page 98.

Secret of Treasure Island, The: the series of films produced by Columbia Pictures, drawn from the L. Ron Hubbard novel *Murder at Pirate Castle.* LRH's screenplays for the serial, written during 1937, became a box office success. Page 116.

Seligman: Edwin Robert Seligman (1861–1939), American economist, professor of political economy and finance at New York's Columbia University. Page 18.

Selkirk, Alexander: (1676–1721) Scottish sailor who, while on an expedition, had a dispute with the captain of his ship. At his own request, he was put ashore in October 1704 on an island off the coast of Chile, where he lived alone until rescued in February 1709. His story served as the background to Daniel Defoe's novel *The Adventures of Robinson Crusoe.* Page 51.

seminal: highly influential in the development of future events. Page 116.

sentinel: one who keeps guard or watches over something; a lookout. Page 76.

sentry: a soldier posted at a given spot to watch out for, and warn of, danger; sentinel. Page 77.

serial: any of the short movies shown as a series of up to fifteen separate installments, often in conjunction with a full-length film. These short films, each with a dramatic ending, drew the audience back each week for the next exciting chapter in the story. Page 116.

set down: recorded in writing or printing. Page 19.

set (oneself) to: applied (oneself) to a piece of work, a task or employment. Page 3.

set piece: an artistic composition, in literature, music, sculpture, etc., designed to give an impressive effect. Page 179.

setting forth: presenting or declaring something; laying something out. Page 3.

Seven Sisters: the seven oil companies that dominated mid-twentieth-century oil production, refining and distribution. These companies were Standard Oil of New Jersey (Exxon), Royal Dutch/Shell, Anglo-Persian Oil Company (BP), Standard Oil Company of New York (Mobil), Standard Oil of California (Chevron), Gulf Oil and Texaco. Page 165.

Seventh Avenue: location of Street & Smith Publications, at Seventh Avenue and 15th Street in the southwestern part of New York City. Page 150.

sf: an abbreviation for *science fiction*. Page 115.

Shadow: a character in pulp magazines and on radio dramas (famous for the introduction "Who knows what evil lurks in the hearts of men? The Shadow knows!"), starting in the 1930s. As described in hundreds of stories by American writer Walter B. Gibson (1897–1985), the Shadow was a crime-fighting hero with psychic powers, in black hat and black, crimson-lined cloak. Page 3.

Shelley, Mary: Mary Wollstonecraft Shelley (1797–1851), English author. Besides her well-known novel *Frankenstein* (1818), she also wrote four other novels, books of travel sketches, stories and poetry. Page 152.

shell out: an informal term meaning hand over (money); contribute; pay. Page 154.

shenanigans: actions that are deceitful, underhanded or otherwise questionable. Page 180.

shine through: appear or stand out clearly; be brilliantly evident or visible. Page 20.

ship of the line: a former sailing warship armed powerfully enough to serve in the line of battle, usually having cannons ranged along two or more decks; battleship. Page 58.

shoals, uncombed: literally, *shoals* are sandy elevations of the bottom of a body of water, constituting a hazard to navigation. If they are *uncombed,* it means they are not flattened or eroded (as by currents passing over them with force) and therefore are a major obstacle for ships, which have to work their way around them. Used figuratively. Page 43.

shoot off (one's) face: talk freely, often in a critical way, without regard to the effect. Page 90.

short: a *short story,* a work of fiction that differs from a novel by being shorter and less elaborate. Page 57.

shotgunned: spread out so as to cover a wide field or area. This is an allusion to the firearm known as a *shotgun,* which is chiefly used in hunting. Shotguns fire a load of metal pellets that spread out over a wide area, making it easier to hit a moving target than when firing a single bullet from a rifle or pistol. Page 9.

shot to the devil: in hopelessly bad condition (shot), likened to going to hell, the residence of the devil. Hence, to everlasting ruin. Page 26.

shows (one) up: reveals something, especially an error. Page 76.

Silverberg, Robert: (1935–) American author of hundreds of science fiction stories and more than a hundred novels. Widely published since the 1950s, he has won five Nebula Awards and five Hugo Awards and was named a Grand Master by the Science Fiction Writers of America in 2004. In addition to his extensive writing career, he has been a Writers of the Future Contest judge since its first year in 1984. Page 185.

sinew: a strong fibrous cord serving to connect a muscle with a bone or other part; a tendon. Page 78.

sitting room: also called *living room,* a room in a house, apartment or the like where people usually relax or entertain guests. Page 35.

Six-Gun Caballero: an LRH story first published in *Western Story* magazine in March 1938. Michael Patrick Obañon, proud owner of a 100,000-acre ranch willed to him by his father, stands to lose his entire inheritance when a band of criminals makes false claims on his property. Page 137.

six-shooter: characteristic of stories involving *six-shooters,* handguns having a revolving cylinder with six cartridges, a long barrel and using relatively large bullets, a kind of gun usually used in the western US in the last half of the nineteenth century. Page 9.

skid by: to get along with a minimum of effort. Page 21.

skittered: moved along rapidly and lightly. Page 70.

slamming: criticizing or insulting harshly. Page 87.

slant(ing): (presenting something from) a point of view, angle or direction toward a particular subject or public. Page 9.

slapstick: of or related to a type of comedy that emphasizes loud, fast physical action and ridiculous, confused situations. From *slapstick,* a device made of two flat, linked pieces of wood, formerly used in comic performances to make a loud, clapping noise, imitating the sound of someone being hit. Page 181.

Slaves of Sleep: an LRH story first published in *Unknown* magazine in July 1939. Jan Palmer witnesses the murder of Professor Frobish by Zongri, an angry demon that the professor had freed from a copper jar. Cursed by the demon with eternal wakefulness, Jan ends up not only jailed for murder, but also struggling to free himself from a nightmare world ruled by the demon. Page 110.

Sleepy McGee: an LRH story first published in *Argosy* magazine in July 1936, the first of the seventeen LRH stories named the "Hell Job" series, each with a setting depicting a dangerous occupation. *Sleepy McGee* portrays how the laziest civil engineer in the world builds a road through ten miles of rain-soaked jungle. Page 9.

slick offices: the offices of publishing companies that produce the slicks. *See also* **slicks.** Page 84.

slicks: magazines printed on paper having a more or less glossy finish and regarded as possessing qualities as expensiveness and sophistication. Page 27.

slur: an insulting remark. Page 149.

smorgasbord: figuratively, a number of things that are combined together as a whole. Literally, a *smorgasbord* is a meal with a large variety of hot and cold dishes from which people serve themselves. Page 168.

snap-ending: characteristic of a *snap ending,* an ending to a story that happens quickly and suddenly. Page 76.

Snark: a two-masted sailing yacht designed by American author Jack London. It was 43 feet (13 meters) long and was launched in April 1907 from San Francisco across the South Pacific. In his book *The Cruise of the Snark* (1911), London describes adventures of his voyage. Page 65.

sob story: an account of personal troubles that is meant to arouse sympathy. Page 25.

sociology: the study of the individuals, groups and institutions that make up human society, including the way the members of a group respond to one another. Page 152.

soldier of fortune: someone who will join any army as a soldier so that he can find profit or adventure. Page 94.

sophomore: of or relating to the second year of college in the United States. Page 2.

S.O.S.: an international coded signal of extreme distress, used especially by ships or aircraft, popularly regarded as an abbreviation for *save our souls*. Page 72.

soul, grizzled: a person of a particular type—in this case, someone with hair that is gray or streaked with gray. Page 70.

sounding board: person or persons whose reactions serve as a measure of the effectiveness of the methods, ideas, etc., put forth. Page 154.

South Seas: the name given by early explorers to the whole of the Pacific Ocean. More usually applied to the islands of the central and South Pacific. Page 63.

space opera: an action-oriented tale of space adventure involving spaceships, spacemen, rockets, flying saucers, wars, conflicts, other beings, civilizations and societies. Space opera was originally a variation of horse opera (a story about the American West) and soap opera (dramas commonly dealing with domestic situations and often characterized by sensation and sentimentality). Page 147.

space race: the competition between nations to be first to achieve various objectives in the exploration of space. Page 109.

spar tree(s): in logging, a tree or other tall structure that supports the rigging used in hauling cut trees out of a forest. The rigging attached to the spar tree consists of overhead cables to which the cut trees are suspended. The cut trees can then be hauled out over the tops of the standing trees, as opposed to being dragged over the ground. Page 57.

speculative: of writing that is usually considered to include fantasy, horror, science fiction and the like, dealing with worlds unlike the real world. Page 1.

spiritualism: the doctrine or belief that the spirits of the dead can and do communicate with the living, especially through a person (a medium). Page 153.

Sportsman Pilot: a monthly American aviation magazine published from around 1930 until 1943. It contained writings on a wide range of subjects, including coverage of aerial sporting events, commentary on current aviation issues, technical articles on flying as well as other articles on topics of general interest. Page 57.

spot, on the: in a difficult situation, one calling for action, a response or the like. Page 73.

spot (something): place or locate something in a certain position, used here in reference to placing an advertisement in a specific publication or in a specific place in a publication. Page 88.

Squad That Never Came Back, The: an LRH story first published in *Thrilling Adventures* magazine in May 1935. Threatened with death, a corporal leads a group of fellow legionnaires to a lost treasure in the Moroccan desert. Originally written by LRH under the pen name Kurt von Rachen, it was published under the pen name Legionnaire 148. Page 123.

stable(s): a group or staff of writers engaged to contribute their services when called upon; pool. Page 11.

staccato: rapid, brief and clipped in sound. Page 72.

stalling for the bell, boxer: someone waiting for something one knows is coming. In boxing, a bell is sounded at the end of each one of the periods, each three minutes in length, that the boxing match is divided into. Page 80.

Standard: the publishing company known as Standard Magazines (also known as Thrilling Publications, Beacon Magazines and Better Publications). The company produced pulp magazines such as *Thrilling Detective, Thrilling Western, Startling Stories* and others. Page 91.

Standard Oil: one of the most powerful businesses in the world during the late 1800s and early 1900s, with a virtual monopoly of the petroleum industry in the United States. It was broken into smaller companies in 1911, many of these companies retaining "Standard Oil" in their names into the 1980s and eventually becoming such industry giants as Exxon Mobil Corporation, Chevron Texaco Corporation and others. Page 18.

standby: something that can always be relied on to be available and useful if needed as a substitute or in an emergency. Page 20.

stands, on the: displayed for sale on *newsstands,* small booths on the street, from which newspapers, magazines and books are sold to passersby. Something *on the stands* has been placed in the newsstands and become available for the public to buy. Page 9.

started: gave an involuntary jerk, jump or twitch, as from a shock of surprise, alarm or pain. Page 124.

steeplejack: a skilled construction worker who performs installations, maintenance and repairs on skyscrapers, towers, steeples, smokestacks and other tall structures. Page 51.

stenog(s): also *steno,* shortened form of *stenographer,* a person who is skilled at or whose job involves writing shorthand and typing up reports and letters from shorthand. (*Shorthand* is a fast method of writing down what someone is saying in symbols that represent letters, words or phrases.) Page 38.

stepchild: something (such as a project, organization or person) that is not properly treated, appreciated or supported. Page 153.

step, in: conforming to what is happening in a related or nearby area or field. Page 86.

Sterling Diesel(s): a type of diesel engine manufactured by the Sterling Engine Company of Buffalo, New York. Sterling built heavy-duty engines for boats and for industrial applications, such as oil pipeline pumping stations. The US Coast Guard installed Sterling engines on 75-foot patrol boats and other vessels. Page 72.

stewardship: conduct of the office of *steward,* someone who manages the property or finances of another; management; control. Page 193.

stewed over: experienced worry or agitation about something. Page 56.

stint: a period of time spent doing something. Page 116.

stock tale: a story of a common or ordinary type. Page 9.

straight-laced: narrowly strict or severe in behavior or moral views. Page 180.

Stranger in a Strange Land: an influential and award-winning science fiction novel by American author Robert A. Heinlein (1907–1988). Published in 1961, the story concerns the events surrounding a human orphaned during the first manned expedition to Mars, who is raised by Martians then brought back to Earth by a second human expedition. Page 146.

Street & Smith: a large American publishing company established in the mid-1800s that put out a large number of periodicals and pulp magazines in the late nineteenth and early twentieth centuries, such as *Astounding Science Fiction* magazine and *Unknown* magazine. Page 107.

stuff, do (one's): perform (one's) duty, function or skill; do what is required or expected. *Stuff* is any unspecified kind of matter and is used here figuratively to mean (one's) actions, movements, duties, functions, etc. Page 57.

stuffing out of, knock the: give a merciless beating to; defeat thoroughly. Page 79.

stylized: characterized by a distinctive and identifiable artistic form or manner of expression. Page 92.

substantive: having practical importance, value or effect; real or actual; essential. Page 68.

sultry: oppressively hot and damp. Page 62.

surmised: concluded or supposed that something was possible or likely. Page 152.

surreal: having the disorienting, hallucinatory quality of a dream; unreal; fantastic. Page 4.

swank: extremely elegant or fashionable. Page 87.

swashbuckling: of or characteristic of a *swashbuckler,* a bold swordsman, soldier or adventurer. Page 116.

swath, cut a: attracted notice or accomplished much. From the literal meaning of *swath,* an area or amount of grass or grain cut in one sweep of a scythe (a farming tool with a long, curved blade fastened to a handle) or in one passage of a mower or other machine. Page 169.

Swift, Jonathan: (1667–1745) English author of *Gulliver's Travels* (1726), one of the most famous satires in English literature. Swift ridicules customs, ideas and actions of the time in highly effective and economical language. While his satire is often bitter, it is also delightfully humorous. Page 169.

swift sock to the medulla oblongata: literally, a blow to the back of the head, used figuratively to refer to being presented forcefully and suddenly with information or data. (The *medulla oblongata* is the lowest part of the brain, continuous with the spinal cord and controlling involuntary vital bodily functions, such as those involved with the heart and lungs.) Page 78.

swipe (something), up and: steal something suddenly. Page 79.

synergy: combined or cooperative action or force. Page 135.

T

taboo: prohibited or forbidden by tradition or convention. Page 25.

Tacoma: a seaport on the west coast of the United States, in the state of Washington. Page 55.

Tah: a story set in China during the 1920s, focusing on a young boy, Tah, who is killed in battle after an all-night march. The first published fiction story by L. Ron Hubbard, *Tah* appeared in the George Washington University literary review magazine in February 1932. Page 1.

Tahiti: an island in the southern Pacific Ocean and part of French Polynesia, an overseas territory of France, known for its pleasant year-round climate. Page 66.

take heart: become encouraged and more confident. Page 147.

take (one) for a buggy ride: help (one) out, as by pointing out the better way to do something, etc., a variation of *thanks for the buggy ride,* an expression of gratitude for having been helped in some way. A *buggy* is a carriage, usually pulled by one horse, and also a slang term for an automobile. Page 73.

take, on the: taking or willing to take bribes. Page 163.

tang, salt: a touch or slight trace of the sea (that is, salty), such as the speech, words and expressions used by sailors. Page 70.

Tarzan: the main character in stories by American writer Edgar Rice Burroughs (1875–1950). First appearing in stories of the early 1900s, Tarzan was the son of an English nobleman, abandoned in Africa in his infancy. He was brought up by apes, learned to speak their language and went through a long series of breathless adventures. Page 3.

teeth, cut (one's): learn how to do something and gain experience from it. Page 74.

teeth, defendant: false teeth that are characterized as being *on trial,* that is, accused in a court of law, a pun on the quoted advertisement for *"False Teeth, 60 Day Trial,"* where *trial* means a test of something in order to determine performance, qualities or suitability. Page 86.

temperament, pretend to: put on an act of being excessively moody, irritable or sensitive. Page 27.

Test Pilot: an LRH story first published in *Argosy* magazine in October 1936. An irresponsible pilot, confronted with the ultimate trial of courage, sacrifices his own life to save his younger brother. Page 51.

thematic: of or pertaining to a *theme,* a subject or topic of discourse or writing. Page 136.

thereby hangs a story: in that connection or relation there is something to tell. Page 93.

Thompson, J. Walter: one of the oldest and largest advertising agencies in the United States, founded (1878) by American advertising executive James Walter Thompson (1847–1928). Page 165.

Thrilling Adventures: a pulp magazine produced by the publishing company of Thrilling Publications (also known as Standard Magazines, Beacon Magazines and Better Publications). The company also produced pulp magazines such as *Thrilling Detective, Thrilling Western, Startling Stories* and others. Page 15.

Thrilling Detective: a pulp magazine produced by the publishing company of Thrilling Publications (also known as Standard Magazines, Beacon Magazines and Better Publications). The company also produced pulp magazines such as *Thrilling Adventure, Thrilling Western, Startling Stories* and others. Page 74.

thud and blunder: a variation of *blood and thunder,* the bloodshed, violence and uproar characteristic of adventure stories. Page 69.

thwart: block or obstruct, as to prevent someone's plans from succeeding. Page 163.

tie into: get to work on vigorously. Page 201.

Tientsin: a city in northeast China, one of the most important commercial cities in that part of the country. Page 9.

tilt field: an enclosed field consisting of two narrow lanes for holding a *tilt,* a contest in which two mounted knights tried to knock each other off their horses. The knights rode toward each other with blunted lances from opposite ends of the tilt field. Each stayed in his own lane, the lanes being separated by a railing to keep the horses from colliding. The winner was the knight who stayed on his horse, but such combat often resulted in injury to one or both knights. Figuratively, a *tilt field* is any area or sphere of contest; a strenuous or forceful struggle between people. Page 44.

time, before (one's): happening earlier than would be expected or before a usual time. Page 27.

time-dilation: of or related to the apparent slowing of time experienced by those observing an object, such as a spacecraft, as it approaches the speed of light, as compared to the passage of time experienced by those in the object itself. For example, a voyage of a spaceship traveling at the speed of light might only seem to last a few weeks to the ship's crew, while to people on Earth the voyage would have lasted many years. Page 116.

tom-tom(s): any of various drums, as of Indian or African tribes, usually beaten with the hands and sometimes used by a medicine man or tribal society to drive demons or evil spirits out of someone's body. Page 85.

tongue in (one's) cheek: in an insincere or ironic manner; mockingly. Page 29.

tooth-and-claw: marked by fierce or savage struggle, such as in the jungle. *Tooth and claw* is a variation of *tooth and nail,* often used in the phrase *to fight with tooth and nail,* with the use of one's teeth and nails as weapons. Page 143.

top brass: the highest-ranking officials of an organization. Page 150.

topliner: a person noted as *topline,* of the highest reputation, quality or importance. From the literal meaning of *topline,* so important as to be named at or near the top of a newspaper item, advertisement or the like. Page 149.

top-notchers: the highest professionals in a field. Page 61.

torch: a valuable quality, principle or cause that needs to be protected and maintained; literally, a stick of wood dipped in wax or with one end wrapped in combustible material, set on fire and carried, especially in the past, as a source of light. Page 97.

torturous: not direct; full of twists and turns. Page 43.

to wit: used to introduce a list or explanation of what one has just mentioned. Originally a phrase used in law, *that is to wit,* which meant that is to know, that is to say. Page 82.

trail, upward: a route followed, thought of as one that goes to a higher or improved level in some activity. Page 29.

transcendent: going beyond or exceeding usual limits; superior. Page 3.

transom: a horizontal beam reinforcing the stern of a boat. Page 70.

transport plane: an airplane for carrying passengers or freight, such as is used on flights that regularly travel between certain points. Page 72.

Tremaine, F. Orlin: (1899–1956) American science fiction editor. As the editor of *Astounding Science Fiction* in the early 1930s, Tremaine built the magazine into a major science fiction magazine of the time period. Page 107.

trendy: deliberately reflecting or adopting fashionable ideas or tastes that are often popular for only a short time. Page 171.

Trenton: the capital of New Jersey, a state in the eastern part of the United States. Trenton is located about 28 miles (45 kilometers) northeast of Philadelphia. It served as a temporary US capital (1784 and 1799) and during the 1800s developed into a major industrial city. Page 181.

tripe: something worthless; nonsense. Page 26.

trough, wallow in the: (of a boat or ship) roll from side to side in the long, narrow hollow or depression between two waves, with the waves headed toward the side of the ship. Page 73.

True West Magazine: a magazine devoted to the history of the American West. Published since 1953, *True West* focuses on articles detailing the history of the Old West, along with travel features and reviews of books and movies. Page 137.

tsar: the title of the ruler or emperor of Russia prior to 1917, also spelled *czar.* Page 97.

tug: short for *tugboat,* a sturdily built, powerful boat designed for towing or pushing ships, barges, etc. Page 70.

turn out: produce or create something, especially in a consistent way with rapidity or skill. Page 23.

turn over: start; used literally in regard to a machine, such as an engine or motor. Page 26.

Twain, Mark: pen name of Samuel Langhorne Clemens (1835–1910), American author and humorist, known particularly for his stories of the West and the Mississippi River, often reflecting the humorous tall tales of the time period, tales filled with hilarious exaggeration. Page 194.

Typewriter in the Sky: an LRH story first published in *Unknown Fantasy Fiction* magazine in November 1940. One of the earliest and most influential fantasies based on a theme of a journey into someone's mind, *Typewriter in the Sky* presents the story of a piano player who suddenly finds that he is part of an adventure novel being written by his friend, and the villain in the story at that! Page 113.

typewriter roller: a cylindrical roll of hard rubber in a typewriter, against which the paper is held while typing is being done. Page 75.

Tyrannosaurus rex: a large, fierce meat-eating dinosaur that walked on powerful hind legs and had small forelegs. It lived about 68 million to 65 million years ago and was one of the largest meat-eating animals that ever existed. Page 181.

U

Ultimate Adventure, The: an LRH story first published in *Unknown* magazine in April 1939. An experiment by an evil scientist sends a young man, Stevie Jepson, into a fantastic Arabian Nights land where a beautiful queen and her subjects are asleep and a wicked spirit nearly kills him before he returns to the real world. Sent back by the scientist for jewels, Jepson rescues the queen and deals with the scientist when he comes searching for the jewels. Page 110.

unbeknownst: without the knowledge (of a specified person). Page 181.

Underwood: a manual typewriter invented in the late 1800s that allowed the typist to see every letter as it was being typed. Page 10.

unfettered: free from restraint; unrestricted. Page 108.

United Nations Society of Writers: an organization of staff of the United Nations who are writers, poets and journalists, that operates with the aim of promoting the written word as a powerful and artistic tool in communication. The society publishes a literary magazine and sponsors an award honoring the work of some of the world's greatest and most inspiring writers. Page 198.

United Press International: a business organization of newspapers in the United States, together with representatives abroad, for the reporting and interchange of news, founded in 1907 by newspaper publisher Edward Wyllis Scripps (1854–1926). Page 169.

University Star, The: a newspaper produced by Texas State University, one of the largest universities in Texas. Published since 1911, *The University Star* has won numerous journalism awards. Page 181.

unsullied: (of the purity, perfection or luster of something) not marred or corrupted; unstained. Page 49.

up and swipe (something): steal (something) suddenly. Page 79.

urchin: a boy who is rude and undisciplined. Page 58.

V

van Vogt, A. E.: Alfred Elton van Vogt (1912–2000), Canadian-born science fiction writer who began his decades-long career during science fiction's Golden Age (1939–1949). Esteemed in the science fiction field, van Vogt was presented the Grand Master Award by the Science Fiction Writers of America in 1995. Page 185.

vapid: without animation; dull or boring. Page 38.

vehicle: 1. a medium of communication, expression or display. Page 3.
2. something such as a play, screenplay or other means of artistic expression regarded as an outlet for creative talent, particularly such a work intended to display the powers of a particular performer. Page 10.

venerable: worthy of respect as a result of great age, wisdom, remarkable achievements or similar qualities. Page 188.

Venetian vase: a humorous reference to the works of detective fiction from the late 1800s and early 1900s, many of which focused on an upper-class world, viewed as similar to a "Venetian vase," from the elegant glassware produced in Venice, Italy. Page 10.

veritable: genuine; actual; properly so called. Page 188.

Verne: Jules Verne (1828–1905), French novelist and the first great specialist of science fiction. He anticipated flights into outer space, submarines, helicopters, air conditioning, guided missiles and motion pictures long before they were developed. Page 152.

Vickers Wellington: a British twin-engine, long-range bomber designed in the mid-1930s. It was widely used as a night bomber in the early years of World War II (1939–1945) and later as an antisubmarine aircraft. Page 110.

Village, the: Greenwich Village, a residential section of Manhattan (the economic center of New York City), inhabited by artists, writers and students. Page 43.

visceral: characterized by or showing deep inward feelings; emotional. Page 159.

Voltaire: (1694–1778) French author and philosopher who produced a range of literary works, often attacking injustice and intolerance. Page 44.

voodoo rites: religious or other solemn ceremonies or acts of *voodoo,* a body of beliefs and practices originally from Africa that includes magic and the supposed exercise of supernatural powers through the aid of spirits. Page 9.

W

wallow in the trough: (of a boat or ship) roll from side to side in the long, narrow hollow or depression between two waves, with the waves headed toward the side of the ship. Page 73.

wanton: causing harm or damage deliberately and for no acceptable reason. Page 165.

War Birds: a pulp magazine featuring aviation stories, published by Dell Publishing Company. Page 57.

wares: articles offered for sale. Page 43.

wasn't anything for it: a variation of *there was nothing for it* or *there was nothing for it but to,* meaning that there was no other course of action open (except that of). The phrase usually precedes a statement of what that course of action ended up being. Page 56.

watering hole: an informal term for a place (such as a restaurant) where people go to eat, drink and socialize. Page 11.

way of, in the: of the nature of, belonging to the class of; as regards to (something). Page 2.

way stop: an intermediate stopping place on a journey. Page 116.

weight of guns: the forcefulness of an attack, as seen in the numbers of cannon used during a battle. Hence *throwing the weight of guns to Nelson* means that the British forces under Nelson had a greater number of cannon than the French (once the French flagship *L'Orient* had blown up) and thus could attack the French during the battle with greater force. Page 58.

Wells: Herbert George Wells (1866–1946), British novelist, historian and author of science fiction stories dealing with themes such as time travel *(The Time Machine),* invasion from Mars *(The War of the Worlds)* and future societies *(The Shape of Things to Come).* Page 152.

Western Action: also called *Western Action Novels,* a pulp magazine that was produced by Columbia Publications of New York. Page 74.

Western Front: during World War I (1914–1918), one of the two main areas of fighting, located in northeastern France. It consisted primarily of trenches many miles in length with German and Austrian troops on one side and the nations allied against them (England, France, the US and others) on the other side. Page 97.

what of it?: a response made to a statement, implying that what is said has no bearing or is not important. Page 43.

wheels, hell on: extremely demanding; aggressive or wild. Page 58.

whereby: in consequence of, as a result of or owing to which; from which (as a cause or reason). Page 20.

whimsical: slightly odd, playful and behaving in such a way as to be hard to predict. Page 113.

white-knuckled: of stories or writing, causing fear or nervous excitement, with reference to the effect caused by gripping tightly to steady oneself. Page 9.

whitewings: workers in New York City automats who wore long-sleeved, white coats. (An *automat* is a type of restaurant where customers served themselves by obtaining food dispensed from small compartments in coin-operated machines.) Page 43.

Williamson, Jack: John Stewart Williamson (1908–2006), American science fiction writer named a Grand Master by the Science Fiction Writers of America. Author of numerous short stories and novels, his writing career spanned more than seven decades. Well known for his teaching and lecturing, Williamson was also an instructor at the original Writers of the Future Workshop held in Taos, New Mexico. For two decades he served as a judge of the Writers of the Future Contest. Page 185.

Williams, Sean: Sean Llewellyn Williams (1967–), award-winning Australian science fiction writer, author of some seventy published short stories and thirty novels. Williams has been published around the world in multiple languages. A Writers of the Future Contest winner in 1992, Williams joined the judges panel in 2003. Page 191.

Williams, Tennessee: (1911–1983) American writer, most of whose works were set in the southern part of the United States. He wrote novels, short stories and plays, nine of which (including well-known works such as *A Streetcar Named Desire* and *Cat on a Hot Tin Roof*) were made into films. Page 3.

wink and nod, a: an expression meaning that one knows about something but will overlook it. From *wink,* an instance of closing one or both eyes (winking) and hence overlooking something, and *nod,* a short, quick downward bending of the head to indicate that one agrees with or gives approval to something. Page 179.

winning way: a very charming manner, to the extent that people are won over (persuaded to do something); also a pun on *winning,* being victorious (as in the humorous reference to using loaded dice to win gambling games). Page 93.

witnesseth: an older way of saying *witness,* used to introduce something that gives evidence of a fact or demonstrates a statement just made. The ending *-eth* is found on some older verbs. Page 59.

wit, to: used to introduce a list or explanation of what one has just mentioned. Originally a phrase used in law, *that is to wit,* which meant that is to know, that is to say. Page 82.

Wolverton, Dave: (1957–) American science fiction and bestselling fantasy writer of some fifty novels whose works have been nominated for Hugo and Nebula Awards. As a 1987 Writers of the Future Contest winner and a judge since the 1990s, Wolverton has also edited the annual anthology and served as an instructor at the Writing Workshop. Page 191.

wordage: the quantity or amount of words written, as over a period of time or for a given text, etc. Page 10.

wordsmith: a person, especially a professional writer, who uses words skillfully. Page 49.

world war, the: a world war is a war involving most of the nations of the Earth, used here in reference to the First World War (1914–1918). Page 23.

worn, nap is a bit: literally, the surface of a fabric, made of small soft fibers sticking up slightly, is showing some signs of wear, as by becoming thin in places. Used figuratively to refer to any method, course of action or the like that is used so much as to no longer be attractive. Page 81.

wrought: brought about or caused. Page 3.

Y

yardstick: a standard used to judge the quality, value or success of something. Page 17.

yarn: an entertaining story of real or fictitious adventures. Page 11.

ye: old form of *you,* as used in the phrase *ye gods,* a mild oath or exclamation expressing contempt, anger, scorn, etc. Page 25.

Z

Zeppelin(s): a rigid cylindrical airship consisting of a covered frame filled with bags containing lighter-than-air gas to provide lift, and a suspended compartment for engines and passengers. Popular in the early 1900s, with the outbreak of World War I (1914–1918), zeppelins were constructed for military purposes, which included the bombing of London, England, by Germany. Page 110.

INDEX

THE
L. RON HUBBARD
SERIES

"To really know life," L. Ron Hubbard wrote, "you've got to be part of life. You must get down and look, you must get into the nooks and crannies of existence. You have to rub elbows with all kinds and types of men before you can finally establish what he is."

Through his long and extraordinary journey to the founding of Dianetics and Scientology, Ron did just that. From his adventurous youth in a rough and tumble American West to his far-flung trek across a still mysterious Asia; from his two-decade search for the very essence of life to the triumph of Dianetics and Scientology—such are the stories recounted in the L. Ron Hubbard Biographical Publications.

Drawn from his own archival collection, this is Ron's life as he himself saw it. With each volume of the series focusing upon a separate field of endeavor, here are the compelling facts, figures, anecdotes and photographs from a life like no other.

Indeed, here is the life of a man who lived at least twenty lives in the space of one.

FOR FURTHER INFORMATION VISIT
www.lronhubbard.org

To order copies of *The L. Ron Hubbard Series*
or L. Ron Hubbard's Dianetics and
Scientology books and lectures, contact:

US and International

BRIDGE PUBLICATIONS, INC.
5600 E. Olympic Blvd.
Commerce, California 90022 USA
www.bridgepub.com
Tel: (323) 888-6200
Toll-free: 1-800-722-1733

United Kingdom and Europe

NEW ERA PUBLICATIONS
INTERNATIONAL ApS
Smedeland 20
2600 Glostrup, Denmark
www.newerapublications.com
Tel: (45) 33 73 66 66
Toll-free: 00-800-808-8-8008